Also by Sylvia Browne

THE TWO MARYS

PSYCHIC CHILDREN

THE MYSTICAL LIFE OF JESUS

INSIGHT

PHENOMENON

PROPHECY

VISITS FROM THE AFTERLIFE

SYLVIA BROWNE'S BOOK OF DREAMS

PAST LIVES, FUTURE HEALING

BLESSINGS FROM THE OTHER SIDE

LIFE ON THE OTHER SIDE

THE OTHER SIDE AND BACK

ADVENTURES OF A PSYCHIC

ALL PETS GO TO HEAVEN

PSYCHIC

SYLVIA BROWNE

written with Lindsay Harrison

End of Days

PREDICTIONS AND PROPHECIES
ABOUT THE
END OF THE WORLD

piatkus

PIATKUS

First published in the US in 2008 by Dutton, a member of Penguin
Group (USA) Inc.
First published in Great Britain in 2008 by Piatkus Books
This paperback edition published in 2011 by Piatkus

3 5 7 9 10 8 6 4 2

A CIP catalogue record for this book
is available from the British Library.

ISBN 978-0-7499-2910-7

Designed by Helene Berinsky

Printed in the UK by
Clays Ltd, St Ives plc

Papers used by Sphere are from well-managed forests
and other responsible sources.

Piatkus
An imprint of
Little, Brown Book Group
Carmelite House
50 Victoria Embankment
London EC4Y 0DZ

An Hachette UK Company
www.hachette.co.uk

www.piatkus.co.uk

From Sylvia & Lindsay
For Kristen, Misty, Crystal, and Willie

CONTENTS

CONTENTS

INTRODUCTION

I'm tired of being scared, and I know you are too. Not that there isn't a lot to be scared of in this world today, between the non-stop headlines about wars and nuclear power plants and terrorists and assassinations and civil unrest and economic uncertainty and political doublespeak and insane weather and an environment that's becoming unhealthier by the day. But a point comes when it's too much to deal with, and thinking about it accomplishes nothing more than sending you to bed with a cold cloth on your head.

Then, just when you're already on enough overload, someone feels compelled to mention that according to the Mayan calendar, the world is going to end in 2012 anyway, so what difference does anything make, really? Or they heard, or read somewhere, that the book of Revelation, or the book of Daniel, or Nostradamus, or something, or someone says we'll all be dead in the next two years, or five, or ten, or whatever, or that there are "obvious signs" that the end of the world is right around the corner. And of course it reminded them of some horrible movie they saw in which only a handful of people are left alive on Earth because of a giant asteroid, and these zombielike survivors are wandering around deserted cities trying to kill each other over a crust of bread.

It's almost enough to make you skip lying down on your bed and to opt for hiding underneath it instead. Almost. But before you do that, I can't encourage you enough to ask a few questions about these dire end-of-the-world predictions. Who were the Mayans, for example, and how did they arrive at a calendar that ends in 2012? What specifically do the books of Revelation and Daniel say that "prove" this impending doom, and what do we know about the circumstances in which they were written in the first place? Who was Nostradamus, why is he credited with any more expertise about the end of the world than the rest of us, and is it true that his writing is so filled with symbolism that it's impossible to tell what he was talking about anyway? What are these "obvious signs" that our time on Earth is almost up—and just out of curiosity, have those same obvious signs ever cropped up before in the history of this planet and maybe been misinterpreted? As for this movie, did it claim to be a documentary? Is there really a legitimate reason to believe that an asteroid gigantic enough to destroy our world is headed toward us, or might be headed toward us any time soon?

Ninety-nine times out of a hundred, the answer to any or all of these questions will be, "I have no idea."

If you've seen my television or personal appearances and/or read my books, you know how strongly I believe that knowledge is power and that the first thing to do when you're afraid of something is to educate yourself about it as thoroughly as possible. I would never say, "Don't be frightened about the end of the world," because, as you'll learn throughout this book, we humans are almost genetically predisposed to thinking about it and worrying about it. But I will say, very enthusiastically, learn all you can, form your own opinions, and maybe above all, find out if there's a choice to be made between ending this planet or saving it.

This book, then, is devoted to replacing fear with fact, to proving that knowledge is power, and to offering the sincere reassurance that, even if the world should end tomorrow (and it won't), God will still keep us safe for all eternity, just as He promised when He created us.

Sylvia C. Browne

End of Days

CHAPTER ONE

The End of Days:
Why This Book Now?

Please don't leap to the conclusion that there's something urgently meaningful about the timing of this book. I promise you have time to read it more than once before the end of life on Earth.

Actually, there are several reasons this book was at the top of my priority list. Many of them I'll discuss as the book progresses, in the context of the chapters themselves. But one of the most important reasons is also one of the most obvious: I've never been asked more often than I have been in the past couple of years about when the end of days is coming. What about the Second Coming of Christ? When should we start looking for Him? Or is He here now? Is the Antichrist here already, and if not, when will he show up and who will he be? How literally should we take the biblical book of Revelation? Is the Rapture really going to happen? Nostradamus made it sound as if the Antichrist is among us right now, and the Mayan calendar specifically says the world will end in 2012, which is right around the corner. Is that true? If not, when *will* it end, and how?

When a subject comes up repeatedly among my clients, I naturally start wondering what's causing the "coincidence." (You do know there's no such thing, right?) And I have a couple of theories. One is that maybe, in the wake of all the millennium Y2K hysteria—and let's face it, *hysteria* is not too strong a word—there's a general feeling of having dodged a bullet, as if we somehow escaped an inevitability of total destruction and we're now living on borrowed time. Another related theory is that apocalyptic books, articles, television specials, and church sermons were wildly popular at the turn of this century, and even though the (imaginary) end-of-the-world crisis has come and gone, the unease from all that information has continued to simmer in people's minds and is finally boiling over. Still another is, as you'll see in upcoming chapters, I know that as this century progresses, the spirituality on our planet is going to grow to unprecedented strength and power, as we humans, at long last, start paying attention to the spirit voices inside us, reminding us that, yes, it actually is time to get our affairs in order. That spiritual growth is already under way, causing more and more of my clients to think beyond their day-to-day lives and search for answers to the bigger questions of their own spirits' futures and the futures of every spirit currently residing on a planet that, according to countless rumors, isn't going to last forever.

Several of these clients were experiencing the same understandable fear: they couldn't get past the feeling that the end of days must be approaching or it wouldn't be on their minds to begin with. For them, and for all of you who share that fear, I'm here to offer concrete proof that we citizens of the world in the year 2008 aren't the first to feel sure that the end is so obviously imminent. Some historically verifiable examples:

In approximately 2800 BC an Assyrian tablet was etched with the words, "Our earth is degenerate in these latter days. There are signs that the world is speedily coming to an end."

The Bible quotes Jesus as saying to his apostles, in Matthew 16:28, "There be some standing here which shall not taste of death till they see the Son of Man coming in his kingdom." And in Matthew 24:34, "This generation shall not pass till all these things be fulfilled." Both statements were taken by some to mean that Jesus would return before the apostles died.

In around AD 90 the fourth pope, St. Clement I, predicted that the end of the world was imminent.

In the second century a Christian sect called the Montanists believed that Christ would return during their lifetime and that the New Jerusalem would "come down out of heaven from God." And one Roman leader was so certain that the end of the world was only two days away that he and his followers disposed of their houses and all other belongings in preparation.

In AD 365 a bishop named Hilary of Poitiers made the public declaration that the world would be ending during that year.

Sometime between AD 375 and 400, a student of Hilary of Poitiers, St. Martin of Tours, braced his followers for a definite end of the world no later than AD 400. He also stated, "There is no doubt that the Antichrist has already been born."

The middle of the first millennium saw a number of doomsday predictions, including that of Hippolytus of Rome, the "antipope," who temporarily defected from the Catholic Church to protest its reformation, whose math convinced him that the Second Coming would occur six thousand years after Creation, or AD 500.

Sextus Julius Africanus, a Roman theologian, was sure that the end of days was destined to occur in AD 800.

Christians annually celebrate the Feast of the Annunciation on March 25, the day on which the Virgin Mary was visited by an angel and told she would give birth to the Christ child. In 992, Good Friday, the acknowledgment of Christ's Crucifixion, coincided with the Feast of the Annunciation, an occasion that for centuries had been anticipated as the arrival of the Antichrist, closely followed by the end of the world according to the book of Revelation.

The year 1000 provided an opportunity for the first official millennium hysteria. It was further fueled by the disinterment of Charlemagne's body, since, according to legend, an emperor would someday rise from the grave to do battle with the Antichrist.

Many authorities who had loudly proclaimed that the world would definitely end in the year 1000 explained their obvious miscalculation by "realizing" they should have added Jesus's life span to their prediction. As a result, the world would now reliably end in 1033.

A priest named Gerard of Poehlde, on the other hand, was sure that Christ's thousand-year reign had actually begun with Constantine's rise to power. Therefore, Satan would escape his bondage in 1147 and overtake the Church.

John of Toledo, a Spanish astrologer, became convinced that a specific alignment of planets in 1186 was a sign that the world would be destroyed by famine, earthquakes, catastrophic storms, and volcanoes.

According to an Italian mystic and theologian named Joachim of Fiore, the Antichrist was already incarnated on Earth and would be defeated by King Richard I of England, heralding the great rebirth of the world in 1205.

In 1260, Brother Arnold, a Dominican monk, predicted an impending end of the world in which he would call upon Jesus to judge Church leaders around the world, during which Jesus would reveal the Pope to be the long-awaited Antichrist.

Pope Innocent III announced 1284 as the end of the world, arriving at that date by adding 666 years, from the book of Revelation, to the date when Islam was founded.

In 1300, a Franciscan alchemist named Jean de Roquetaillade published such predictions as the arrival of the Antichrist in 1366, to be followed no later than 1370 by a millennial Sabbath, and Jerusalem becoming the center of the world.

A society called the Apostolic Brethren, which believed that they were the new Roman Church authority, were sure that in 1307 all Church clergy, including the Pope, would be killed in a great war that would lead to the Age of the Spirit.

Czechoslovakian archdeacon Militz of Kromeriz insisted that the Antichrist would reveal himself by 1367, ushering in the end of the world.

In 1496, many Church leaders began anticipating the Apocalypse based on the fact that it would soon be fifteen hundred years after the birth of Christ.

Astrologers predicted a massive global flood that would destroy the world in 1524.

Reformist Hans Hut made it his business to round up 144,000 elect saints to prepare for Jesus's return in 1528.

A German visionary named Melchior Hoffman prophesied the Second Coming of Christ in 1533 and the reestablishment of Jerusalem in Strassburg, Germany. Following the lead of the book of Revelation, he believed that 144,000 faithful would be saved, but the rest of the world would perish in flames.

Astrologer Richard Harvey foresaw the Second Coming of Christ at noon on April 28, 1583.

According to Dominican monk, poet, and philosopher Tomasso Campanella, the sun and Earth were destined to collide in 1603.

In 1661, a group called the Fifth Monarchy Men decided that by trying to overtake parliament they could prove to God that faith was alive and well on Earth and it was time for Jesus to return and claim his rightful millennial kingdom.

Christopher Columbus wrote *The Book of Prophecies* in the late fifteenth and early sixteenth centuries, including a prediction that the end of the world would happen in 1658.

When the Russian Orthodox Church went through a reformation, a group that called itself the Old Believers broke from the Church and began its own ultraconservative, ultratraditional faith. Included in that faith was a belief that the world would end in 1669. Between 1669 and 1690 nearly twenty thousand Old Believers burned themselves to death rather than be faced with the Antichrist.

Seventeenth-century Baptist Benjamin Keach saw the end of the world happening in 1689, as did French prophet Pierre Jurieu.

Puritan minister and renowned witch hunter Cotton Mather predicted the end of the world three separate times, the first being 1697.

On October 13, 1736, many braced for a great global flood predicted by William Whitson, a British theologian and mathematician.

The renowned mystic Emanuel Swedenborg was told by angels that the world would end in 1757.

Charles Wesley, one of the founders of Methodism along with his brother John, was sure that doomsday would occur in 1794. John Wesley disagreed with his brother about the timing of the world's end and stated that it was actually in 1836 that the "beast of

Revelation" would rise from the sea and the new age of peace would begin.

Presbyterian minister Christopher Love braced his followers for a massive earthquake that would destroy the earth in 1805.

In 1814, a sixty-four-year-old prophet named Joanna Southcott claimed to be pregnant with the baby Jesus and that he would be born on December 25, 1814. It so happened that instead of giving birth that day, she died, and an autopsy revealed, to no one's surprise, that she wasn't pregnant after all.

Margaret McDonald, a fifteen-year-old Christian prophet, declared in 1830 that the Antichrist was Robert Owen, a cofounder of socialism.

It was a widely held belief that the Crimean War of 1853–56, during which Russia and France fought over which nation would seize Palestine from the Ottoman Empire, was actually the great battle of Armageddon prophesied in Revelation.

Sixteenth-century British prophetess Ursula Southeil, who became famous and/or infamous as Mother Shipton, is quoted as saying, "The world to an end shall come/in eighteen hundred and eighty-one." It's since been theorized that the majority of Mother Shipton's prophecies were actually written and attributed to her after she died, and that "her" 1881 prediction was the work of her publisher, Charles Hindley.

Joseph Smith, founder of the Church of Jesus Christ of Latter-day Saints, aka the Mormon Church, is quoted as saying, "I prophesy in the name of the Lord God, and let it be written—the Son of Man will not come in the clouds of heaven till I am eighty-five years old." Smith would have turned eighty-five years old in 1890. As luck would have it, he'd been dead for almost fifty years by then.

At the end of the nineteenth century, physicist William Thomson, aka Lord Kelvin, asserted that there was only enough oxygen in the atmosphere to last humankind for three hundred years, and therefore the human race was destined to be suffocated to death.

In anticipation of the November 13, 1900, doomsday they predicted, more than one hundred members of a Russian cult called the Brothers and Sisters of the Red Death killed themselves on that date.

On December 17, 1919, according to seismologist and meteorologist Albert Porta, a specific conjunction of six planets would create a magnetic current so powerful that it would cause the sun to explode and engulf the earth.

Herbert W. Armstrong, who founded the Worldwide Church of God in the early 1930s, believed the Rapture would occur in 1936 and that only members of his church would be drawn into Jesus's arms in the sky to be saved. When 1936 came and went with no Rapture, he shifted his prophecy to the year 1975.

Bible teacher Leonard Sale-Harrison toured North America to lead a series of prophecy conferences during the 1930s, assuring his audiences that the world would end in 1940 or 1941.

When the state of Israel was founded in 1948, there were many Christians who believed that the final predicted event leading to the Second Coming of Christ had been satisfied.

Astrologer Jeane Dixon predicted that this planet would be destroyed on February 4, 1962, by the force from a planetary alignment.

Moses David, founder of a religious group called the Children of God, predicted that, probably in 1973, a comet would hit the earth and eliminate all life in the United States. He then revised that prediction to include a battle of Armageddon in 1986 and the Second Coming of Christ in 1993.

In 1987, author and educator José Argüelles warned that unless 144,000 people gathered in specific places throughout the world on August 16–17 to honor the Harmonic Convergence, Armageddon was inevitable.

NASA scientist Edgar C. Whisenant's book entitled *88 Reasons Why the Rapture Could Be in 1988* sold more than four million copies.

Fundamentalist author Reginald Dunlop predicted that since September 23, 1994, was the last encoded date in the Great Pyramid of Giza, the world was clearly not meant to survive beyond that date.

The year 1999 was thought to be the definite end of the world by, to name just a tiny handful, the Seventh-day Adventists, the Jehovah's Witnesses, linguist Charles Berlitz, spiritual historian Father Charles Moore, retired electronics engineer Gerald Vano, spiritualist Eileen Lakes, rocket scientist Hideo Itokawa, "Messianic Rabbi" Michael Rood, televangelist Jack Van Impe, former NASA consultant Richard C. Hoagland, and former businessman, politician, and cult leader Joseph Kibweteere.

Michael Travesser, born Wayne Bent, is a former sailor and now the spiritual leader of a New Mexico sect called The Lord Our Righteousness Church. Travesser claims to be the long-awaited messiah and predicted that the world would end with an apocalyptic event at midnight, October 31, 2007.

The Lord's Witnesses, a British sect, after an intricate series of calculations based on biblical prophecies, concluded that the United Nations would take over the world in the lunar month preceding April 24, 2001, which happens to be 666 Hebrew months following the founding of the United Nations. Since that didn't happen, it's probably safe to assume that we don't need to worry about their second prediction—that after the United Nations gains global control, Armageddon will begin on March 21, 2008, killing three-quarters of the world's population.

We'll be discussing many more end-of-days prophecies throughout this book, and even then we won't have scratched the surface of the human search for just one reliable hint about what's to become of us. I'll be weighing in with my own predictions as well, not to add to the confusion but because I do think there are aspects to the end of days that aren't addressed often enough, while other aspects get far more attention and credibility than they deserve.

Three General End-of-the-World Categories

While it's not true in each and every theory of the end of days that we're about to explore, it's certainly true in general that end-of-the-world theories and prophecies fall into one of three categories: millennialism, apocalypticism, and messianism.

Millennialism, which is obviously a derivation of the Latin word for one thousand years, revolves around a belief that the earth will be subjected to a series of devastating catastrophes after which the "saved" of humankind will spend eternity in the bliss of paradise. At first glance it might appear that millennialism means we should all fly into an end-of-days panic at the turn of a millennium, as if there's some implied doom in any calendar date that has three zeroes in it. And according to history, we weren't the first global population to fall into that mental and emotional trap.

In reality, though, as we'll explore in depth in Chapter 3, millennialism has its roots in the biblical book of Revelation, the apostle John's prophecy (or nightmare, or political essay) on the end-time. In chapter 20 John writes:

> *Then I saw an angel coming down from heaven, holding in his hand the key of the bottomless pit and a great chain. And he seized the dragon, that ancient serpent, who is the Devil and Satan, and bound him for a thousand years, and threw him into the pit, and shut it and sealed it over him, that he should deceive the nations no more, till the thousand years were ended ... Then I saw thrones, and seated on them were those to whom judgment was committed. Also I saw the souls of those who had been beheaded for their testimony to Jesus and for the word of God, and who had not worshiped the beast or its image and had not received its mark on their foreheads or hands. They came to life again, and reigned with Christ a thousand years. The rest of the dead did not come to life again until the thousand years were ended ... And when the thousand years are ended, Satan will be loosed from his prison and will come out to deceive the nations ... to gather them for battle ... And they marched up over the broad earth and surrounded the camp of the saints and the beloved city; but fire came down from heaven and consumed them, and the devil who had deceived them was thrown into the lake of fire and brimstone where the beast and the false prophet were, and they will be tormented day and night for ever and ever.*

It's not hard to read those verses and understand why the cultural significance of a thousand-year period exists to this day, whether or not those who believe in that significance and are concerned about it have any awareness of the Bible at all.

11

Apocalypticism is a theory of the end of days that involves God channeling His wrath toward the earth with a series of cataclysmic events, then judging each human according to their deeds on Earth and finally taking His rightful place again as the Creator and Supreme Ruler of heaven and Earth.

Probably the deepest roots of apocalypticism are found in the Old Testament book of Daniel, as illustrated in the following excerpts:

I saw in my vision by night, and behold, the four winds of heaven were stirring up the great sea. And four great beasts came up out of the sea. The first was like a lion and had eagle's wings. Then as I looked its wings were plucked off, and it was lifted up from the ground and made to stand upon two feet like a man; and the mind of man was given to it. And behold, another beast, a second one, like a bear. It was raised up on one side; it had three ribs in its mouth between its teeth, and it was told, "Arise, devour much flesh." After this I looked and lo, another, like a leopard, with four wings of a bird on its back; and the beast had four heads; and dominion was given to it. After this I saw in the night visions, and behold, a fourth beast, terrible and dreadful and exceedingly strong; and it had great iron teeth; it devoured and broke in pieces, and stamped the residue with its feet . . .

A king of bold countenance, one who understands riddles, shall arise. His power shall be great, and he shall cause fearful destruction, and shall succeed in what he does, and destroy mighty men and the people of the saints . . .

An anointed one shall be cut off, and shall have nothing; and the people of the prince who is to come shall destroy the city and the sanctuary. Its ends shall come with a flood, and to the end there shall be war; desolations are decreed . . . and upon the wing of abominations shall come one who makes desolate, until the decreed end is poured out on the desolator . . .

And there shall be a time of trouble . . . and many of those who sleep in the dust of the earth shall awake, some to everlasting life, and some to shame and everlasting contempt. And those who are wise shall shine like the brightness of the firmament; and those who turn many to righteousness, like the stars for ever and ever.

And then there's messianism, which revolves around the premise that at the end, a messiah (from the Hebrew word meaning anointed), or savior, will appear on Earth to lead the faithful and devout people of God from the suffering and oppression they've endured into an eternity of divine, peaceful joy. While the most obvious examples of messianism are found in the Christian and Jewish faiths, we'll discover that there are other great religions as well that continue to look for a messiah to arrive before the end-time and deliver them safely into God's arms.

Among the reasons I believe humankind has been historically fascinated with the subject of the end of the world is that, despite God's promise over and over again that we're all genetically eternal, our conscious minds find the earthly pattern of "beginning, middle, and end" much easier to grasp than the concept of eternity. We hear the fact that on the Other Side there is no such thing as time, that nothing exists but a perpetual "now," and we understandably find it impossible to imagine, since on Earth we're virtually obsessed with time. We're told by brilliant theologians and spiritual leaders that this planet is not our real Home at all, that our blissful, sacred

Home is waiting patiently for us to leave our bodies and get back there where we belong, but we can't consciously remember having lived anywhere else, so how can somewhere else be "Home"?

All things considered, then, it can't be too surprising that a "beginning, middle, and end"–oriented society—consumed with the notion of time-related questions like "when?" and "how much longer?" and clinging fiercely to Earth in the mistaken belief that it's the only Home we know—wants answers, always has and always will.

Whether or not the following chapters provide answers or simply raise more questions, at least we'll know that just by asking, we're expressing curiosity about a subject as timeless as humankind itself.

CHAPTER TWO

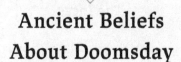

Ancient Beliefs
About Doomsday

It's an undeniable facet of human nature that we somehow feel more secure if we know the end of a story, especially when it's *our* story. We don't like loose threads. We don't like unanswered questions or unsolved mysteries or uncertainty. We don't like not knowing what's waiting for us around the corner and, if it might hurt us, what we can do to avoid it or prepare for it. It's the inherent belief of humankind that "forewarned is forearmed." And we've held that belief for as long as humankind has existed on Earth.

Ancient civilizations were every bit as determined as we are to piece together the puzzle of the end of our story on this earth, and the story of this earth itself. They used the same tools we use today to figure it out: some combination of their religious beliefs, their bodies of experience, and the information they had at hand. Their doomsday scenarios ranged from the optimistic to the truly depressing—again, no different from our current "sophisticated, educated" theories except for the vocabularies and details. But when it's

15

all said and done, they were as earnest as we are to come up with the truth about what may be the first question ever asked on this planet: "How does our story end?"

The Incas

The Inca empire of South America was once the largest nations on Earth, sprawling two thousand five hundred miles along the Andes mountain range. The origins of the Incan civilization are cloaked in myth and mystery, preserved mostly through the spoken word from one generation to the next when their recorded history was destroyed, and their vast wealth pirated, by Spanish conquistadors in 1532.

The earliest Inca were artisans, hunters, farmers, and indisputably brilliant builders and engineers. Before the invention of the wheel, they built fourteen thousand miles of roads intended for nothing but foot travel, and there was such integrity to the roads' construction that some of them are still intact today. Probably the most extraordinary monuments to the architectural genius of this ancient society are the Incan pyramids, temples, observatories, and other structures that continue to fascinate visitors from all over the world—also still intact, impeccably designed, and, in many cases, incomplete, mute reminders of a civilization suddenly decimated for the sake of power and greed.

The heart of Incan lives, language, and religion was their sense of oneness with nature. Nature, they believed, was the handiwork of the Sun God, of whom they considered themselves to be direct descendants. With elaborate festivals they thanked the Sun God for their harvests, they prayed to the Sun God for bountiful crops, and they implored the Sun God not to leave them, his children, during solstices when the earth and the sun are farthest from each other. They believed in reincarnation and, when the holiest of rituals were being held, carried mummies of their ancestors to the ritual sites so they could share their most reverent moments with those who preceded them.

When the Incan civilization was destroyed by the Spanish invasion in the 1500s, a small tribe of refugees known as the Q'ero escaped to isolated villages in the high Andes. They live there to this day, with their elders and shamans teaching their ancient language, history, traditions, and prophecies to generation after generation of heirs to the once vast and brilliant Incan world.

In 1996, a Q'ero tribal leader, a revered shaman, and other tribal elders honored the United States with a historic visit in which they shared a wealth of information about the Inca, including the prophecies of their ancestors. Among those prophecies is an eloquent passage describing the Incan beliefs about the end of the world:

The new caretakers of the Earth will come from the West, and those that have made the greatest impact on Mother Earth now have the moral responsibility to remake their relationship with her, after remaking themselves.

The prophecy holds that North America will supply the physical strength, or body; Europe will supply the mental aspect, or head; and the heart will be supplied by South America.

The prophecies are optimistic. They refer to the end of time as we know it—the death of a way of thinking and a way of being, the end of a way of relating to nature and to the earth.

In the coming years, the Incas expect us to emerge into a golden age, a golden millennium of peace.

The prophecies also speak of tumultuous changes happening

in the earth, and in our psyche, redefining our relationships and spirituality.

The next pachacuti, or great change, has already begun, and it promises the emergence of a new human after this period of turmoil.

As if to guide their listeners toward this prophesied golden age, the Q'ero added the following in parting:

Follow your own footsteps.
Learn from the rivers,
the trees and the rocks.
Honor the Christ,
the Buddha,
your brothers and sisters.
Honor your Earth Mother and the Great Spirit.
Honor yourself and all of creation.
Look with the eyes of your soul and engage the essential.

The Maya

The Mayan civilization is thought to have been born in the Yucatan Peninsula in about 2600 BC and thrived through approximately AD 1300. They excelled brilliantly in astronomy, hieroglyphic writing, science, mathematics, art, farming, weaving, architecture, and creating highly technical, intricate calendar systems, to name only a handful of their gifts. Their society was formed around a hierarchy of class distinctions, with kings and priests of clearly defined territories as their ruling class and a vast peasant population as the lowest class providing slave labor, and the Maya ultimately spread throughout what is now Mexico, El Salvador, Belize, Honduras, and Guatemala.

Almost as fascinating as the Mayan civilization itself is the mysterious abruptness with which it vanished. It was as if a complex, sophisticated society of fifteen million people simply walked away from their lives one day and never came back, leaving nothing but deserted cities and abandoned architectural masterpieces in their wake. To this day there are no definitive answers but many theories about what happened so suddenly and with such finality. Some believe a series of droughts forced the population into a choice between relocating or starving to death. Some believe a revolt of the peasants/slaves left a handful of nobility to work the land with no experience or expertise, and as a result the society essentially imploded from its inability to support itself. Some believe that the overzealous agricultural pursuits of the Maya led to everything from severely depleted soil to an ultimately destructive "slash and burn" approach to clearing the rich Central American forests for farmland, so that this civilization literally robbed their land of its ability to sustain them. Some believe deadly viruses destroyed the Maya, while others believe that overpopulation was to blame. Again, the only thing about the vanishing of the Maya that experts seem to agree on is that no one knows with any certainty what really happened to those fifteen million people around AD 1300. And, because the Spanish conquistadors made it their practice to kill the Mayan priests and nobility and to burn Mayan books and records when they invaded Central and South America, it's likely that no one ever will.

What has survived after all these centuries is the fascinating and very complicated Mayan calendar, which consisted of cycles of 260 days, each day having one of twenty names represented by its own symbol. The days of the Mayan calendar were numbered one through thirteen, but since there are twenty names, after a thirteen-day period was finished, the next day was numbered "one" again. The calendar also kept track of a solar year in which the months were named, and following the eighteen months of their solar year, they included a five-day month in which the days were thought to be unlucky and, as a result, were not given names.

I won't pretend to be able to decipher the intricacies of the Mayan calendar. Instead, I'll focus on an element of it that everyone can decipher: it ends on December 21, 2012, which has been a source of concern for those who are aware of it and are determined to find specific "doomsday" predictions to be fearful of. But the Mayan culture never intended to imply that a cataclysmic end of the world would be happening on 12/21/12, or the winter solstice of 2012. Their prophecy is that on that date the world will be making a transition from one age into another, and it is humankind's choice whether that transition will involve violently dramatic changes or will simply evolve with graceful, peaceful tranquility.

Every 5,125 years, the Maya say, one cycle on Earth ends and another begins. There are five cycles, each of them with characteristics roughly corresponding to our passage through a twenty-four-hour day. The first of Earth's cycles is comparable to a galactic morning, when our solar system is just approaching the central light of the universe. The second cycle, midday, is our solar system's closest proximity to the universal central light. The galactic afternoon, or third cycle, occurs as our solar system begins moving away from the central light. The fourth cycle corresponds to the night, when our solar system is at its farthest from the central light. And the fifth cycle is that "darkest before the dawn" period, as our solar system pulls away from being devoid of light and moves toward its first cycle of morning again.

The prophecy of the Mayan calendar is that our solar system was slowly ending its fifth cycle, its "darkest before the dawn," in 1987, moving toward the morning of the first cycle that will officially arrive in 2012. And how we use the brief years between now and then will determine whether the impending birth of the "morning" is destructive or productive. Negativity, violence, greed, cruelty, the lust for power, and the systematic desecration of nature and its sacred inhabitants will guarantee a catastrophic transition from the fifth cycle back to the first, while a global nurturing of kindness, respect, unity, charity, and a celebration of the sanctity of our natural planet and all its living creatures can, by our choice, create a cyclical transition into a truly golden age. So 2012, the Maya promise, will mark a profound change among us on Earth. What kind of change it will be is entirely up to us.

ATLANTIS

According to the Maya, the end of the Fourth World (cycle) and the beginning of the Fifth occurred on August 12, 3113 BC, with the sinking of the great continent Atlantis.

Atlantis was first referred to in literature by the brilliant Greek writer and philosopher Plato (428–348 BC). His dialogues *Timaeus* and *Critias* include characters who refer to Atlantis as a place "somewhere outside the Pillars of Hercules" that was destroyed by a tsunami or an earthquake about nine thousand years earlier. According to the dialogues, Socrates had been talking about ideal societies, in response to which both Timaeus and Critias tell Socrates a story that is "not a fiction but a true story," about a conflict between the ancient Athenians and the Atlanteans.

Literally since Plato, the Atlanteans, their origins, and their civilization have been the subject of exhaustive legend, research, and exploration. A variety of sources are convinced that they were extraterrestrials who came to Earth more than fifty thousand years ago. They were of human shape, fair skinned, and were giants, averaging from seven to ten feet tall. Excavations have unearthed skeletons that confirm the existence of a race that grew to and exceeded that height.

The life span of the Atlanteans was said to be about eight hundred years, which might explain how they had time to develop their astonishing technology, light-years beyond ours even today.

They were able to achieve perfect control of the weather. And because they were virtually addicted to stimulation, they took particular delight in conjuring violent storms for their amusement. They could also create geological "special effects," from volcanic fountains to geysers to mineral venting, and, possibly most breathtaking of all, they invented something called "threshold technology"—a device that converted what we think of as the time-space continuum into a source of energy.

One of the most common sources of energy on Atlantis, though, was the crystal, which we know has the ability to both transfer and amplify a beam of light directed at its facets. The Atlanteans simply expanded on that premise, using crystal energy not only for basic energy needs similar to ours but also to enhance their crops, their own physical development, their mental capacity, and their youthful appearance despite their dramatically advanced ages.

Atlantis held a great fascination for the brilliant psychic and prophet Edgar Cayce, whom we'll discuss at length in a later chapter. In one of his many detailed descriptions of life on Atlantis, he referred to a Tuaoi Stone, or Firestone, a great crystal that was housed in a building with a retractable roof so that it could be "charged" by the sun, moon, stars, general atmosphere, and Earth itself. It was able to transmit energy to power all forms of craft on, above, and below the continent; send audio and video transmissions over vast distances; and wirelessly provide heat and light anywhere they were needed throughout Atlantis.

According to Cayce and other scholars, the Great Crystal that had so blessed the Atlanteans ultimately led to their demise. As they became more obsessed with their own power, and the power of this unprecedented energy source they'd created, they began "tuning" the crystal to higher and higher frequencies, until it literally caused mountains to implode, volcanos to erupt, and the continent to fall in on itself and submerge into the Atlantic Ocean.

While there won't be unanimous agreement that Atlantis existed until it rises again during this century—and it will—there have certainly been indications that it wasn't as imaginary as skeptics prefer to believe.

A 1954 issue of *Geologic Society of America Bulletin*, for example, reporting on the exploration of the summit of the submerged Mid-Atlantic Ridge, reads:

The state of lithification of the limestone suggests that it may have been lithified under subaerial (i.e., above water, on land surface) conditions and that the sea mount (summit) may have been an island within the past 12,000 years.

And then there was a series of satellite photographs shown and described in the March 1996 issue of *Discover* magazine:

*The Midatlantic Ridge snakes down the center of that ocean off
Greenland to the latitude of Cape Horn . . . Under South Africa,
the Southwest Indian Ridge shoots into the Indian Ocean like a
fizzling rocket, or perhaps like the trail of some giant and car-
toonish deep-sea mole.*

But maybe the Maya gave the existence of Atlantis all the confirmation it will ever need by considering its demise so historically
monumental that, in their most sacred beliefs, it ended a world.

The Aztecs

Another powerful and now extinct civilization of warriors was the
Aztec empire, centered in the Valley of Mexico beginning in approximately the twelfth century AD. Their early history wasn't
committed to paper but was passed along from one generation to
the next through word of mouth, so there's no way of tracing their
inception with any great accuracy. Legend suggests that the Aztecs
came from the island of Aztlan. But there is speculation about
whether or not Aztlan is a place that actually existed; it is as shrouded
in myth and mystery as Camelot and, some would say, the lost
continent of Atlantis. And further speculation suggests that Aztlan
was very real and that it was located in Utah, or perhaps Colorado.
If that were proven to be true, it would mean that the Aztecs
may have arrived in the Valley of Mexico from what is now the
western United States, and the whole notion of undocumented im-
migrants from south of the border might have to be rethought—
they might have a case that they're descendants of native Americans
who are even more entitled to be here than the rest of us. The Aztec

Migration Scrolls describe Aztlan as an island in a lake, inhabited by great flocks of herons, with seven temples in the center of the island. Some say the seven caves of Utah's Antelope Island might confirm its identity as the ancient Aztlan, while others are convinced Aztlan will ultimately be found in or near Florida. But Jesus Jauregui of the National Institute of Anthropology and History in Mexico, states without equivocation, "Aztlan is a mythical place, not a historical one." So the debate and occasional search expeditions continue.

What's not in doubt is that the Aztecs were led into the Valley of Mexico in the fourteenth century by Tenoch, their chieftain. He was subsequently ordered by the war god Huitzilopochtli to take his uncivilized, barbaric people to the refuge of a marshy island in Lake Texcoco, where they were to build a city and honor Huitzilopochtli with human sacrifices, a practice not uncommon among the Aztecs. Tenoch's city was built under these swampy, difficult conditions, and it was called Tenochtitlan. From those harsh beginnings the Aztec empire took root and thrived until around 1520, when the Spanish conquistadors, led by Cortez, invaded and conquered the Aztecs and virtually every other civilization in their path, destroying every trace of the Aztecs in the process.

Like the Maya, the Aztecs developed a very complex calendar system based on astronomy, designed not only to mark their holidays and short periods of time but also to track the cycles of humankind through our progress on Earth. They embraced what they referred to as the Legend of the Five Suns, each of which represented periods in their own history. During the life of each sun, the earth thrives in peace, prosperity, and new life. But when a sun dies, the world descends into catastrophic turmoil, with the gods renewing the earth through the process of first destroying it.

The first sun was called the Sun of Precious Stones, and it was destroyed by jaguars at the command of Tezcatlipoca, the god of night and god of the north. Because he was believed to carry a magic mirror that emitted smoke and killed his enemies, Tezcatlipoca was also called "god of smoking mirror."

The second sun was known as the Sun of Darkness, upon whose death life was destroyed by a massive hurricane that was summoned by Quetzalcoatl, the creator and god of the sky.

The third sun, the Sun of Fire, and all life it nourished, was exterminated by fire sent by Tezcatlipoca.

The fourth sun was the Sun of Water, at whose death a huge flood destroyed the world. This flood came from Tlaloc, the god of rain and fertility, whom the Aztecs so feared that they sometimes drowned their children as sacrifices to him.

According to the Aztec calendar, we're now in the Sun of Movement, presided over by Tonatiuh, the Sun God and the Rising Eagle, who will ultimately cause earthquakes so cataclysmic that they will split the world in half.

Native Americans

It's been said of the true Native Americans for thousands of years, and it's still true today: ask them to tell you their story, and they'll tell you about nature and their reverent relationship with Mother Earth.

The origin of Native Americans is a subject of debate, and there's no real consensus among experts about where they came from. Theories range from a prehistoric migration from Asia via the Bering Strait to an escape from the destruction of the lost continent

Atlantis. But there's no question that in 1492, when Christopher Columbus arrived by mistake on San Salvador Island, the natives who greeted him, with their brown skin and black hair, convinced him that he'd successfully completed his journey to India. He referred to them as "Indios," Spanish for Indians, and the cultural name was born.

The many tribes of the Native American nations each have their own histories, languages, rituals, and prophecies. But they all revolve around their spiritual connection to the earth and their belief that the survival of our planet is dependent on humankind's learning to treat all things in nature with nothing short of reverence.

THE HOPI PROPHECIES

There's a wonderful story that's been circulating since 1959, and was told in part in a 1963 publication called *Book of the Hopi*. The story goes that in 1958 a minister named David Young was driving through the stifling heat of the desert when he saw a Native American elder beside the road. The Reverend Young stopped to offer the elder a ride, and the elder silently accepted. The two rode along wordlessly for a few miles, until the elder began to speak.

"I am White Feather," he said, "a Hopi of the ancient Bear Clan . . . I have followed the sacred paths of my people, who inhabit the forests and many lakes in the east, the land of ice and long nights in the north, and the places of holy altars of stone built many years ago by my brothers' fathers in the south . . . I have heard the stories of the past, and the prophecies of the future. Today, many of the prophecies have turned to stories, and few are left. The past grows longer, and the future grows shorter."

The Reverend Young listened raptly as the extraordinary man continued:

My people await Pahana, the lost White Brother [whose return to Earth marks the beginning of the Fifth World, according to Hopi legend], as do all our brothers in the land. He will not be like the white men we know now, who are cruel and greedy. We were told of their coming long ago. But still we await Pahana . . .

The Fourth World shall end soon, and the Fifth World will begin. This the elders everywhere know. The Signs over many years have been fulfilled, and so few are left.

This is the First Sign: we are told of the coming of the white-skinned men, like Pahana, but not living like Pahana men who took the land that was not theirs. And men who struck their enemies with thunder.

This is the Second Sign: our lands will see the coming of spinning wheels filled with voices. In his youth, my father saw this prophecy come true with his eyes—the white men bringing their families in wagons across the prairies.

This is the Third Sign: a strange beast like a buffalo, but with great long horns, will overrun the land in large numbers. These White Feather saw with his eyes—the coming of the white men's cattle.

This is the Fourth Sign: the land will be crossed by snakes of iron.

This is the Fifth Sign: the land shall be crisscrossed by a giant spider's web.

This is the Sixth Sign: the land shall be crisscrossed with rivers of stone that make pictures in the sun.

This is the Seventh Sign: you will hear of the sea turning black, and many living things dying because of it.

This is the Eighth Sign: you will hear of many youth, who

wear their hair long like my people, come and join the tribal nations to learn their ways and wisdom.

This is the Ninth and Last Sign: you will hear of a dwelling place in the heavens, above the earth, that shall fall with a great crash. It will appear as a blue star. Very soon after this, the ceremonies of my people will cease.

These are the Signs that great destruction is coming. The world shall rock to and fro. The white man will battle against other people in other lands—with those who possessed the first light of wisdom. There will be many columns of smoke and fire such as White Feather has seen the white man make in the deserts not far from here. Only those which come will cause disease and a great dying.

Many of my people, understanding the prophecies, shall be safe. Those who stay and live in the places of my people also shall be safe. Then there will much to rebuild. And soon—very soon afterward—Pahana will return. He shall bring with him the dawn of the Fifth World. He shall plant the seeds of his wisdom in their hearts. Even now the seeds are being planted. These shall smooth the way to the emergence into the Fifth World.

The Reverend Young and White Feather the elder never saw each other again after they parted ways that day, but the extraordinary experience and the prophecies that emerged from it have become a part of the modern Hopi legends. And according to most interpreters, the signs White Feather prophesized are imagery of the following:

The First Sign: "thunder" is a reference to guns.

The Second Sign: an obvious reference to the arrival of settlers in covered wagons.

The Third Sign: "strange beast like a buffalo but with great long horns" is a reference to the proliferation of longhorn cattle in the newly settled Southwest and West.

The Fourth Sign: "snakes of iron" is a reference to railroad tracks.

The Fifth Sign: "a giant spider's web" is a reference to power lines.

The Sixth Sign: "rivers of stone" are concrete highways, and "pictures in the sun" are very likely the mirages created by the hot sun beating down on the pavement.

The Seventh Sign: "the sea turning black" is a reference to the destructive rash of oil spills.

The Eighth Sign: "youth who wear their hair long" and "join the tribal nations to learn their ways and wisdom" is a reference to the hippie movement of the late 1960s and early 1970s, and the hippies' interest in both Native American and Indians and their cultures.

The Ninth Sign: "a dwelling place . . . above the earth that shall fall with a great crash" is a reference to the 1979 disaster of the space station Skylab plummeting to Earth.

THE NAVAJO END OF DAYS

The wonderful Navajo writer Ray Baldwin Louis beautifully described his people's prophecies and beliefs in a short story called "When All Things Come to an End." It reads, in part:

> *The birds will all settle to the ground; the badger will grow horns, the wind will blow without ceasing; the people will intermarry with other tribes as well as within clans; there will be*

voices, but they will be too weak for many to hear; the enemy will penetrate the stronghold of The People, the Navajo. And this will be when all things come to an end, when all generations come to meet.

But first, four major events will occur; a mule will give birth of its own kind; a baby with white hair and with teeth will be born speaking; there will be a famine and many will suffer; lightning will whip across the sky from the east to the west. These things will be signs that all things are coming to an end . . .

Old men and women who foresaw the future taught their children to hold on to their traditions and not forsake their religion, for the day was coming when they would lose it if they were not careful . . .

I heard [the medicine man's] prophecy that his medicine bag will no longer have strength as in the past, there will be no regard for it, and it will be thrown away. The People will be lost without its presence, and they will have no power against the enemy.

According to interpretations of ancient Navajo chants, the "Time of the End" won't bring the destruction of this planet. Instead, when the Great Spirit returns to Earth, His arrival will mean the dawn of a new day. He will breathe new life into the spirit of the people; all people on Earth will "melt into one" and love each other; humankind will no longer be threatened or affected by the world's afflictions and perils; and a joyful new religion will spread throughout the planet that is devoid of all the prejudices and arbitrary laws of the previously existing religions that have been passed along through the ages.

THE LAKOTA

Humankind's imperative need to begin cherishing our planet in order to avoid its destruction is beautifully expressed in an excerpt from a Lakota prophecy. It refers to the Star People, whom many tribes believe to be their ancient extraterrestrial ancestors, and to the Sacred Mother, their name for the earth:

The Star People that you call meteorites will come to this earth in answer to the Mother's call for help. You see, we are all relations. So the Star People are beings, and they are the planets, and the other bodies in the heavens as well.

The Sacred Mother is screaming for life and the meteorites will hear her cries and answer her call for help. They will hit the earth from the heavens with such force that many internal things will happen as well as external. The earth will move as a result of the impact. This will cause the sacred fire that is the source of all life to the Mother to move through her body.

The rains will change their fall and the winds will alter their course and what has existed for three hundred years will no longer exist. And where there is summer, there will be fall. And where there is fall, there will be winter. And where there is winter, there will be spring.

The animals and plants will become confused. There will be great plagues that you do not understand. Many of these plagues are born from your scientists whose intentions have gone awry. Your scientists have let these monsters loose upon the land. These plagues will spread through your waters and through your blood and through your food because you have disrupted the natural chain through which your Mother cleanses herself.

Only those who have learned to live on the land will find

sanctuary. Go to where the eagles fly, to where the wolf roams, to where the bear lives. Here you will find life because they will always go to where the water is pure and the air can be breathed. Live where the trees, the lungs of this earth, purify the air. There is a time coming, beyond the weather. The veil between the physical and the spiritual world is thinning.

THE LOWER BRULE SIOUX TRIBE

Brave Buffalo of the Brule Sioux offers an eloquent prophecy about the sanctity of nature and how we're endangering ourselves by compromising it, and about the eternal cycle of life in this universe:

It is time for the Great Purification. We are at a point of no return. The two-legged are about to bring destruction to life on earth. It's happened before, and it's about to happen again. The Sacred Hoop shows how all things go in a circle. The old becomes new; the new becomes old. Everything repeats. White people have no culture. Culture is having roots in the earth. People without culture don't exist very long because Nature is God. Without a connection to Nature, the people drift, grow negative, destroy themselves.

In the beginning we had one mind, and it was positive, a thing of beauty, seeing beauty everywhere.

THE CHEROKEE PROPHECIES

The Cherokee are an intensely spiritual civilization who believe that each morning humankind should give thanks to the Creator, to Mother Earth, to Father Sky, to all their relatives and to the four sacred directions: the East, guardian of the nourishment and healing that grows from the earth; the South, guardian of the wind, sky, and air; the West, guardian of the life-giving element of water; and the North, guardian of fire. To the Cherokee, all things are connected, all things have a purpose, and all things contain the divine spark of life. They believe that when we die, our souls may be selected to keep living as ghosts in the earthly dimension, who can be seen when needed. There is no death, in other words, just an eternal cycle bestowed by our Creator, the Great Spirit.

The Cherokee deeply treasure the prophecies of their elders, passed along from one generation to the next in their rich oral tradition by the revered tribal elders. Among those prophecies:

+ A black ribbon would be built across the land, and a bug would begin to move across the ribbon—a sign that very soon the earth would shake so violently that the bug would be thrown into the air and begin to fly. (The black ribbon is thought to be the first roadways, and the bug moving across it is thought to be the first automobile, mass-produced for the first time in 1908. Soon after, the violent shaking of the earth, the First World War, "threw the bug into the air," i.e., initiated the widespread usage of the airplane.)

+ A cobweb would be built across the world through which people would talk. (A few hundred years after this prophecy, telephone lines reached into virtually every corner of the globe.)

+ A sign of life in the east would turn on its side and be surrounded by death, and one day the sun would rise in the west, bringing a second violent shaking of the earth even worse than the first. (The cross, a sign of life, was turned on its side to form the Nazi swastika, the symbol of the Japanese empire was the rising sun, and the earth's "violent shaking" in the Second World War was indeed even worse than the first.)

+ Gourds of ashes would fall from the sky, creating more ash from all living things in their path and preventing new growth for years to come. (The atom bomb fit that description perfectly.)

+ The eagle would someday fly in the night and land on the moon. (In 1969 the safe arrival on the moon of the Apollo 11 spacecraft was announced by astronaut Neil Armstrong to the NASA control room with the simple words, "The eagle has landed.")

+ A house would be built in the east that would welcome all the peoples of the earth, and it would sparkle like the sun reflecting off the desert mica. (The United Nations, founded in 1945, moved its original headquarters from San Francisco to a shimmering golden glass monolith in New York City in 1952.)

+ If we miss our opportunities after the first two shakings of the earth to come together as a human family of brothers and sisters—as we have—the earth will be shaken for a third time, more violently than ever before.

At the core of the Cherokee prophecies, though, is the belief that their souls come from the stars in the form of Starseeds to be born into the human race and bring light and knowledge, and that those same souls return to the heavens to become stars when they die. In fact, some Cherokee elders teach that all their ancestors were travelers from the legendary star cluster Pleiades, a cluster of stars that form the "eye" of the "bull" formed by the Taurus constellation.

The six stars of the Pleiades that are visible to the naked eye are said to be lost boys who, according to Cherokee myth, were severely punished by their mothers for returning home from playing later than their curfew allowed. The seven boys, deciding their angry mothers must no longer love or want them, ran away from home again, returning to the hills outside the village where they always played. They began to dance in a circle, for hours on end, chanting, "Spirits of our people, take us into the sky so blue. Our mothers no longer want us, and we wish to be with you."

Back in the village, the boys' mothers discovered their sons were missing and quickly headed to the hills to retrieve them. They arrived to see the boys dancing and chanting, and suddenly one of the mothers cried out, "Look! They're leaving the ground! If we don't hurry they'll be gone forever!"

The boys were dancing above their mothers' heads by the time their frantic mothers reached them. Each mother jumped in panic, trying to grab and hold onto her son, but only one was successful, barely getting a grip on her boy's foot. She pulled him to the ground so hard that a hole formed where he landed and the earth closed around him. She fell to her knees beside him, weeping, and then looked up to see that the other six boys were dancing into the clouds and disappearing into the sky.

Legend says that every day for the rest of their lives the seven mothers, who never smiled or laughed again or knew another moment of joy, returned to the spot where they lost their sons. Six mothers looked to the heavens for their sons, while the seventh knelt to the ground, soaking the earth with her tears.

And then one day six mothers saw that stars had formed in the sky exactly where their sons had vanished. Those stars, they say, are the Pleiades. The seventh mother looked to the spot where the earth had swallowed up her son and gaped at the tiny pine tree than had begun to grow.

To this day the Cherokee consider the pine to be one of their most sacred trees, and it is their custom to look to the Pleiades to pray.

The Pleiades star system is also prominent in one of the most treasured and famous Cherokee prophecies, the Prophecy of the Rattlesnake, a sign in the heavens that is evolving toward the end of the Cherokee calendar in the year 2012. Needless to say, it's no coincidence that the Cherokee and Mayan calendars end in the same year. It's simply the result of the northern migration of the Mayans and the Aztecs from Central and South America to settle in the United States. But the heart of the Prophecy of the Rattlesnake is rooted in the wisdom and teachings of the ancient Cherokee elders.

Just as all cultures interpret the stars and their movement into zodiac systems and prophecies, the Cherokee see a zodiac of their own, ancient and cherished, the story of eternity, or Time Untime, written across the face of the universe. The universe itself is made of crystal, and four rawhide ropes hang from it to suspend the great island known as Earth. While the outline of the heavens retains its shape in the sky, there is movement within the Cherokee zodiac that makes it seem alive, breathing and transforming itself to foretell the fate of Earth against the backdrop of the eternal cycle of life.

There are thirteen constellations in the Cherokee zodiac, most of them designs of animals. And prominent among them is the Constellation Rattlesnake, in which a prophecy is written. The Rattlesnake has a head, and the tip of its tail is the revered Pleiades system. Between the head and the tail is a body that twists and slithers in a kind of sidewinding movement. There are fifty-two scales on its mouth, the number fifty-two being an essential part of the very sophisticated Cherokee calendar. The outline of the Rattlesnake remains stationary, but various forms and shapes that appear and disappear on the snake itself are read as signs of the past, present, and future of the universe.

From July 16 to 22, 1994, astronomers around the world were mesmerized as more than twenty fragments of a comet called Shoemaker-Levy 9 collided with the planet Jupiter's southern hemisphere, a phenomenon predicted in the Cherokee calendar. In their mythology, these comet fragments were actually an attack on Jupiter by the fingers of a fearsome, bloodthirsty witch named Spearfinger. Spearfinger was forty feet tall, had skin made of stone that no weapon could penetrate, and brandished a long, razor-sharp finger with which she could stab her victims in the back, remove their livers without leaving a single mark, and eat them in one gulp. Whether it was a fragmented comet crashing into Jupiter or a cruel assault by Spearfinger, this spectacle was considered to be a sign for the Cherokee nation to wake up from its complacency and become vigilant.

This collision with Jupiter was also prophesied to wake Orion, the celestial hunter, who would resume his pursuit of the maidens of the Pleiades, while Jupiter and Venus would do battle against each other, signalling the time of the Cherokee UKU's, or high priests. In the years 2004 through 2012, a phenomenon is foreseen in the heavens in which feathers will appear on the head of the Rattlesnake. Its glowing eyes will open. It will grow wings, hands, and arms, and its hands will hold a bowl of blood. The seven rattles of its tail will resemble the roots of a tree, "the Pleaides Tree of the Beginning." This will correspond to the transit of Venus, a very rare alignment of Earth, Venus, and the sun in which it appears from Earth as if Venus is crossing the face of the sun. A Venus transit occurred on June 8, 2004, and astronomers predict it will happen again on June 5-6, 2012.

And it's in the year 2012 that the Cherokee calendar, like the Mayan calendar, comes to an end.

To some ancient Indian civilizations of South America, "the end" marks the coming of Quetzalcoatl, the God of Creation, often depicted as a feathered Serpent much like the feathered Rattlesnake the Cherokee watch for in the night sky as a sign that the end is near.

To the Cherokee, "the end" in the year 2012 signifies that all will be reborn.

THE SIOUX NATION AND THE WHITE BUFFALO WOMAN

To the Sioux, there is no more sacred living thing than a white buffalo. On the rare occasions when a white buffalo calf is born—most recently in 1994, 1996, and 2005—Native Americans from throughout the North American continent make pilgrimages to pay homage to what they consider to be a newborn sign of hope and healing and fulfilled prophecies. "For us," they've said, "this would be something like coming to see Jesus lying in the manger."

The legend of the White Buffalo Woman is a beautiful and significant cornerstone of the Sioux heritage itself. Crow Dog, a Sioux medicine man, described her importance by saying, "Before she came, people didn't know how to live. They knew nothing. The Buffalo Woman put her sacred mind into their minds."

The story has passed from one Sioux generation to the next through their elders and medicine men for countless hundreds of years, expressing the deeply spiritual nature of a traditionally warrior tribe and their prophecies for the earth and all its people.

Legend has it that one summer, longer ago than anyone can trace, the sacred council of the Sioux nation, called the Oceti-Shakowin, gathered to camp together out of concern for their people. Despite a steady bright sun, there was no game for the braves to hunt, and people throughout the land were starving. Each day the council sent out scouts to search for game animals, but none could be found.

Among the assembled council was Chief Standing Hollow Horn, in his own camp circle with his tribe, the Without Bows, or Itazipcho. One morning as dawn broke Standing Hollow Horn dispatched two of his young braves to hunt. The Sioux had no horses, so the two braves proceeded on foot, and after finding nothing in the surrounding area, they decided to climb a high hill nearby for a better view of the vast countryside.

As they scaled the green hill they noticed a figure moving toward them from very far away. Because it seemed to be floating rather than walking, they were sure a holy person was approaching them. The closer it came the more clearly they could see that the small form was a radiantly beautiful woman. Her dark eyes seemed electrified with power. Her long black hair cascaded freely down her back, with the exception of a single strand tied gracefully back with buffalo fur. Circles of red were painted onto her cheekbones, dramatically contrasting with her transluscent brown skin. Her gleaming white buckskin clothing was embroidered with sacred designs in colors that were unearthly in their intensity. She carried a large bundle in her hands.

The two braves stared at her, transfixed. Then one of them, overwhelmed by her beauty and wanting to possess her, reached to touch her. But she was far too sacred to tolerate being an object of earthly desire, and the young impulsive man was suddenly consumed by a black fiery cloud and reduced to nothing but a pile of incinerated bones.

The other scout remained silent, in pure respectful awe, as the

White Buffalo Woman turned her dark eyes to him and said, "I bring your people a message from the Buffalo Nation, along with sacred gifts for this difficult time. Return to your camp and help prepare for my arrival. Your chief should construct a medicine lodge, supported by twenty-four poles, and make it holy to receive me."

The young brave hurried back to Chief Standing Hollow Horn and the others at the camp circle, breathlessly repeating the instructions of the White Buffalo Woman. Excited, they built the medicine lodge with twenty-four poles for support, performed rituals to sanctify it, and then waited eagerly for the most reverent arrival.

Four days later they saw the sun glinting off of the radiant white dress of a small approaching form, and before long they found themselves in the divine presence of the White Buffalo Woman. They respectfully bowed their heads as Chief Standing Hollow Horn stepped forward to greet her, his voice hushed with awe. "Sister," he said, "we are honored that you have come to help us."

She motioned for them to follow her into the medicine lodge and taught them to build a sacred altar of earth in the center of the circle of twenty-four poles. At her direction they smoothed the red earth of the altar, in which she traced a holy emblem. She then stood before the chief and opened the bundle she'd brought with her. She reached into it and withdrew a sacred pipe, called a *chanunpa*, which she held out to the gathered crowd. Its stem was in her right hand. Its bowl was in her left. The *chanunpa* has been held in that exact way by the Sioux people since that day.

The White Buffalo Woman filled the bowl of the pipe with tobacco made of bark and walked around the medicine lodge four times, representing the sacred circle that does not end, like the path of the great sun. Next she lit the pipe with a dry buffalo chip she ignited from the altar fire, creating the flame that does not end, known as *petaowihankeshini*, which would forever be passed on from one Sioux generation to the next.

Again she held the pipe toward the gathered crowd. "This holy pipe," she told them, "holds all of us together, the Sacred Beneath and the Sacred Above. As your feet stand planted in the earth and the stem of the pipe reaches toward the sky, you become a living prayer, a bridge that joins the earth, the sky and all living things, with two legs and four, with wings and with no limbs at all, as well as the trees, the wildflowers and the grasses that bend in the moving spirit of the wind. All are related. All are one family, joined together in the form of this pipe. The stone of its bowl is both the buffalo and the flesh and blood of the red man. The buffalo stands on four legs, honoring the four directions of the universe and the four ages of man. He was created in the west to hold back the waters when the Great Spirit made the world. Each year he loses a hair. In each of the four ages he loses a leg. The Sacred Circle will be done when the hair and legs of the buffalo are gone and he can no longer stop the waters from covering the earth."

She then presented the pipe to Chief Standing Hollow Horn and said, "Respect this sacred pipe and it will see you safely to the end of the road. I shall come back to see you once in every generation."

With that she left the camp in the same direction from which she had come. The chief and his people watched in reverence as she floated toward the setting sun. Suddenly, some distance away, they saw her stop and roll over, turning into a black buffalo. She rolled over a second time and became a brown buffalo. Rolling over again, she changed to a red buffalo. The fourth time, she rolled over and was transformed into a beautiful white buffalo calf before she disappeared beyond the horizon.

The moment she had vanished, great herds of buffalo miraculously appeared, sacrificing themselves to the Sioux hunters so that the people would be nourished and survive. From that day forward, the buffalo, beloved kin of the Sioux nation, provided all that was needed, from the meat to feed them to the skins to clothe and house them to the bones from which tools could be made.

Many Native American tribes embrace and revere a list of Sacred Instructions given to them by the Great Spirit at the time of Creation. It's their belief that following these instructions can perpetuate the Sacred Hoop, the Creator's intended cycle of life, that will end only if we allow it. This list is so eloquently simple that I can't help but think—shame on any of us who can't be bothered to follow these instructions, no matter what our culture or religion, because they're so little to ask in exchange for the possibility of saving our Earth:

+ Take care of Mother Earth and the other colors of man.
+ Respect Mother Earth and creation.
+ Honor all life, and support that honor.
+ Be grateful from the heart for all life. It is through life that there is survival. Thank the Creator at all times for all life.
+ Love, and express that love.
+ Be humble. Humility is the gift of wisdom and understanding.
+ Be kind with one's self and with others.
+ Share feelings and personal concerns and commitments.
+ Be honest with one's self and with others.
+ Be responsible for these sacred instructions and share them with other nations.

The Aborigines

The Aborigines of Australia are believed to have been on this earth for more than eighteen thousand generations. They've been nomadic hunters and gatherers since their ancient beginnings, traveling and living in clans, orally passing along their culture, traditions, and beliefs to their progeny. The Aborigines revere nature. They revere their elders and their ancestors. They're deeply committed to maintaining a balance between the practical and the spiritual aspects of their lives. And they embrace a gorgeous mythology called the "Dreamtime," which lies at the heart of their faith.

The Dreamtime, woven through their lives in the most sacred and the most mundane ways, is at its core that time of creation when the Aborigines' spirit ancestors moved through bare, unsanctified land and gave it its physical form and its sacred laws.

There was the Rainbow Serpent, who slithered across the earth forming rivers and valleys with its massive body.

There was Bila, the Sun Woman, whose fire lit the world.

There were Kudna and Muda, two lizardlike creatures who destroyed Bila. They were then so frightened by the darkness they'd created by killing the Sun Woman that they began hurling boomerangs into the sky in all directions, trying to bring back the light. Kudna's boomerang flew into the eastern sky and a brilliant ball of fire appeared. The ball of fire slowly crossed the sky and vanished again beyond the western horizon, and day and night were born.

The countless spirits and stories of the Aborigines' mythology form the exquisite foundation on which this ancient civilization built its reverence for all of nature and their belief that it is humankind's privilege to live among and serve such hallowed creations.

Dreamtime is a reality of the Aborigines' past, present, and future. It isn't something that happened and was completed a very long time ago. It's a continuing consciousness and responsibility, with tragic consequences if it's ignored.

A prophecy from an Australian Aborigine tribal elder named Guboo Ted Thomas, orally preserved until it was finally committed to writing, reflects their profoundly simple faith and their vision of the end of days.

> *I was in Dreamtime.*
> *I see this great wave going.*
> *I tell people about this wave.*
> *It wasn't a tidal wave.*
> *This was a spiritual wave.*
> *So, to me, I believe that the Dreamtime is going to be that.*
> *I believe the revival is going to start in Australia when we're Dreaming.*
> *It's the hummingbee that I'm talking about.*
> *And love.*
> *We've got to learn to love one another.*
> *You see, that's really what's going to happen to the earth.*
> *We're going to have tidal waves.*
> *We're going to have earthquakes.*
> *That's coming because we don't consider this land as our Mother.*
> *We've taken away the balance, and we're not putting back.*
> *I look at the bush, and those trees are alive.*
> *They're not dead, they're alive.*
> *And they want you to cuddle them.*

Norse Mythology

There are few more colorful and more intricate doomsday visions than the Norse mythology of the end of the universe, or Ragnarok, which means "doom of the gods." Norse mythology had its origins in the pre-Christian northern Germanic, European, and Anglo-Saxon beliefs of Scandinavia. And when it came to Ragnarok, the "doom" in "doomsday" was an understatement.

First, the legend goes, Fimbulvetr arrives—a three-year nonstop blast of the most brutal winter imaginable. During Fimbulvetr, probably because of their relentless misery, people begin feuding and fighting with each other and abandoning any semblance of morality. It's the first sign that the end is on its way.

Next, a wolf arrives. The wolf's name is Skoll, and upon his arrival he devours the sun. His brother Hati promptly eats the moon, and the whole world is plunged into darkness.

Three cocks crow, summoning the gods and the earth's giants and even waking the dead.

The earth begins rumbling with massive earthquakes, toppling mountains and freeing a ship of the dead from the bowels of hell, with Loki at its helm, his son Fenrir, another wolf with a massive mouth, at his side.

The sea roils violently and Jormungand, a colossal, venomous serpent, writhes enraged as he heads toward the Norwegian battleground called Vigrid, where the final war on Earth will be fought by the gathering combatants. Jormungand poisons the sea, the land, and the sky with his venom and he makes his way to Vigrid.

The tsunami waves of the sea liberate the ship *Naglfar* from its moorings, and, commanded by the giant Hymir, the vessel full of giants sails toward the battlefield.

From the south comes another army of giants, led by Surt the fire giant, who carries a sword hotter than the sun that scorches everything in his path as he and his legions march to Vigrid.

Heimdall, the Viking god of light, sees the warriors approaching from all directions and sounds his horn to summon the gods. Odin, the supreme Norse deity; Thor, the god of thunder; Odin's sons; and the other heroic gods of the heavens arrive on the battlefield in golden armor, riding magnificent white steeds.

The assembly continues until all the gods, giants, and demons have arrived for mortal combat on the massive, doomed Norwegian expanse.

Odin and Fenrir instantly attack each other, a fight that continues for a very long time.

Thor attacks Jormungand, the venomous serpent, and kills him. But the serpent's poison slowly and very surely kills Thor.

Surt the fire giant finds the unarmed god of sun and rain, Freyr, and quickly destroys him.

Tyr, the one-handed god of heroic glory, does battle with the monstrous hound Garm, who guards the entrance to the underworld. They both die in combat.

Loki and Heimdall, mortal enemies for as long as anyone can remember, square off, and neither survives.

Finally the battle between Odin and Fenrir ends, with the vicious wolf managing to seize and swallow Odin.

Enraged, Odin's son Vidar kills Fenrir with his bare hands.

Surt, in a final insane explosion of violence, begins hurling fire all around him until the entire world is burning and anyone still living dies in the flames.

And all the land on Earth sinks into the sea.

But that's not quite the end.

There's a very special tree in heaven, the World Tree, or Yggdrasil. This tree possesses the essence of every living thing that ever was and ever will be on Earth. And while the world was being destroyed, two people—Lif and Lifthrasir—managed to survive by hiding in the welcoming branches of Yggdrasil. A few of the gods survive as well, including Odin's brother and sons and Thor's sons.

So that when a beautiful, cleansed new world rises from the sea, and the sun and moon are reborn, Lif, Lifthrasir, and the surviving gods are there to welcome it and happily take up residence there. This new world, devoid of evil and thriving in peaceful harmony, is gradually repopulated with Lif and Lifthrasir's descendants.

As for the inhabitants of the previous world, who either died in Surt's fire or drowned as countries and continents sank, their souls never ceased to exist. They might be living among the gods in Grimli, or in the splendor of Brimir, if they were good people during their lifetimes. If they weren't, they'll be exiled to Nastrond, a hideous nightmare of a dungeon, the walls and roofs of which are made entirely of live, very poisonous snakes.

I have to admit, I chuckled more than once about the preposterous series of events the Norse came up with to describe the end of the world. Then I remembered what I was taught about the Apocalypse in Catholic school and wondered if the Norse might have chuckled a little themselves at stories about locusts wearing crowns, pouring out of a bottomless pit to torture anyone who didn't have the sign of God on their forehead. Suddenly I didn't feel I had as much room to laugh about giant tsunami-causing snakes, and wolves that could eat the sun, and I realized we humans always have been and always will be just trying to piece together the unknowable as best we can.

CHAPTER THREE

Christians, Jews, and Catholics on the End of Days

World religions are among my passions. I studied them in college, and I've studied them ever since. I'm sure the seeds of this passion were planted during my childhood, when the family influences of Christianity, Judaism, and Catholicism blended to create my open-minded, loving curiosity about the variety of ways in which humankind defines, reaches out to, and worships our Creator. The differences between these three beautiful faiths are every bit as fascinating as the similarities, from their traditions to their interpretations of historic events to their beliefs about how, or if, life on Earth will end.

Christianity

The word *eschatology* is defined in the *Merriam-Webster's Collegiate Dictionary* as "a branch of theology concerned with the final events in the history of the world or of humankind; a belief concerning death, the end of the world, or the ultimate destiny of humankind; specifically, any of various Christian doctrines concerning the Second Coming, the resurrection of the dead, or the Last Judgment." And several aspects of Christian eschatology are still being debated by theologians around the world, millennia after the Bible was written.

Both the Old Testament and the New Testament of the Bible are filled with prophecies about the end of days, so it might seem logical that such a wealth of information would lead to clarity. But a lot of the Bible's apocalyptic verses and passages were deliberately disguised in imagery and symbolism because the atmosphere in which they were written wasn't exactly welcoming to "seers and soothsayers." There might also have been some reluctance to be specific about the date and time of the end of days because of Jesus's words in Matthew 24:36:

But of that day and hour no one knows, not even the angels of heaven, nor the Son, but the Father alone.

So there are almost as many interpretations of the apocalyptic passages in the Bible as there are scholars who've studied them.

For one of a hundred examples, it's very common these days to read and hear "experts" warning that, because of the current wars, the frequency of natural disasters, and the general (perceived) decline of morality and religion, the end of days is obviously right around the corner. What else could all these "unmistakable signs" possibly mean?

Saint Cyprian of Carthage felt exactly the same way, and wrote about it, in approximately AD 250. Before him, in the first century

AD, Christians were sure the end of the world would occur during their lifetime because the world had become so self-destructive. It's probably safe to say that at least a few "experts" in every generation since before Christ have managed to find and interpret enough unmistakable signs of the impending end of days to attract an audience.

I should mention, I guess, that I've not just read, I've *studied* all twenty-six versions of the Bible. Based on those studies, I've put together a very simplistic list of what I'll call the "highlights" (for lack of a better term) of the biblical end-of-days prophecies:

- All good Christians who've devoted their lives to the Lord will be risen from the earth to be embraced in the sky and saved for eternity by Jesus. This joyful reunion with Christ among the clouds is called the Rapture.

- A powerful Antichrist will sign a seven-year covenant of peace with Israel. This covenant launches God's punishment for all the evil on Earth, and the world is afflicted with wars, plagues, natural disasters, and other forms of great suffering. This period of terrible chaos is called the Tribulation.

- The Antichrist, in total disregard of his own peace treaty, gathers his militia and attacks Israel. He has an image of himself sculpted in the temple and demands that it be worshipped in his honor.

- The seven-year Tribulation ends with an attack on Jerusalem by the Antichrist and his armies. In what the Bible refers to as the battle of Armageddon, Jesus now returns and destroys the Antichrist along with all his soldiers and all his followers.

- Ultimately, the Antichrist is defeated forever, and Christ makes way for the New Jerusalem and a world where there is no more evil, no more suffering, and no more death.

One of countless debates about that sequence of events, by the way, is whether the Rapture takes place before, during, or after the Tribulation. Please don't interpret my list of highlights as an effort to weigh in on that debate. In fact, in my opinion, I think the biblical references to the Rapture were meant to be taken symbolically, not literally. For example:

For the Lord himself will descend from heaven with a cry of command, with the archangel's call, and with the sound of the trumpet of God. And the dead in Christ will rise first; then we who are alive, who are left, shall be caught up together with them in the clouds to meet the Lord in the air; and so we shall always be with the Lord. (1 Thessalonians 4:16–17)

Again, beautiful imagery, but as long as the outcome is the same—that "we shall always be with the Lord"—I don't know that any of us will be disappointed if our trip Home doesn't actually involve being caught up in the clouds to meet the Lord in the air.

The biblical book of Revelation is most often associated with the prophesied end of days. It's filled with similar imagery, much of which has become legendary but not clearly understood, and none of which, I'm convinced, is meant to be taken literally. A perfect example is the mythical Four Horsemen of the Apocalypse.

According to the sixth chapter of Revelation, at the end of days, God will exact a series of judgments on humankind, each series more devastating than the one before it. The first series is the "seven seals," and the first four of those seven seals are the horsemen.

And I saw when the Lamb opened one of the seven seals . . . And I saw, and behold, a white horse: and its rider had a bow; and a crown was given to him, and he went out conquering and to conquer . . .

When he opened the second seal . . . out came another horse, bright red; its rider was permitted to take peace from the earth, so that men should slay one another; and he was given a great sword . . .

When he opened the third seal . . . I saw, and behold, a black horse, and its rider had a balance in his hands; and I heard what seemed to be a voice . . . saying, "A quart of wheat for a denarius, and three quarts of barley for a denarius; but do not harm oil and wine!"

When he opened the fourth seal . . . I saw, and behold, a pale horse, and its rider's name was Death, and Hades followed him; and they were given power over a fourth of the earth, to kill with sword and with famine and with pestilence and by the wild beasts of the earth. (Revelation 6:1–8)

The most common translation: the first of the four horsemen, the white horse, brings the Antichrist. The second incites devastating warfare. The third inflicts famine. And the fourth kills with more warfare and famine, plagues, and vicious animal attacks. The Four Horsemen of the Apocalypse, all part of the prelude to the end of days, more dramatic imagery but clearly not intended to be read literally.

The fifth of the seven seals, I should add, is the martyred souls of Jesus's followers; the sixth seal unleashes a massive, devastating earthquake; and the seventh seal contains the seven trumpets, which cause:

- ✦ fire and hail that destroys plant life
- ✦ "something like a great mountain, burning with fire" (Revelation 8:8) crashing into the sea, destroying marine life and ships at sail
- ✦ similar destruction of the earth's lakes and rivers
- ✦ the darkening of the sun and the moon
- ✦ a plague of "demonic locusts"
- ✦ an equally demonic army
- ✦ the arrival of seven angels holding the seven bowls containing the wrath of God

Again, this series of punishments from God leading to the end of days is progressive. So the seven bowls of the seven angels are the most dire of all:

Then I heard a loud voice from the temple telling the seven angels, "Go and pour out on the earth the seven bowls of the wrath of God."

So the first angel went and poured his bowl on the earth, and foul and evil sores came upon the men who bore the mark of the beast [Antichrist] and worshiped its image.

The second angel poured his bowl into the sea, and it became like the blood of a dead man, and every living thing died that was in the sea.

The third angel poured his bowl into the rivers and the fountains of water, and they became blood.

The fourth angel poured his bowl on the sun, and it was allowed to scorch men with fire. Men were scorched by the fierce heat, and they cursed the name of God who had power of these plagues, and they did not repent and give him glory.

The fifth angel poured his bowl on the throne of the beast, and its kingdom was in darkness . . .

The sixth angel poured his bowl on the great river Euphrates, and its water was dried up . . .

The seventh angel poured his bowl into the air, and a great voice came out of the temple, from the throne, saying, "It is done!" And there were flashes of lightning, loud noises, peals of thunder, and a great earthquake such as had never been since men were on the earth. (Revelation 16:1–17)

Again, in the end, following this terrifying series of events (the Tribulation), and the battle of Armageddon that is the ultimate, bloody war of good versus evil, and Satan being bound and sealed in the bottomless pit for a thousand years, there is, according to Revelation 21:1, "a new heaven and a new earth; for the first heaven and the first earth had passed away, and the sea was no more."

A FEW WORDS ABOUT THE BOOK OF REVELATION

Whatever your beliefs about the end of days, I hope that if they're primarily based on the biblical book of Revelation, you'll keep those potentially disturbing pages in accurate historical context.

There's not even unanimous agreement among scholars and theologians about the actual author of the book of Revelation. But for the sake of argument, let's assume it was written by the apostle John, who's most often given credit for it.

John was born in Galilee around AD 10 to 15, the son of Zebedee and Salome. He and his brother, James, were pursuing their father's trade as fishermen when they became disciples of Jesus. It was John who stayed with Jesus in the Garden of Gethsemane on the eve of the Crucifixion, John who stayed with the dying Christ when all the other disciples had left, and John to whom Jesus entrusted the care of his mother Mary after Jesus died.

It was also John who, along with the apostle Peter, was convicted of "activities subversive to the authority of the land"—specifically, the Roman emperor Nero and his successor Domitian, who declared themselves "lord and god" and persecuted anyone who refused to comply with that declaration. Nero, in fact, was responsible for the first documented case of governmentally supervised persecution of Christians. John was sentenced to a four-year banishment to Patmos, an island in the Aegean Sea. It was in a cave in the Patmos prison that John is said to have written the book of Revelation.

So there was John, locked away in what was undoubtedly a torturous dungeon. He was in the later years of his life. His brother James and his friend Peter, both fellow disciples of Christ, had been martyred. His existence must have been bleak, cruel, and desolate from one day to the next. Assuming he really did author the book of Revelation, how surprising can it be that much of its imagery is every bit as bleak, cruel, and desolate?

It's worth adding that John's temper was a widely known facet of his generally passionate personality, and he was enraged about the politics of the day. He'd seen a transition from a tolerant atmosphere toward the fledgling religion of Christianity to such violent intolerance that Christians who refused to disavow their faith were routinely executed, crucified, or fed to the lions for sport. So why would a man imprisoned for heresy against a political regime that demanded to be worshipped write a book meant to be taken literally, exalting the ultimate power of God, that could only make his life even more of a nightmare?

One of the analyses of Revelation I have the least patience with is the exercise of reducing its symbolism to a word game. For example, Revelation 13:2 reads, "And the beast I saw was like a leopard, its feet were like a bear's and its mouth was like a lion's mouth." I've heard more than one theologian point out the "obvious" reference to Russia because of the phrase "its feet were like a bear's." Now, admittedly, Revelation wasn't added to the Bible until three hundred years after the fact, but even then I doubt that anyone was starting the preliminary plans for a country called Russia, let alone deciding that its symbol would be a bear. Why John would be making even a subtle reference to Russia for the benefit of readers in the first century AD I can't begin to imagine.

Let's also remember that none of the original manuscripts of the New Testament, including Revelation, still exist. And no written manuscript of Revelation from the first century still exists. Much of what we know of the New Testament comes from Greek manuscripts dating from the second to the eighth centuries, translated again and again, including writings from early theologians recording from memory what they'd read or been told about the actual text of the New Testament. Revelation is one of several books that exists only in fragments, heavily edited passages, and translations of translations. I'm not sure how taking it literally is even a consideration without John's original manuscript to work with—again, assuming John is its author to begin with.

As you read or reread the book of Revelation, I hope you'll keep all of that in mind, and consider a couple of other theories as well:

Many biblical scholars consider it to be a fiery political essay—understandable considering John's circumstances and his temperament.

Others theorize that it was a series of tortured dreams committed to paper.

"The beast" referred to so often throughout the book of Revelation, and associated with the number 666 that has come to symbolize evil, is commonly thought to be Nero, whose name, in the Hebrew form of numerology called gematria, translated to the number 666.

The wonderful prophet and clairvoyant Edgar Cayce interpreted Revelation to have nothing to do with outward battles but instead to be an expression of the spiritual struggle between good and evil that every one of us experiences.

In the end, I think the greatest danger in examining Revelation too literally is the likelihood of missing its ultimate message: that no matter how vicious and powerful the "beast" or how deadly the battle, in the end the victory, glory, and joy belong to God.

> *And I heard a great voice from the throne saying, "Behold, the dwelling of God is with men. He will dwell with them, and they shall be His people, and God himself will be with them; he will wipe away every tear from their eyes, and death shall be no more, neither shall there be mourning nor crying nor pain and more, for the former things have passed away."* (Revelation 21:3-4)

A FEW WORDS ABOUT THE BOOK OF DANIEL

The book of Daniel is often referred to as the Old Testament version of Revelation because of its apocalyptic prophecies. And, like Revelation, it's surrounded by its share of controversy.

The young Daniel was captured by the Babylonian army during its attack on Jerusalem in 605 BC. He spent the rest of his life in Babylon, serving the royal court—primarily King Nebuchadnezzar—throughout the seventy-two-year duration of the Babylonian empire as a seer, prophet, and dream interpreter.

Jesus spoke of Daniel to his disciples on the Mount of Olives, written of in Matthew 24:15–16:

So when you see the abomination of desolation of which the prophet Daniel spoke, standing in the holy place (let the reader understand), then let those who are in Judea flee to the mountains.

The "abomination of desolation" to which Jesus referred two hundred years after it occurred was a specific reference to the Greek ruler Antiochus Epiphanes who, in 167 BC, erected an altar to Zeus, the supreme ruler of the Greek gods, in the Jewish temple in Jerusalem, then sacrificed a pig on the altar in Zeus's honor. Daniel 9:27 refers to that same event:

And he shall make a strong covenant with many for one week; and for half of the week he shall cause sacrifice and offering to cease; and upon the wing of abominations shall come one who makes desolate, until the decreed end is poured out on the desolator.

The general concensus among theologians is that the "desolator" who will perform the abomination of turning a sacred temple of God into a place of worship for himself will be revealed as the Antichrist. The "covenant of one week" will actually be a seven-year peace treaty with Israel, which the Antichrist will break before it ends with his own form of the abomination of desolation in a Jerusalem temple. It's no coincidence that that same broken seven-year covenant of peace by the Antichrist is referred to in the book of Revelation as one of the signs that the Second Coming of Christ is at hand and the end of days is imminent.

In fact, there are many similarities between the imagery of the Old Testament book of Daniel and the New Testament book of Revelation, all of them referring to the same sequence of apocalyptic events or, as Daniel put it, the "end of history": the resurrection of the dead, the judgment of humankind according to the deeds they accomplished on Earth, and the embrace into heaven or the banishment to hell of humankind based on that judgment.

You'll read in the chapter on prophets that Sir Isaac Newton, brilliant mathematician and student of the Bible, calculated a year for the end of days based on the information alluded to in Daniel 12:6–13:

> *And I said to the man clothed in linen, who was above the waters of the stream, "How long shall it be 'til the end of these wonders?" The man . . . raised his right hand and his left hand toward heaven; and I heard him swear by him who lives forever that it would be for a time, two times, and half a time; and that when the shattering of the power of the holy people comes to an end all these things would be accomplished . . . And from the time that the continual burnt offering is taken away, and the abomination that makes desolate is set up, there shall be a thousand two hundred and ninety days. Blessed is he who waits and comes to the thousand three hundred and thirty-five days. But go your way 'til the end; and you shall rest, and shall stand in your allotted place at the end of days.*

There are those who believe that the book of Daniel was written in the sixth century by Daniel himself. Others argue that it was actually written many centuries later, by an anonymous author or series of authors, and attributed to Daniel to lend credibility to the work. The skeptics raise such issues as:

+ The text of the book of Daniel contains several Greek words. The Greek occupation of Israel occurred in the fourth century BC, while the book of Daniel is generally thought to have been written in the sixth century AD.

+ The last chapter of Daniel states that after the final judgment, humankind will ascend to heaven or descend into hell. But at the time of Daniel's life and writings, the Jewish belief was that all the dead went directly to Sheol. In Hebrew, Sheol is a grave or pit beneath the earth where the dead would exist in a conscious eternal limbo of hopeless, joyless separation from God. The Greek concepts of heaven and hell weren't introduced into Israel until hundreds of years after Daniel's life and purported writing.

Whether the book of Daniel is a work of fiction written under a pseudonym or the true work of a prophet acknowledged by Christ on the Mount of Olives, its ultimate message, identical to that of Revelation, is that in the end, evil will be defeated and God will reign eternally over all who worship Him.

A FEW WORDS ABOUT THE APOSTLE PAUL

An extraordinary example of Jesus's ability to redirect a life is the story of Saul, whose Latin name was Paul. In Acts 22:1–8 and Acts 26: 4–11 he shares his history:

I am a Jew, born at Tarsus in Cilicia, but brought up [in Jerusalem] at the feet of [the renowned teacher] Gamaliel, educated according to the strictest party of our religion. I have lived as a Pharisee, in the manner of the law of our fathers, being zealous for God as you all are this day.

Accordingly, I was convinced I ought to do many things opposing the name of Jesus of Nazareth for which reason I persecuted the Way [the original name for the body of the followers of Jesus] to the death, binding and delivering to prison both men and women, as the high priest and the whole council of elders bear me witness. When they were put to death, I cast my vote against them.

From the high priest and council of elders, I received letters to the brethren, and I journeyed to Damascus to take those who were there and bring them in bonds to Jerusalem to be punished. As I made my journey . . . a great light from heaven suddenly shone about me. And I fell to the ground and heard a voice saying, "Saul, Saul, why do you persecute me?" And I answered, "Who are you, Lord?" And he answered, "I am Jesus of Nazareth."

Saul was blinded by that light from heaven. For three days he was without sight and abstained from food and drink. The disciple Ananias was instructed where to find him and told to lay hands on him to restore his sight, then inform him of his mission: to "carry my name before the Gentiles [with whom it was unlawful for Jews to associate—Acts 10:28] and kings and the sons of Israel" (Acts 9:15). This divine assignment led to Paul's three missionary journeys and the establishment of the churches to whom his letters in the New Testament are addressed.

One of Paul's primary messages involved the return of Jesus, promised by the angels in Acts 1:11, which describes the Ascension:

This Jesus who was taken up from you into heaven will come in the same way as you saw him go into heaven.

And that event, Paul said, would herald the end of the world. Paul believed the end of days was imminent in the first century, which is apparent throughout his letters but especially in those written to the church in Thessalonica, and he urged them to prepare:

When the Lord Jesus is revealed from heaven with his mighty angels in flaming fire, inflicting vengeance upon those who do now know God and upon those who do not obey the gospel of our Lord Jesus. They shall suffer the punishment of eternal destruction and exclusion from the presence of the Lord and from the glory of his might when he comes on that day to be glorified in his saints, and to be marveled at in all who have believed.
(1 Thessalonians 1:7–10)

Respect those who labor among you and are over you in the Lord, esteem them very highly in love because of their work. Be at peace among yourselves . . . admonish the idle, encourage the faint-hearted, help the weak, be patient with them all. See that none of you repays evil for evil, but always seek to do good to one another and to all. Rejoice always, pray constantly, give thanks in all circumstances . . . Do not quench the Spirit, do not despise prophesying, but test everything; hold fast to what is good, abstain from every form of evil.   (1 Thessalonians 5:12–19)

We hear that some of you are living in idleness, mere busybodies, not doing any work. If anyone will not work, let him not eat. Such persons we command and exort in the Lord Jesus Christ to do their work in quietness and to earn their own living. Brethren, do not be weary in well-doing.   (2 Thessalonians 3:10–13)

And finally, Paul's description of the end of days, and his words of hope, found in 1 Thessalonians 4:13–5:11:

But we would not have you be ignorant concerning those who are asleep, that you may not grieve as others do who have no hope. For since we believe that Jesus died and rose again, even so, through Jesus, God will bring with him those who have fallen asleep. For this we declare to you by the word of the Lord, that we who are alive, who are left until the coming of the Lord, shall not precede those who have fallen asleep. For the Lord himself will descend from heaven with a cry of command, with the arch-angels' call, and with the sound of the trumpet of God. And the dead in Christ will rise first; then we who are alive, who are left, shall be caught up together with them in the clouds to meet the Lord in the air; and so we shall always be with the Lord.

But as to the times and the seasons, you have no need to have anything written to you. For you yourselves know well that the day of the Lord will come like a thief in the night. When people say, "There is peace and security," then sudden destruction will come upon them as travail comes upon a woman with child, and there will be no escape. But you are not in darkness, for that day to surprise you like a thief. For you are all sons of light and sons of the day; we are not of the night and of darkness . . . So since we belong to the day, let us be sober, and put on the breastplate of faith and love, and for a helmet the hope of salvation . . . Encourage one another and build one another up just as you are doing.

Judaism

The Torah is the first five books of the Bible, the law books of the Jewish faith. The Talmud is the collection of Jewish law and tradition and describes how to apply the rules of the Torah to a variety of circumstances.

According to the Talmud, the world as we know it will exist for a total of six thousand years, counting from God's creation of the world. Based on the Jewish calendar, the year 2008 is calculated to be the 5,765th year of the world's existence, with the end of days to occur in 2240.

The end of the world, called *acharit hayamim* in Judaism, will be catastrophically violent and deadly. In fact, a wise man of the Talmud has written, "Let the end of days come, but may I not live to see them." This time of great suffering, though, will usher in an era of peace, holiness, and global spiritual enlightenment.

Jewish tradition about the end of days anticipates:

+ a return to Israel of Jewish exiles from around the world;
+ an attack of Israel by Gog, the king of Magog. While there's no definitive explanation of those terms, Gog is described as the prince of a land north of Israel, or "northern barbarians," possibly Russia or China. The battle between Israel and Magog, the true Armageddon, will be so terrible that it will take seven months to bury the dead;
+ the revival of the dead, or Resurrection;
+ the defeat of all of Israel's enemies
+ the building of the third Jewish temple in Jerusalem
+ the coming of a messiah, or anointed one.

The messiah, a human being who will be the anointed king of Israel, will obviously play an essential, divine role in the events that will follow Armageddon and usher in the seventh millennium of purity and the worldwide worship of the One God. His return is taken so seriously and literally that special preparation has been made for him in Jerusalem.

In one of the walls of the Old City is an entrance called the Golden Gate, also known as the Gate of Mercy and the Gate of Eternal Life. According to Jewish tradition, it's through the Golden Gate that the messiah will enter Jerusalem when he returns. But in 1541 the reigning Ottoman sultan, Suleiman, ordered the gate sealed, allegedly to block the messiah's entrance. The Golden Gate remains sealed today.

Among the Jewish prophecies about the messiah and his handiwork:

- He will be descended from King David.
- He will come in human form, and will be an "observant Jew."
- Evil and tyranny will be vanquished due to his presence.
- His embrace will enfold all cultures and nations.
- He will dispel hunger, suffering, and death forever and re-place them with eternal joy.
- The ancient ruins of Israel will be restored.
- Jews will know the Torah without studying, and all the world will know God.
- Barren land will become fruitful.
- Weapons of war will be destroyed.

The book of Isaiah holds many of the prophecies at the center of the Jewish beliefs about the end of days, particularly Isaiah 2:1–5:

And it shall come to pass in the last days, that the mountain of the Lord's house shall be established in the top of the mountains, and shall be exalted above the hills; and all nations shall flow unto it. And many people shall go and say, "Come ye, and let us go up to the mountain of the Lord, to the house of the God of Jacob; and he will teach us his ways, and we will walk in his paths: for out of Zion shall go forth the law, and the word of the Lord from Jerusalem." And he shall judge among the nations, and shall rebuke many people: and they shall beat their swords into plowshares, and their spears into pruninghooks: nations shall not lift up sword against nation, neither shall they learn war any more.

The prophet Joel was also an important part of the Hebrew scripture and its views on the end of times. Joel lived approximately four centuries after Moses had led the Israelites out of slavery in Egypt and sent them off to be settled in the land that was then called Canaan.

The Israelites confronted many complex problems when they arrived in Canaan. The country was occupied, and there was no security, so there was never a question of if they would be attacked, the only question was when. The Israelites themselves were disorganized, with no experience at self-rule. The climate was arid, water was scarce, and the soil was hard and rocky, making the successful planting and growing of edible crops virtually impossible.

During Joel's time, between 835 and 800 BC, the southern area of Canaan, called Judah, had been devastated by locusts, which ate the sparse crops. The plague of locusts was followed by a severe drought, prompting Joel to speak out to an omnipotent God who was ultimately in charge and responsible for all that happens.

The explanation Joel received for this disastrous succession of hardships was that the nation was receiving divine judgment for its sins. He symbolically described the locusts as a marching human army and goes on to one of his prophecies in Joel 1:13–14 and Joel 2:1–2:

Lament, O priests, wail, O ministers of the altar ... Call a solemn assembly ... Gather the elders to the house of the Lord your God and cry to the Lord; for unless they change their ways, the enemy armies will devour the land as did the natural elements. Awake, you drunkards, and weep!

Alas for the day of the Lord! For the day of the Lord is near, and as destruction from the Almighty it comes ... Let all the inhabitants of the land tremble, for the day of the Lord is coming ... a day of darkness and gloom, a day of clouds and thick darkness.

Like most prophetic writings, Joel's offer a word of hope:

"Yet even now," says the Lord, "return to me with all your heart, with fasting, with weeping and with mourning; and rend your hearts, not your garments." Return to the Lord, your God, for He is gracious and merciful, slow to anger, and abounding in steadfast love, and repents of evil. (Joel 2:12–13)

Following Jesus's days on Earth, after the feast of Pentecost at which the spirit of Jesus was manifested, the disciple Peter quoted from Joel 2:28–32 in Acts 2:17–21:

And in the last days it shall be, God declares, that I will pour out my Spirit upon all flesh, and your sons and your daughters shall prophesy. And your young men shall see visions, and your old men shall dream dreams . . . I will pour out my Spirit and they shall prophesy, and I will show wonders in the heaven above and signs on the earth beneath, blood, and fire, and vapor of smoke; the sun shall be turned into darkness and the moon into blood, before the day of the Lord comes, the great and manifest day. And it shall be that whoever calls on the name of the Lord shall be saved.

According to Judaism, the coming of the messiah and the divine worldwide era of peace, joy, and spiritual purity will by definition be preceded by unspeakable suffering. It's understandable, then, that many Jewish leaders have suggested that the Godless, obscene persecution of the Jews during the Holocaust might be historically perceived as the early dawn of the messiah's impending arrival.

Catholicism

While Catholics see no value in trying to predict the date or year of the end of days, take it from a woman who was raised in a Catholic school and once had her heart set on becoming a nun, they most definitely believe in the end-time and its biblically designated sequence of events:

1. The Resurrection of the Dead
The Catholic Church believes in not only a resurrection of the spirit but a resurrection of the body as well, as specified in the Apostles' Creed:

I believe in God, the Father Almighty,
the Creator of heaven and earth,
and in Jesus Christ, His only Son, our Lord,
Who was conceived of the Holy Spirit,
born of the Virgin Mary,
suffered under Pontius Pilate,
was crucified, died and was buried.
He descended into hell.
The third day He arose again from the dead.
He ascended into heaven
and sits at the right hand of God the Father Almighty,
whence He shall come to judge the living and the
    dead.
I believe in the Holy Spirit, the holy catholic [universal]
    church,
the communion of saints,
the forgiveness of sins,
the resurrection of the body,
and life everlasting.
Amen.

2. The Universal Judgment

Following the resurrection of all earthly flesh, Christ will sit upon the throne of judgment and, one by one, each of us will be given the justice our works in the world deserve.

For the Son of man is to come with his angels in the glory of
his Father, and then he will repay every man for what he has
done.   (Matthew 16:27)

3. The World's Destruction

At the command of Jesus Christ, the world will be destroyed, not by man's handiwork or by geological destruction or a cosmic collision but by purely supernatural means.

4. The Victory and Reign of the Church

Christ and every one of his faithful believers live and reign together forever, while all who pursue evil and give their allegiance to the devil are damned for all eternity.

The Catholic Church fully anticipates the second physical manifestation of Christ, often called the Parousia, which is Greek for presence, or coming. But it also emphasizes that it's not as if Jesus left the earth after His Resurrection and has been absent ever since. His spirit is among us every minute of every day of every year, as He promised when He appeared to His disciples at Galilee after the death of his body:

> All authority in heaven and on earth has been given to me. Go therefore and make disciples of all nations, baptizing them in the name of the Father and of the Son and of the Holy Spirit, teaching them to observe all that I have commanded you; and lo, I am with you always, to the close of the age. (Matthew 28:18–20)

> I will not leave you desolate. I will come to you. Yet a little while, and the world will see me no more, but you will see me; because I live, you will live also. In that day you will know that I am in my Father, and you in me, and I in you. (John 14:18–20)

Three of the most famous and controversial prophecies about the end of days had their origins in the Catholic Church. And the voices who uttered them are as fascinating as the prophecies themselves.

PADRE PIO

On June 16, 2002, Padre Pio, an Italian priest born in 1887, was elevated to sainthood by the Roman Catholic Church. He was renowned for his piety, his charitable works, his suffering, his occasional severity, and his divinely directed, controversial supernatural powers, from healings to prophesying. Perhaps most extraordinary and controversial of all was Padre Pio's bearing of the stigmata—wounds in his hands and feet that corresponded with the wounds inflicted on Christ at his Crucifixion.

The day after his birth, Padre Pio was baptized Francesco Forgione, and he was raised by an intensely devout Catholic family. He was ten years old when he was drawn to a young Capuchin friar who was traveling through the area, who inspired him to announce to his parents, "I want to be a friar with a beard." His ecstatic parents pursued their son's passion with a lot of traveling and a private tutor, and on January 22, 1903, at the age of fifteen, Francesco Forgione became Padre Pio, selecting his name in honor of Saint Pius V.

Seven years later he became an ordained priest. One morning shortly after his ordination, as legend has it, he was deep in prayer when Jesus and the Holy Mother appeared to him and bestowed on him the stigmata. He prayed that the wounds disappear, saying, "I do want to suffer, even to die of suffering, but all in secret." The stigmata disappeared, but only temporarily.

Padre Pio suffered from chronic poor health, and he was in and out of the religious community for several years, continuing his daily Mass and life of piety wherever he went and eventually becoming the spiritual director of an agricultural community called San Giovanni Rotondo on the Italian Gargano Promontory. There he developed and followed five rules for spiritual growth:

weekly confession
daily communion
spiritual reading
meditation
examination of conscience

And he created his motto: Pray, Hope and Don't Worry.

It was during a period of heightened intensity of prayer among all Christians in 1918 to end World War I that Padre Pio's stigmata returned. First came a vision during which Christ came to him and pierced his side, leaving a visible wound. Weeks later, Christ appeared again and left visible wounds in his hands and feet, and this time the five wounds of Jesus's Crucifixion stayed with him for the rest of his life.

Word spread of Padre Pio's stigmata and his recurring visions of Christ, and he was examined by countless physicians and questioned endlessly by both devotees and detractors, within and outside the Catholic Church. For better or worse, he became a phenomenon, and a source of such celebrity that huge crowds began gathering in the small community of San Giovanni Rotondo. The church was forced to restrict the public's access to him to prevent riots, and he was ultimately ordered to cease all church-related responsibilities and practices with the exception of private Mass. The more famous he became, the more the accusations against him escalated. To name just a few:

+ insanity, largely due to his claims of visions
+ deception, especially that he used acid to create and maintain the stigmata
+ immorality toward women, including allegations of intercourse with women in the confessional
+ "perverting the fragile lives and souls of boys," as a result of which he was forbidden to teach the male youth at the monastery
+ misappropriation of funds

Many of his accusers were high-ranking Catholics, and in 1933 Pope Pius XI began taking his own look at the ugly controversy swirling around the celebrity priest. In a declaration that almost single-handedly restored order and dignity to the situation, he finally announced, "I have not been badly disposed toward Padre Pio, but I have been badly informed." Padre Pio's duties and privileges were restored and expanded, and in 1939 Pope Pius XII even encouraged visitations and pilgrimages by the priest's throngs of devotees.

In 1940, Padre Pio initiated plans for a hospital in San Giovanni Rotondo that would be called Home to Relieve Suffering. It officially opened its doors in 1956 and to this day is considered to be one of Europe's most efficient hospitals. Home to Relieve Suffering gave Padre Pio's enemies yet another opportunity to hurl accusations at him of misappropriation of funds. But this time it was Pope Paul VI who resoundingly declared a dismissal of all indictments against him.

Padre Pio's chronic ill health finally claimed his life on September 23, 1968. More than one hundred thousand people attended his funeral, and thirty-four years after his death he was canonized by

Pope John Paul II and the Roman Catholic Church that so deeply treasured him and, on occasion, allowed some of its archbishops and bishops to try to destroy him.

Incidentally or not, those who were with Padre Pio in the hours immediately before and after his death claim that the stigmata disappeared without a trace as he took his last breath.

Much of Padre Pio's fame and infamy came from his gifts of healing and prophecy. A handful of the countless healing stories give a glimpse of his divine and sometimes unique power:

A woman of very modest means traveled some distance to bring her deaf child to Padre Pio, who instantly restored the child's hearing. In awe and gratitude, the woman removed a gold chain, her only possession of value, from her little girl's neck and presented it to Padre Pio in the name of the Blessed Virgin. The next morning, back in her own home, the woman awoke to find the gold chain on her bed table.

A blind child who'd been born with no pupils was brought to Padre Pio by her grandmother. During her time with Padre Pio she began to see and identify objects for the first time in her life. Ocular specialists who'd examined the child before and after her healing had no explanation for how pupils had managed to generate themselves in the little girl's eyes.

A man with a desperately ill child, who'd been given no hope by any number of doctors, took the child to Padre Pio. But as he entered the monastery, Padre Pio chased him back out the door again, yelling that because the man was a Communist and therefore a nonbeliever, he had no business presenting himself to "God's tribunal." Heartsick, the man was preparing to return to

Moscow with his child when he happened across a local professor to whom he told his story. The professor persuaded the man to go back to Padre Pio, confess his sins, and renounce the Godless beliefs he'd been taught throughout his life. He took the professor's advice and went with his child to the monastery again the next day. On seeing Padre Pio, he immediately and very sincerely fell to his knees, weeping. Padre Pio helped him to his feet, saying, "You have done the right thing and your son will get well. Now, come to confession." The man did as he was told and experienced a full spiritual awakening, while his child was completely healed.

One of Padre Pio's most famous prophecies was allegedly delivered through him by Jesus Christ and describes the coming Apocalypse. It reads, in part:

My Son, My love for man is very great, especially for those who give themselves to Me . . . The time is near at hand in which I shall visit my unfaithful people because they have not heeded the time of My grace. My judgment shall come upon them suddenly and when least expected—not one shall escape My hands. But I shall protect the just. Watch the sun and moon and the stars, when they appear unduly disturbed and restless, know that the day is not far away.

Stay united in prayer and watching until the angel of destruction has passed your doors. Pray that these days will be shortened. My children, have confidence. I am in the midst of you. My kingdom shall be glorified and My name shall be blessed from the rising of the sun unto the setting. My kingdom shall have no end.

Pray! Men are running toward the abyss of hell in great rejoicing . . . Assist Me in the salvation of souls. The measure of sin is filled! The day of revenge, with its terrifying happenings is near! Nearer than you can imagine! And the world is sleeping in false security! The Divine Judgment shall strike them like a thunderbolt! These godless and wicked people shall be destroyed without mercy . . .

Keep your windows well covered. Do not look out. Light a blessed candle, which will suffice for many days. Pray the rosary. Read spiritual books. Make acts of love which are so pleasing to Us. Pray with outstretched arms, or prostrate on the ground, in order that many souls may be saved . . .

Take care of the animals during these days. I am the Creator and Preserver of all animals as well as man. I shall give you a few signs beforehand, at which time you should place more food before them. I will preserve the property of the elect, including the animals, for they shall be in need of sustenance afterwards as well . . .

A most dreadful punishment will bear witness to the times. My angels, who are to be the executioners of this work, are ready with their pointed swords! Hurricanes of fire will pour forth from the clouds and spread over the entire earth! Storms, bad weather, thunderbolts and earthquakes will cover the earth for two days. An uninterrupted rain of fire will take place! It will begin during a very cold night. All this is to prove that God is the Master of Creation.

Those who hope in Me, and believe in My words, have nothing to fear because I will not forsake them, nor those who spread My message. No harm will come to those who are in the state of grace and who seek My Mother's protection. That you may be prepared for these visitations . . . Talk to no one outside the house. Kneel down before a crucifix, be sorry for your sins, and beg My Mother's protection. Those who disregard this advice will be killed instantly. The wind will carry with it poisonous gases which will be diffused over the entire earth. Those who suffer and die innocently will be martyrs and they will be with Me in My kingdom.

Satan will triumph! But in three nights, the earthquake and fire will cease. On the following day the sun will shine again, angels will descend from Heaven and will spread the spirit of peace over the earth. A feeling of immeasurable gratitude will take possession of those who survive this most terrible ordeal, the impending punishment, with which God will visit the earth since creation . . .

The weight of the Divine balance has reached the earth! The wrath of My Father shall be poured out over the entire world! I am again warning the world as I have so often done heretofore. The sins of men have multiplied beyond measure. The world is filled with iniquity . . .

I Myself shall come amidst thunder and lightning. The wicked shall behold My Divine Heart. There shall be great confusion because of this utter darkness in which the entire earth shall be enveloped. And many, many shall die of fear and despair. Those who shall fight for My cause shall receive grace from My Divine Heart; and the cry: "WHO IS LIKE UNTO GOD!" shall serve as a means of protection to many. However, many shall burn in the open fields like withered grass! The godless shall be annihilated, so that afterwards the just shall be able to start afresh . . .

The darkness shall last a day and a night, followed by

another day and a night, and another day—but on the night following, the stars will shine again, and on the next morning the sun shall rise again, and it will be springtime! . . .

Hell will believe itself to be in possession of the entire earth, but I shall reclaim it . . .

Pray! Pray! My dear Mother Mary and the saints and holy angels shall be your intercessors. Implore their aid. Be courageous soldiers of Christ! At the return of light, let everyone give thanks to the Holy Trinity for their protection! The devastation shall be very great. But I, your God, will have purified the earth. I am with you, have confidence. Again and again I have warned men, and often have I given them special opportunities to return to the right path. But now, wickedness has reached its climax, and the punishment can no longer be delayed. Even though My heart does suffer and bleed, yet for My name's sake I must deal this blow.

Tell all men that the time has come in which these things shall be fulfilled.

THE FATIMA PROPHECIES

On May 13, 1917, three children—Lucia, age eleven; Francisco, age nine; and Jacinta, age seven—took the family sheep to graze in the Cova da Iria, a hollow near the town of Fatima, Portugal. The sheep were quietly grazing and the children were playing when suddenly what appeared to be a flash of lightning blazed from the cloudless sky. Confused and frightened, the children began gathering the sheep to hurry home when a second flash of lightning appeared, and a lady, dressed in brilliant, radiant white, materialized above a small tree.

"Don't be afraid," the lady assured the terrified children. "I come from Heaven, to ask that you come here for six months in succession, on the thirteenth day, at this same hour. At that time I will tell you who I am and what I want."

After a few more messages and instructions, the lady seemed to vanish into a cloud of light.

The children raced home to tell their parents about their amazing experience. Their mother punished them, first for lying and then for refusing to admit the lie. Word of the children's preposterous story spread through the village of Fatima, and they were subjected to relentless ridicule.

But each month, on the thirteenth day, the children obediently made their way to the Cova da Iria, and the lady never disappointed them. Slowly but surely, with each passing month, larger and more curious crowds began following the children to the site of the apparition, despite the fact that no one except the children could see or hear the lady as she shared important secrets with them. Finally, she promised a miracle in October, the sixth month of her appearances to them, that would make everyone believe.

On the 13th of October, 1917, a crowd of nearly seventy thousand followed Lucia, Francisco, and Jacinta through a hard steady rain to the Cova da Iria. At the stroke of noon the lady appeared and, as promised during her first appearance, she revealed to the children who she was and what she wanted.

"I am the Lady of the Rosary," she said, "and I would like a chapel built on this site in my honor."

She ascended again, opening her hands toward the sky. And in the sky the children saw the Mysteries of the Rosary, followed by Joseph, Mary, and the baby Jesus, who blessed the crowd. Then came a vision that only Lucia saw, the sacred sight of the Virgin Mary beside her resurrected Son.

In the meantime, the throngs nearby were transfixed by the spectacle in the sky that was simultaneously playing out before their eyes: the rain suddenly stopped, and the sun appeared. Impossibly, the moment it broke through the clouds, the sun began dancing, whirling, erupting in a rainbow of fire that reflected prisms of color on the faces of the crowd. Then, with no warning, in one swift, blinding thrust, the sun appeared to be hurtling out of the sky toward the seventy thousand witnesses, terrifying them and convincing many of them that the end of the world had come. But in a matter of seconds, it reversed its direction and returned to its proper, benign place in the heavens. It was only when the crowds had begun to recover from their panic and their confused awe that they noticed how completely dry their clothing and the ground around them were, despite the relentless rain they'd stood in for hours.

As the Blessed Mother had requested, a shrine was built on the site of the visions. Francisco and Jacinta tragically died in an influenza plague that swept through Portugal within three years of that miraculous October day in 1917. Lucia entered a convent and continued receiving occasional visits from the Virgin Mary who, in 1927, gave her permission to reveal two of the three prophecies she'd given to the children. The third prophecy, she said, was not to be made public before 1960.

In the first prophecy, shared with the children on July 13, 1917, Mary told the children that the war—World War I—would end soon, as it did, the following year. She went on to say that same day that "a night illuminated by an unknown light" would precede a "worse war." On January 25, 1938, a stunning aurora borealis stretched across the northern sky with such unprecedented brilliance that it was visible across Europe. World War II began in 1939.

In her second prophecy the Lady of Fatima warned that Russia would "spread her errors throughout the world, promoting wars . . . Various nations will be annihilated. If people attend to My request for the consecration of Russia to My immaculate heart, Russia will be converted." In 1984 Pope John Paul II consecrated Russia, which many believe fulfilled the prophecy and led to the subsequent collapse, or conversion, of the Soviet Union.

As for the third prophecy, Lucia wrote it down and sealed it in an envelope. She gave it to a Portuguese bishop with instructions that it wasn't to be opened and read until after 1960. That bishop in turn presented it to the Vatican.

When 1960 came, Pope John XXIII reportedly unsealed the envelope but refused to reveal its contents, with the cryptic explanation that "this prophecy does not relate to my time." His successor, Pope John Paul II, is said to have read the prophecy as well. Rumor had it that it referred to a "bishop clothed in white," i.e., the Pope, who, as he makes his way through throngs of the faithful, falls to the ground, seemingly dead from a burst of gunfire.

On May 13, 1981, sixty-four years to the day after Our Lady of Fatima's first appearance to the three children in the Cova da Iria, a Turkish gunman in St. Peter's Square attempted to assassinate Pope John Paul II. The Pope thanked the Mother Herself for saving his life by "guiding the bullet's path," and the potentially fatal bullet was given by the Pope to the bishop of Leiria-Fatima, who had it set in the crown on the statue of Our Lady of Fatima at her shrine.

On May 13, 2000, Pope John Paul II visited Sister Lucia dos Santos, who by then was ninety-three years old and a Carmelite nun. He also beatified her cousins, Francisco and Jacinta, who are buried near the Virgin's shrine. Never before or since has the Roman Catholic Church beatified children who weren't martyrs.

And finally, on June 26, 2000, the Vatican released the complete forty-page text of the third Fatima prophecy, which had been committed to paper in Portuguese by Sister Lucia on January 3, 1944, and eventually translated into English, French, Italian, Spanish, German, and Polish.

The third prophecy from the Blessed Virgin of Fatima, reads, in part:

At the left of Our Lady and a little above, we saw an Angel with a flaming sword in his left hand; flashing, it gave out flames that looked as though they would set the world on fire; but they died out in contact with the splendor that Our Lady radiated towards him from her right hand. Pointing to the earth with his right hand, the Angel cried out in a loud voice: "Penance, Penance, Penance!"

And we saw in an immense light that is God: "something similar to how people appear in a mirror when they pass in front of it" a Bishop dressed in White "we had the impression that it was the Holy Father." Other bishops, priests, men and women Religious going up a steep mountain, at the top of which there was a big Cross of rough-hewn trunks as of a cork tree with the bark. Before reaching there the Holy Father passed through a big city half in ruins and half trembling with halting step, afflicted with pain and sorrow, he prayed for the souls of the corpses he met on his way. Having reached the top of the mountain, on his knees at the foot of the big Cross he was killed by a group of soldiers who fired bullets and arrows at him, and in the same way there died one after another the other Bishops, Priests, men and women Religious, and various lay people of different ranks and positions. Beneath the two arms of the Cross there were two

Angels each with a crystal aspersorium [basin meant to hold holy water] in his hand, in which they gathered up the blood of the Martyrs and with it sprinkled the souls that were making their way to God.

Cardinal Joseph Ratzinger, the Roman Catholic Church's prefect of the Sacred Congregation for the Doctrine of the Faith, interpreted the third prophecy of Our Lady of Fatima as being perfectly summed up by the "triple cry, 'Penance, Penance, Penance!'" In its entirety, he says, he believes it to be

a consoling vision, which seeks to open a history of blood and tears to the healing power of God. Beneath the arms of the cross angels gather up the blood of the martyrs, and with it they give life to the souls making their way to God. Here, the blood of Christ and the blood of the martyrs are considered as one: the blood of the martyrs runs down from the arms of the cross. The martyrs die in communion with the Passion of Christ, and their death becomes one with his . . . Since God himself took a human heart and has thus steered human freedom toward what is good, the freedom to choose evil no longer has the last word. From that time forth, the word that prevails is this:

> *In the world you will have tribulation, but take heart;*
> *I have overcome the world.*

John 16:33

The message of Fatima invites us to trust in this promise.

MARIA ESPERANZA

Maria Esperanza was considered to be one of the world's most gifted contemporary mystics and seers. Born in Venezuela in 1928, she was five years old when she received a vision of Saint Therese, "the little flower of Jesus," who threw a rose to her, a rose that materialized in the child's hand. At the age of fourteen, when she was plagued with pneumonia and heart problems and not expected to live, Maria had the strength of faith to pray to Jesus for either a happy death or a complete healing, whichever was her Father's will. The Blessed Mother Mary instantly appeared to her, and at that moment Maria was miraculously and completely healed.

In 1954, Maria traveled to a Venezuelan convent to pray for guidance in the direction her life should take. It was there that Saint Therese appeared to her again and tossed her a second rose. This time when Maria reached for it, her hand was pricked by a thorn. It was a minor injury, but it foreshadowed the fact that Maria would bear the stigmata, the visible wounds of Christ on the cross, every Good Friday for the rest of her life.

Maria received the blessings of Pope Pius XII in Rome in 1954, and the Blessed Mother appeared to her again during her stay with another message, which concluded:

You will be the mother of seven children: six roses and one bud.

Maria was married in 1956 to a member of the Vatican's President of the Republic's Guard, a marriage that produced one son and six daughters.

In 1984 Maria Esperanza and almost five hundred witnesses were given an appearance of the Blessed Mother Mary in a place called Betania near Caracas, Venezuela. The witnesses were interviewed by the Most Reverend Pio Bello Ricardo, a bishop and psychologist, who, after discussions with the Vatican, declared the visions authentic and declared Betania to be "sacred ground."

Before her death on August 7, 2004, Maria Esperanza offered her prophecies on the Second Coming and the end of days during an interview with Michael H. Brown, a writer and biographer:

> It will be very different than what people think. He [Jesus] is going to come in silence. People will realize He is among us little by little . . . In those days an innocent person whom He loves a lot will die, an innocent person. This will shock the world, will move the world. Many people will believe. He will disappear for some days and appear again.

> And when he disappears, people will go back again to the mess, to the disordered things. He will bilocate, He will multiply Himself, to assist everyone, in their homes, because this will be a definite thing. He will come and knock on every door. And then people will realize it is truly Him. He will let Himself be seen for a little while and then will disappear until God decrees what has to be done.

> The same way He resurrected, that is how God is going to appear to you, to me . . . as an apparition . . . He already is among us but is not letting us see Him. With our brains, in this physical reality, we can only see what God wants us to see, but it only needs a little touch from God to open another little door in our brains to see Jesus whenever He wants us to see Him . . .

> When He comes in glory is the Final Judgment, it is the end of this world. If He comes now, the ones who will receive Him

will be the Pope and all the faithful souls in the world, no one else, because they are expecting Him and waiting for Him.

The years before such a manifestation there will be a special light from Heaven. Many natural and political events will take place as well, to purify and prepare.

CENTURIES OF CATHOLICS ON THE END OF DAYS

Take it from a Catholic school graduate, the legacy of the end-of-days prophecies is a rich, treasured tradition in the church. Some of the prophecies were biblical in origin, while others were said to be divinely channeled.

Saint Malachy, for example, born in 1094, was the first Irish saint canonized by a pope, Clement III. He reportedly possessed the God-given powers of levitation, healing, clairvoyance, and prophecy. Probably his most famous vision appeared to him during a trance when he saw the entire line of popes from his day until the end of time. He wrote brief descriptions of each of them and presented the writing to Pope Innocent II. The manuscript wasn't unearthed again until 1950, and it's been a source of controversy ever since. The last of the popes, according to Saint Malachy's early twelfth-century prophecy, will be:

+ "The Flower of Flowers," as Saint Malachy named him, thought to be Paul VI (1963–78), whose coat of arms bears three fleurs-de-lis.
+ "Of the Half Moon," thought to be John Paul I, who was born in the diocese of Belluno, which translates to "beautiful moon," and was elected Pope during a half-moon on August 26, 1978. He died a month later, shortly after a lunar eclipse.

+ "The Labor of the Sun," which would correspond to Pope John Paul II, whose papal reign lasted from 1978 until 2005. On the morning he was born in 1920 there was an almost total eclipse of the sun over Europe, obviously including Pope John Paul II's native Poland. As for the "labor" reference, he was the most widely traveled Pope in the history of the church.

+ "The Glory of the Olive," who would be Pope Benedict XVI, the 265th Pope, elected in 2005. The Order of Saint Benedict, also known as the Olivetans, declared that the penultimate Pope would come from their ranks and would "lead the Catholic Church in its fight against evil."

+ "Peter the Roman." According to Saint Malachy, the final Pope will be Satan, in the form of a man named Peter, who will inspire great worldwide loyalty and adoration. He'll be the long-anticipated last Antichrist, who will "feed his flock amid many tribulations, after which the seven-hilled city [Rome] will be destroyed and the dreadful Judge will judge the people. The End."

An Austrian monk named Johannes Friede (1204–57) wrote the following prophecy that continues to be studied and debated more than seven centuries later:

When the great time will come, in which mankind will face its last, hard trial, it will be foreshadowed by striking changes in nature. The alternation between cold and heat will become more intensive, storms will have more catastrophic effects, earthquakes will destroy great regions, and the seas will overflow many lowlands. Not all of it will be the result of natural causes, but mankind will penetrate into the bowels of the earth and will reach into the clouds, gambling with its own existence. Before the powers of destruction will succeed in their design, the universe will be thrown into disorder, and the age of iron will plunge into nothingness. When nights will be filled with more intensive cold and days with heat, a new life will begin in nature. The heat means radiation from the earth, the cold the waning light of the sun. Only a few years more and you will become aware that sunlight has grown perceptibly weaker. When even your artificial light will cease to give service, the great event in the heavens will be near.

Saint Vincent Ferrer (1350–1419) was a Dominican missionary whose following was once said to number more than ten thousand. He lived an austere, disciplined life of self-sacrifice, ministering to countless children, healing countless troubled souls and plague-infested bodies, and was ultimately canonized by Pope Calixtus III. According to his prophecy:

In the days of peace that are to come after the desolation of revolutions and wars, before the end of the world the Christians will become so lax in their religion that they will refuse to receive the Sacrament of Confirmation, saying, "It is an unnecessary Sacrament."

Pope Pius X (1835–1914) first declined the papal nomination because he felt unworthy of the honor. It speaks volumes about how wrong he was that he was ultimately canonized in 1951 by Pius XII.

One day in 1909, during an audience for an order of Franciscans, Pius seemed to go into a trance. After several moments, during which everyone around him watched in silent alarm, the Pope opened his eyes, stood, and called out, "What I have seen is terrifying! Will I be the one, or will it be a successor? What is certain is that the Pope will leave Rome and, in leaving the Vatican, he will have to pass over the dead bodies of his priests!" He then asked that everyone in the room keep the whole incident secret until after he died.

His vision seemed to clarify itself shortly before his death, through a second vision, which he described:

I have seen one of my successors, of the same name, who was fleeing over the bodies of his brethren. He will take refuge in some hiding place; but after a brief respite, he will die a cruel death. Respect for God has disappeared from human hearts. They wish to efface even God's memory. This perversity is nothing less than the beginning of the last days of the world.

CHAPTER FOUR

Other Great Religions and the End of the World

Please don't let it enter your mind that the "other" in the title of this chapter even remotely implies "less important." As most of you may already know, I was born into a Catholic/Jewish/ Lutheran/Episcopalian family, and I've studied world religions throughout my life. All of them are fascinating, all of them include aspects that are utterly beautiful, and all of them, whether or not you agree with each and every detail of their beliefs, warrant our awareness and respect.

Islam

Muslims, as followers of the Islamic faith are called, believe that in AD 570, God, or Allah, sent the last of His prophets to Earth to deliver His message among humankind. That prophet was Muhammad, who was born in Makkah (Mecca), in what is now Saudi

Arabia. Muslims consider Muhammad to have been human, not a part of divinity, and they never refer to him as Allah. Allah is the one God, our Creator, all-powerful, all-knowing, all-merciful, supreme and sovereign, the only entity in the universe worthy of worship.

Muhammad was orphaned at a very young age and raised by his uncle, Abu Talib. Early in his life he was already being recognized for his wisdom, honesty, generosity, and sincerity. He was forty years old, on one of the meditative retreats he often took to the cave of Hira, close to Mecca, when the angel Gabriel appeared to him and delivered the first of what would evolve into twenty-three years of revelations. And those twenty-three years of revelations, given to Muhammad from God through the angel Gabriel, became the Qur'an (Koran), the Holy Book of the Islam faith.

Muhammad was sixty-three when he died. Within a hundred years of his death, Islam had spread throughout Europe and across Asia as far east as China. Muslims cherish Muhammad as God's final messenger and prophet. Again, though, their worship is devoted strictly to Allah.

Nothing sums up the Islamic view of the Apocalypse more gracefully than the Final Signs of Qiyaamah (Islam), one of the most famous of the Islamic prophecies:

> *The Ground will cave in:*
> *one in the east,*
> *one in the west,*
> *and one in Hejaz, Saudi Arabia.*
> *Fog or smoke will cover the skies for forty days.*
> *The nonbelievers will fall unconscious,*
> *while Muslims will be ill [develop colds].*
> *The skies will then clear up.*

A night three nights long will follow the fog.

It will occur in the month of Zil-Hajj after Eidul-Ahja,***

and cause much restlessness among the people.

After the night of three nights,

the following morning the sun will rise in the west.

People's repentance will not be accepted after this incident.

One day later, the Beast from the earth will miraculously

emerge from Mount Safaa in Makkah, causing a split in the ground.

The Beast will be able to talk to people and

mark the faces of people,

making the believers' faces glitter, and

the nonbelievers' faces darken.

A breeze from the south causes sores in the armpits of Muslims,

which they will die of as a result.

*The Ka'aba**** will be destroyed by a non-Muslim African group.*

Kufr [Godlessness] will be rampant.

Haj [the pilgrimage to Makkah] will be discontinued.

The Qur'an will be lifted from the heart of the people,

thirty years after the ruler Muquad's death.

The fire will follow people to Syria, after which it will stop.

*Zil-Hajj—the last month of the Islamic calendar

**Eidul-Ahja—the Festival of Sacrifice

***The Ka'aba—an oblong stone building in the center of the Holy City of Makkah that houses the sacred Black Stone given to Abraham by the angel Gabriel

> *Some years after the first,*
> *Qiyaamah [Islam] begins with the Soor [trumpet] being*
>   *blown.*
> *The year is not known to any person.*
> *Qiyaamah will come upon the worst of creation.*

It's very much worth adding that Muslims have enormous respect for Jesus and never say his name without adding the homage "Peace be upon him." The Qur'an refers to the immaculate birth of Christ, acknowledges His miracles, and predicts his Second Coming. In fact, the Islam faith believes that in the final days both Jesus and the prophet Imam Mahdi, a descendant of Muhammad, will come to Earth to combine forces of good against evil and usher in the Apocalypse.

Hinduism

Hinduism is the third largest religion in the world, with more than 750 million followers. It is thought to have been born in northern India between 4000 and 2200 BC. There's some disagreement about the origin of its beliefs, whether it was brought by invading Indo-Europeans who practiced a religion called Vedism or it grew from the already established Vedic culture in India.

But there is no disagreement on the many unique aspects of this ancient religion compared to the other great religions of the world. Hinduism isn't the result of any one messiah, leader, or group of leaders. There are no prophets in its rich history and no specific sequence of events that led to its creation.

Instead, Hinduism seems to have evolved into reality, with

sacred texts—the Vedas and the Upanishads—that were committed to paper between 800 and 400 BC. It worships one supreme God, the principle of Brahman, a singular divine entity who is both at one with the universe and transcends it at the same time. Brahman exists as three separate aspects:

+ Brahma the Creator, who perpetually creates new realities;
+ Vishnu, or Krishna, the Preserver, the protector of the creations; when eternal order is threatened, Vishnu travels to Earth to restore it;
+ Shiva the Destroyer.

Hindus believe that everything becomes nothing, which becomes everything again, in cycle after cycle. In other words, Brahma creates the universe, Vishnu takes over as its caretaker, and then Shiva destroys it so that Brahma can begin the cycle again. A cycle is very, very long—current Hindu wisdom suggests that the universe has approximately 427,000 years left before this cycle ends and a new one begins. These cycles are thought of as ages, and there are four ages in orthodox Hinduism, ranging from an age of absolute purity to an age of absolute corruption. This fourth, corrupt age is the Kali Age, or Iron Age, characterized by the spiritual decline of civilization, violence, plagues, and a tragic desecration of nature. The Kali Age immediately precedes complete destruction, which then evolves into the purity of the Golden Age, when the cycle begins again. According to Hinduism, when evil and chaos in the world reach their peak of intolerable obscenity, an avatar—incarnation of the Supreme Being—appears on Earth and restores righteousness and purity to humankind.

The Hindu Puranas, which are a written interlacing of mythology and history, contain a list of prophecies involving this cyclical concept that is as close as Hinduism comes to other religions' concept of the end of times:

+ Apocalypse for the Hindu is the natural ending of the world in the fourth age, the Kali Age, the age of Darkness and Discord.

+ It is one of a series of apocalypses, each of which marks the end of one cycle and the beginning of another creation. The central figure in these transitions is Vishnu, the Preserver God, into whom the world is absorbed before being born again.

+ Vishnu has already saved humanity on a number of occasions, symbolically appearing as a savior in many different forms. It is said that He will appear again soon, as Kalki, a white horse, destined to destroy the present world and to elevate humanity to a higher plane.

+ All kings occupying the earth in the Kali Age will be wanting in tranquility, strong in anger, taking pleasure at all times in lying and dishonesty, inflicting death on women, children, and cows, prone to take the paltry possessions of others, with character that is mostly vile, rising to power and soon falling.

+ They will be short-lived, of little virtue, and greedy. People will follow the customs of others and be adulterated with them; peculiar, undisciplined barbarians will be vigorously supported by rulers. Because they go on living with perversion, they will be ruined.

+ Dharma [eternal order, righteousness] becomes very weak in the Kali Age. People commit sin in mind, speech, and actions.

- Quarrels, plague, fatal diseases, famines, drought, and calamities appear. Testimonies and proofs have no certainty. There is no criterion left when the Kali Age settles down.
- People become poorer in vigor and luster.
- They are wicked, full of anger, sinful, false, and avaricious.
- Bad ambitions, bad education, bad dealings, and bad earnings excite fear.
- The whole batch becomes greedy and untruthful.
- Many sudras [Godless ones] will become kings, and many heretics will be seen.
- There will arise various sects, sannyasins [elevated ones, gurus] wearing clothes colored red.
- Many will profess to have supreme knowledge because, thereby, they will easily earn their livelihood.
- In the Kali Age, there will be many false religionists.
- India will become desolated by repeated calamities, short lives, and various diseases.
- Everyone will be miserable owing to the dominance of vice and Tamoguna [apathy, inaction].
- Earth will be valued only for her mineral treasures.
- Money alone will confer nobility.
- Power will be the sole definition of virtue.
- Pleasure will be the only reason for marriage.
- Lust will be the only reason for womanhood.
- Falsehood will win out in disputes.
- Being dry of water will be the only definition of land.
- Praiseworthiness will be measured by accumulated wealth.
- Propriety will be considered good conduct, and only feebleness will be the reason for unemployment.
- Boldness and arrogance will be equivalent to scholarship.

- ✦ Only those without wealth will show honesty.
- ✦ Just a bath will amount to purification, and charity will be the only virtue.
- ✦ Abduction will be marriage.
- ✦ Simply to be well-dressed will signify propriety.
- ✦ Any hard-to-reach water will be deemed a pilgrimage site.
- ✦ The pretense of greatness will be the proof of it, and powerful men with many severe faults will rule over all the classes on Earth.
- ✦ Oppressed by their excessively greedy rules, people will hide in valleys between mountains, where they will gather honey, vegetables, roots, fruits, birds, flowers, and so forth.
- ✦ Suffering from cold, wind, heat, and rain, they will put on clothes made of tree bark and leaves.
- ✦ And no one will live as long as twenty-three years.
- ✦ Thus, in the Kali Age humankind will be utterly destroyed.

Is it me, or does a whole lot of this description of the Kali Age sound awfully familar?

Buddhism

According to legend, twenty-five hundred years ago Queen Maha Maya, wife of King Suddhodana of northern India, had a dream one night. In this dream a beautiful white elephant encircled her and entered her right side. Wise men interpreted the dream as a sign that a magnificent son would be born to the queen and king, a prince who, if he remained in the palace, would become a great ruler. If he declined his royal lineage, however, he would become a Buddha, or an Awakened One.

A son was born to the queen and king. They named him Siddhartha, which meant "all wishes fulfilled." High walls were built around the exquisitely beautiful perfection of the palace to prevent Prince Siddhartha from being exposed to anything that might devastate his privileged isolation—it was ordered that he should never be exposed to the seriously ill, the very old, the dying, or most definitely not any wandering holy men.

Prince Siddhartha lived in palatial luxury until he was twenty-six, happily married to Princess Yasodhara for half of those years. But he felt that something about his life was missing and incomplete, and he became consumed with curiosity about what the world was like beyond those high palace walls. And so, with the help of his charioteer Channa, he began a series of secret excursions beyond the walls into the streets of northern Indian villages.

For the first time in his life Prince Siddhartha saw the sick, the dying, the dead, and the starving, and he was shattered by them. He was told about the belief that birth and death were simply part of an eternal cycle that could only be stopped by somehow escaping the trap of continual rebirth, and he became consumed by the tragic inevitability of that cycle when it included the profound deprivation and illness that surrounded him in the poverty-stricken villages.

It was during what would become the prince's final excursion that Siddhartha's life was transformed forever. He came across what he first thought to be yet another beggar, a small, barefoot, seemingly starving man with a shaved head, draped in a yellow robe, and holding a bowl to receive any kindness a stranger might be moved to extend. But when Prince Siddhartha looked more closely, he saw that the man's face was almost radiant with peace and dignity. Deeply moved, the prince commented to his charioteer about the amazingly transcendent little man, and Channa explained that the man was a monk, one of the quietly devout who found great spiritual happiness in a life of simplicity, purity, discipline, and meditation on his journey to be delivered from suffering.

Irrevocably moved by this experience, Prince Siddhartha, in a decision that would come to be known as the Great Renunciation, left behind his beloved family, his heritage, and his life of unlimited wealth and, at the age of twenty-nine, began a solitary search for a way to end the constant cycle of suffering and rebirth and then, somehow, be of real help to the sad afflicted world around him.

After six brutal years of pain, self-mortification, punishing discipline, and deprivation, Siddhartha came to the conclusion that an exhausted, neglected, malnourished body was hardly a welcoming environment for a healthy, enlightened mind and spirit. He began to nourish himself, and to rebuild his strength and vitality. His companions abandoned him, scornful of his inability to maintain his disciplines of sacrifice, and he found himself as alone as he'd been on the day he'd walked away from the palace.

On his thirty-fifth birthday, Siddhartha was wandering in a beautiful forest when a woman appeared and presented him with a bowl of milk rice.

"Venerable sir," she said, "whoever you may be, god or human, please accept this offering. May you attain the good which you seek."

Later that day he met a groundskeeper who offered him a cushion of fresh-cut grass beneath a magnificent spreading fig tree, which came to be known as the Bodhi Tree, or Tree of Enlightenment. As he rested beneath that tree he began contemplating his life and his near-death through the futility of his abusively extreme self-discipline.

In the shade of the Bodhi Tree he vowed, "Though my skin, my nerves and my lifeblood go dry, I will not abandon this seat until I have realized Supreme Enlightenment." And he remembered a similar moment from his childhood, when, while resting beneath a tree, he discovered that by sitting cross-legged, with his eyes closed and his mind focused on nothing but breathing in and out, he could reach a state of mental bliss. The peace of that simple, private exercise came flooding back to him that day beneath the Bodhi Tree, and he crossed his legs, closed his eyes, and cleared his mind of everything but his silent, rhythmic breathing.

He sat still as a thousand doubts, fears, memories, cravings, and temptations raged inside him, waging war with all the good he was longing to accomplish. He sat still through a violent storm that thundered all night through the forest. He felt his resolve strengthen and his meditative serenity engulf him. Finally he reached out with his right hand and touched the ground, which quaked and trembled and roared at his touch, asking Mother Earth for confirmation of the worth of his lonely pilgrimage with the words, "I, Earth, bear you witness!"

Throughout the night, as his deep meditation continued, he came to know how darkness of the mind is born, and how it is destroyed forever. He dispelled past, present, and future spiritual ignorance, and his delusion was transformed into total clarity. He gained complete understanding of "things as they are," and when dawn broke, Prince Siddhartha had become Buddha Shakyamuni, the Enlightened One, whose ensuing teachings and divine revelations gave birth to Buddhism, with a current following that exceeds 665 million devotees.

The religion that Buddha's life and enlightenment inspired involves being as active, self-propelled, and personally responsible as Buddha was in his quest for understanding "things as they are." Followers are taught that if depth, meaning, and substance are missing from their lives, they're not to look to Buddha for answers, or to the people around them. They're to look to themselves and find their transformation within their own souls.

Buddha predicted that someday another Buddha would be born. Buddha Maitreya, who currently resides in the Tutshita, or heaven, waiting to be born again for one final time on earth. Before Buddha Maitreya's arrival, Buddha Shakyamuni's teachings would vanish, all memory of him would disappear, and even his sacred relics would be destroyed by fire. Only then would Buddha Maitreya appear, to renew Buddhism in the world and light the path to Nirvana, or the extinguishing of ignorance, hatred, and earthly suffering. Buddhist prophecies describe him:

> He will have a heavenly voice which reaches far; his skin will have a golden hue; a great splendor will radiate from his body; his chest will be broad, limbs well developed, and his eyes will be like lotus petals. His body is eighty cubits high, and twenty cubits broad . . . Under Maitreya's guidance, hundreds of thousands of living beings shall enter upon a religious life.

The time preceding Maitreya, according to the scriptures, would be recognizable by its hedonism, its sexual depravity, its general social chaos, and its widespread lack of physical health. And only a force as powerful as Buddha Maitreya will be able to shift the world into its next inevitable cycle.

Buddhists, in other words, don't believe in an end of times. Instead, they agree with a universal cycle of creation, destruction, and then creation again, ushered in by a new Enlightened One who will bring peace and well-being, or Nirvana, to humankind right here on Earth.

The Baha'i Faith

In 1844 an Iranian merchant named Sayyid Ali Muhammad Shiraz, said to be a descendant of the prophet Muhammad, founded a religious movement that evolved into what we now know as the Baha'i Faith. Taking the title of the Bab, which translates to "the gate," he gathered eighteen disciples around him, whom he called Letters of the Living, and sent them throughout the lands to share his message.

The Bab gained thousands of followers in the next few years, and attracted the attention of a few powerful detractors, including the Iranian prime minister, who had him imprisoned for fear that the Bab's expanding power might interfere with the prime minister's religious influence over the shah. It was during the Bab's imprisonment in 1848 that he wrote *The Bayan*, his most important book of teachings. In the meantime, the Babis, as the Bab's followers were called, were being attacked by various local armies whose religious leaders found them disruptive and threatening to their own beliefs.

Finally, in 1850, the prime minister and the shah decided that the most effective way of stopping this divisive new movement would be to eliminate its founder, the Bab himself. He was brought to Tabriz in northern Iran and suspended in front of a firing squad in a square where the public could witness his execution.

On command, the squad of soldiers fired at the Bab. In what the Baha'i regard as a great miracle of their faith, not a single bullet struck the Bab, and he actually seemed to vanish into thin air. He was discovered later, committing his final words to writing, and was brought back to the public square. The first firing squad refused to participate in another attempt at executing the Bab, so a replacement firing squad was summoned. They tragically succeeded, and the Bab was killed. His body was spirited away by a few of his followers and eventually interred in a shrine at Mount Carmel in the city of Haifa.

One of the Bab's primary missions on Earth was to prepare humankind for the impending arrival of another great prophet and teacher who would lead the world into a new era of global peace. In 1863 a follower of the Bab named Mirza H'usayn Ali Nuri, whose father was an Iranian nobleman, declared that he himself was that prophet and teacher. He took the title Baha'u'llah, which translates to "the glory of God," and was the leader to whom the Bab's followers turned after the Bab's execution.

The Babis were still being tortured and killed when Baha'u'llah took charge of the Bab's faithful, and he was arrested and severely beaten many times. It was while imprisoned in an underground pit that he had a vision considered in the Baha'i Faith to be equivalent to the Burning Bush that transformed Moses and to the enlightenment of Siddhartha beneath the Bodhi Tree that elevated him to the great Buddha:

While engulfed in tribulations I heard a most wondrous, a most sweet voice, calling above My head. Turning My face, I beheld a Maiden—the embodiment of the remembrance of the name of My Lord—suspended in the air before Me. So rejoiced was she in her very soul that her countenance shone with the ornament of the good-pleasure of God, and her cheeks glowed with the brightness of the All-Merciful. Betwixt earth and heaven she was raising a call which captivated the hearts and minds of men. She was imparting to both My inward and outer being tidings which rejoiced My soul, and the souls of God's honoured servants. Pointing with her finger unto My head, she addressed all who are in heaven and all who are on earth, saying: "By God! This is the Best-Beloved of the worlds, and yet ye comprehend not. This is the Beauty of God amongst you, and the power of His sovereignty within you, could ye but understand. This is the Mystery of God and His Treasure, the Cause of God and His glory unto all who are in the kingdoms of Revelation and of creation, if ye be of them that perceive."

—from *God Passes By* by Shoghi Effendi

Before he died in 1892, Baha'u'llah had created the Baha'i Faith based on the teachings of the Bab. The Baha'is believe in one God, the Supreme Being who sent such divine teachers and prophets as Buddha, Abraham, Jesus, Moses, Krishna, Zarathustra, and Muhammad—in addition to the Bab and Baha'u'llah—to educate humankind on the religious revelations that will guide "an ever-advancing civilization." They believe in unity, expressed in Baha'u'llah's writings with the statement that "the earth is but one country, and mankind its citizens." This global civilization must and will include such principles as the total elimination of prejudice; a uniting of the world's great religions based on the fact that they share one omnipotent Source; elimination of both extreme poverty and extreme wealth; mandated worldwide education; a cooperative harmony among the religious and scientific communities;

and the teaching that every person is responsible for their own search for truth and wisdom.

The Baha'i belief about "sin" has nothing to do with an external evil power or even necessarily with the concepts of "right" and "wrong." Instead, sin is anything that interferes with spiritual progress, while right or good is anything that is helpful and encouraging to spiritual progress. One of the greatest hindrances to spiritual progress, they believe, is pride, since it creates illusions of overimportance and superiority over other people, neither of which perpetuates God's intended global unity. Salvation doesn't involve God's judgment but instead is a journey toward nearness to God, who is the only source of true, complete happiness. Nearness to God is the Baha'i definition of "heaven," which they don't believe is an actual physical place, and "hell" is the soul existing in distance from Him through its own ill-conceived choices.

The general Baha'i belief about the end of the world is that there will be no literal cataclysmic destruction of this planet but that instead there will be a major global transformation to the divine unity God intended when He created us. This transformation began in the middle of the nineteenth century, when the Prophetic Cycle evolved into the Cycle of Fulfillment—the era in which the apocalyptic prophecies of the world's great religions would be fulfilled and God's kingdom would come to pass.

"One day the earth will be changed to a different earth, and so will be the heavens," the Baha'i scriptures read. "And the earth shineth with the light of her Lord . . . Praise be to Allah, Who hath fulfilled His promise unto us and hath made us inherit the earth." And from the tablets of Baha'u'llah, "The day is approaching when we will have rolled up the world and all that is therein, and spread out a new Order in its stead. The day is approaching when [civilization's] flame will devour the cities, when the tongue of Grandeur will proclaim: 'The Kingdom is God's, the Almighty, the All-Praised.'"

The Baha'i Faith is one of the world's most widespread religions, with more than six million followers, or adherents, worshipping from India to Iran to Vietnam to the United States to the Baha'i headquarters in Haifa, Israel.

Jehovah's Witnesses

TEOTWAWKI. An acronym for The End Of The World As We Know It. The Watchtower Society, founded in the early 1870s by Charles Taze Russell, predicted a variety of dates for TEOT-WAWKI. Not once have their predictions been accurate, so they've now begun stating simply that it will occur "in the near future."

Also known as Jehovah's Witnesses, the Watchtower Society believes that The End Of The World As We Know It—which they actually prefer to call "the conclusion of a system of things"—will be heralded by Jesus Christ reappearing to claim his kingdom on Earth. Other biblical prophets, including Abraham, Jacob, Elijah, and Isaac, will be resurrected to participate in the glorious perfecting of humankind. God, in the meantime, will wage the great war of Armageddon, a global genocide in which billions of people will die. The only survivors of God's war will be adults who are in good standing with the Jehovah's Witnesses, which by definition requires obedience to the teachings of Pastor Charles Russell. Whether or not children and adults who are mentally and psychologically challenged survive the genocide will be God's decision on a case-by-case basis. Disenfranchised Jehovah's Witnesses, the vast majority of Christians, Jews, Buddhists, Hindus, Muslims—in other words, all other religions—will be eliminated and never experience the Rapture of ascending to meet Jesus in the clouds.

Pastor Russell, as he was called by his followers, never claimed to be the messiah and, for that matter, never claimed to have founded a religion. Instead, he considered himself to be utterly and wholly committed to God's service and, because of that, he was granted divine permission to fully understand the Bible and to fulfill the Lord's promise that the devoutly obedient, restored to the perfection of mind, body, and character, will spend eternity in paradise.

Pastor Russell's intensive studies and interpretations of the Bible, combined with his studies of such spiritually historic wonders as the Great Pyramid, resulted in a variety of predictions about the date of Armageddon, or TEOTWAWKI. At the core of his calculations was Daniel 4:13–16:

I saw in the visions of my head on my bed, and, behold, a watcher and a holy one came down from the sky. He cried aloud, and said thus, "Hew down the tree, and cut off its branches, shake off its leaves, and scatter its fruit: let the animals get away from under it, and the fowls from its branches. Nevertheless leave the stump of its roots in the earth, even with a band of iron and brass, in the tender grass of the field; and let it be wet with the dew of the sky: and let his portion be with the animals in the grass of the earth: let his heart be changed from man's, and let an animal's heart be given to him; and let seven times pass over him."

Pastor Russell interpreted the word *time* in that passage to be equal to 360 days. Seven "times" gave him a total of 2,520 days, which he translated to actually mean 2,520 years. Using 607 BCE as a start date and adding 2,520 years, Pastor Russell arrived at the conclusion that TEOTWAWKI would happen in October of 1914. The Watchtower Bible, written in the late 1800s, states, "The final end of the kingdoms of this world, and the full establishment of the Kingdom of God, will be accomplished by the end of A.D. 1914."

Obviously 1914 came and went without God exterminating billions of people. Still believing in Pastor Russell's prophecy about its being a significant year, the Watchtower Society simply redefined its importance. The End Of The World As We Know It would undoubtedly be preceded by a series of transitional events, rather than a mass genocide and the reappearance of Jesus Christ on Earth happening with no prelude at all, and what more likely prelude to the war of Armageddon than 1914, the start of World War I? And with Pastor Russell's statement that those transitional events could take a number of years to occur, the date of the ultimate Armageddon was moved to 1915 and then 1918.

Pastor Russell passed away in 1916, and the newly appointed president of the Watchtower Society, J. E. Rutherford, decided to make a few adjustments in Pastor Russell's calculations and prophecies. The Jehovah's Witnesses had come to accept it as fact "beyond a doubt" that Jesus Christ appeared on Earth in 1874. Working both backward and forward from that date, with the help of the Bible and other spiritually charged sources on earth, Rutherford arrived at the conclusion that Pastor Russell's initial TEOTWAWKI date of 1914 could reliably be changed to 1925. Not that he was ready to stake his reputation on it, though—as New Year's Day of 1925 approached, he wrote, "The year 1925 is a date definitely and clearly marked in the Scriptures, even more clearly than that of 1914; but it would be presumptuous on the part of any faithful follower of the Lord to assume just what the Lord is going to do during that year."

It goes without saying that the Lord clearly decided not to commit mass genocide in 1925 either. Undeterred, the Jehovah's Witnesses kept right on calculating their way to such TEOTWAWKI years as 1932 and 1966, and then arriving with some certainty on the fall of 1975. "Our chronology," they wrote in the Watchtower publication, "which is reasonably accurate (but admittedly not infallible), at best only points to the autumn of 1975 as the end of 6,000 years of man's existence on earth."

Obviously, 1975 wasn't it either, which sent the Jehovah's Witnesses back to their calculations and resources. And in Psalms 90:9–10 they found a possible clue:

> For all our days pass away under thy wrath,
> our years come to an end like a sigh.
> The years of our life are threescore and ten,
> or even by reason of strength fourscore.

Fourscore, they reasoned, translates to eighty years. And the beginning of TEOTWAWKI was still believed to be 1914. Eighty years from 1914, then, or 1994, was apparently the date they'd been looking for when Armageddon would occur. The church leaders were understandably reluctant to make any dramatic announcements about the significance of 1994, and, as we all know now, even we non-Jehovah's Witnesses survived that year as well.

To this day the devout membership of the Jehovah's Witnesses, who number more than six million worldwide, continues to believe that the end of the world is quickly approaching and to behave accordingly: since they can only be saved from extermination in God's mass genocide by being His perpetually active witnesses, they preach His word and the impending TEOTWAWKI each and every day in His service.

The Mormons: The Church of Jesus Christ of Latter-day Saints

In the book of Matthew, chapter 24, verses 35–36, Jesus says:

Heaven and earth shall pass away, but my words shall not pass away. But of that day and hour knowest no man, no, not even the angels of heaven, but my Father only.

That biblical passage may be the reason why some religions, including the Latter-day Saints, believe in the inevitable Second Coming of Christ and the ensuing end of the world but avoid predicting the exact date or year when it will happen. In the case of the Latter-day Saints, also known as the Mormons, they teach that we're now living the last days of life on this earth, and that our only way to prepare is to watch for but not be afraid of the signs that Armageddon is at hand.

According to Mormon history, it was 1823 when an eighteen-year-old Vermont boy named Joseph Smith was visited by the angel Moroni, who told him about the existence and location of a series of Golden Plates. The plates, written in a form of hieroglyphics and translated by Smith with Moroni's help, became the Book of Mormon. In 1830, at the age of twenty-five, Joseph Smith, with his published Book of Mormon in hand, founded what would become the Mormon Church and settled with his followers in Kirtland, Ohio, and subsequently in Nauvoo, Illinois.

In June of 1844 Joseph Smith was killed, attacked by an angry mob in Carthage, Illinois, who disapproved of his claim of having contact with the dead. Brigham Young, a member of Smith's Council of Twelve Apostles, succeeded Joseph Smith as the leader of the Mormon Church and, in 1846, led the Mormons west from Illinois to a site in Utah that became Salt Lake City.

The Latter-day Saints believe that their church leaders are prophets, and that those prophets are given ongoing information from God. Included in that information is the concept that God gave the earth seven thousand years to survive when He created it, and that we're currently existing in about its six thousandth year. Preceding the Second Coming of Christ in the seven thousandth year, the earth will be plagued by wars, earthquakes and other natural disasters, global epidemics, and economic collapse.

The Mormon temple in Salt Lake City features two large doors facing east, which are considered sacrosanct and are never used. Mormons believe that when Jesus comes to Earth again he will enter through those hallowed doors, initiating a thousand years of peace called the Millennium. During the Millennium the wicked will be destroyed, while the righteous, led by Jesus, will live in peace on this earth. The righteous who have died throughout the ages will be resurrected, or, in the language of the Latter-day Saints, "caught up to meet him." (1 Thessalonians 4:17) In fact, by the end of the Millennium, everyone including the wicked will be resurrected. Only those who insist on denying the sanctity of Christ will be denied their place in heaven. Instead, they'll be banished to a place called the Outer Darkness, which is the ultimate destination of Satan.

According to the Latter-day Saints, among the specific signs that will indicate the impending return of Jesus are the darkening of the sun and moon, with resulting darkness covering the earth; Israel gathering power; all nations gathering to do battle against Jerusalem; two prophets being killed and then resurrected in Jerusalem; and Babylon rising and falling.

It's worth adding that more than thirteen million Mormons around the world are currently keeping an eye out for the signs of the Second Coming, and there's every reason to believe they'll be compassionate enough to warn the rest of us when the time comes.

The Rastafarians

In the early 1900s a Jamaican Christian named Marcus Garvey founded the African Orthodox Church to provide his countrymen with an alternative to white churches. An activist leader and nationalist, Garvey spoke with eloquent passion about a movement called Back to Africa, or an exodus to the "homeland" of Ethiopia, and the crowning of a king in Africa who would be revealed as the black messiah.

In 1930, Leonard Howell, another Jamaican, initiated a religious movement based on Marcus Garvey's beliefs (to Garvey's great displeasure, by all accounts). This movement held that Marcus Garvey was a full-fledged prophet and that Haile Selassie, the newly crowned Ethiopian emperor, was the black messiah, the king of kings and lord of lords, that Garvey had prophesied. Selassie was formerly known as Ras Tafari Markonnen, and those who worshipped him as the Second Coming of Christ began calling themselves the Rastafari, which colloquially evolved into the name Rastafarians.

The Rastas, as they're also called, don't actually consider their belief system a religion. Instead, they consider it an ideology, simply a way of life. There are no clergy, and there are no actual churches. They typically worship in small gatherings in the privacy of their homes, studying their Holy Piby, an edited version of the Christian and Hebrew bibles. The other book of intense importance to the Rastafarians is called the Kebra Negast, which outlines the lineage that, in their opinion, establishes Haile Selassie as a direct descendant of King Solomon. They strongly believe in the Hebrew Ten Commandments, the importance of simplicity and purity, the potential corruption of materialism, and the simultaneous worship and dread of Jah, their name for God.

Rastafarians are prohibited from interfering with the natural growth and course of their hair—classic Rastafarian dreadlocks are a natural progression rather than a cultured, manufactured style. The orthodox diet is pure and free of additives and preservatives, and they consume no tobacco or alcohol or coffee, nor salt, seafood, and meat of any kind.

Their famous or infamous relationship with marijuana, which they call ganja, is based on their belief that it aids them in an enlightened knowledge of Jah's true will. A typical gathering of the faithful will invariably include the passing of a ceremonial pipe, known to Rastafarians as the Chalice, which is filled with the sacramental ganja. The most comparable ritual in the Christian world is the sacrament of Communion.

In 1966, Haile Selassie paid a visit to Jamaica to offer an audience to his faithful believers. He died in 1980, although it's not an uncommon Rastafarian belief that his death never really happened and instead he left this earth very much alive and ascended to heaven.

Both Selassie's birthday and the date of his arrival in Jamaica are celebrated as important holidays.

As for Marcus Garvey's Back to Africa movement/prophecy, Emperor Selassie told his Jamaican worshippers that they shouldn't return to Africa until Jamaica was liberated.

Rastafarians have created their own fascinating beliefs about the Apocalypse. The end of days, in their view, began in 1930, when Haile Selassie was crowned Ethiopia's emperor. Very soon he'll reveal himself as the true king of kings and proclaim a day of judgment. The forces of good and evil will collide, and Selassie, the incarnate God, will gather the righteous and return with them to Zion, the promised land, where they'll live eternally in a paradise where there is no oppression, no wickedness, and none of the earthly materialistic corruption in present society, which they refer to as Babylon.

The late great reggae musician Bob Marley is generally credited with bringing the Rastafari movement to mainstream culture following his conversion to it in 1967. You're probably more familiar with his music than you might think—the song for the television commercial "Come to Jamaica" that begins "One love, one heart" is a Bob Marley composition called "One Love." In it are lyrics that beautifully capsulize the Rastafarian view of the end of days:

> *Let's get together*
> *to fight this Holy Armageddon,*
> *so when the man comes*
> *there will be no, no doom.*

Zoroastrianism

It was around 8000 BC that a man named Zarathustra was born in an area of the world we now know as Iran. His followers are called Zoroastrians, and a legion of theological scholars considers Zoroastrianism to be the predecessor and core of contemporary world religions. With good reason, I might add.

Zarathustra is credited with being the first prophet to embrace and advocate the concept that there is one and only one God, or monotheism. His name for this one God, this Supreme Being, was Ahura Mazda, a combination of words that translate to "Lord Creator" and "Supremely Wise." He also believed, several millennia before the birth of Jesus, that a messiah was coming who would be born to a virgin.

Zarathustra believed that Ahura Mazda, or God, created humankind with the freedom to choose throughout life between good and evil, and with the obligation to face the consequences of those choices. In other words, we humans are the cause of the good and the evil in our lives. No more blaming it on Ahura Mazda, and certainly no blaming it on an evil being of some kind—Zarathustra didn't believe in Satan, or the devil.

He believed that our purpose in life is to participate in renewing the world as it progresses toward perfection. Just as the way to combat darkness is by spreading light, and the way to fight evil is by spreading goodness, the way to fight hatred is by spreading love and reflecting the essence of God that is our birthright. Each of us possesses the divine within ourselves, he preached, and it is our obligation to honor and act on our own divinity by respecting the natural and moral laws of the universe.

Asha is the fundamental law of the universe, the natural course and pattern of heavens, the four seasons, the reliable repetition of such phenomena as the tides, the setting of the sun, and the rising of the moon. Everything in physical creation is governed by that fundamental law, Ahura Mazda's divine plan and order. To denigrate that law is to denigrate what Ahura Mazda created, which is to denigrate Ahura Mazda Himself.

The Zoroastrian concept of the battle between opposite forces on Earth isn't limited to the classic good versus evil conflict. The battle of opposites that disrupts the order of Ahura Mazda's creations, which is called *druj*—the ongoing battle of *asha* versus *druj*, in other words—extends to lies versus truth, chaos versus order, the destruction of the planet versus creation, love versus hate, war versus peace, and so on.

Zarathustra taught that when we leave life on Earth, our essence departs our body on the fourth day after death. If we've made good, God-centered choices throughout our lives, treating ourselves and others with love, compassion, and thoughtfulness, our essence goes to the House of Songs, often called the Realm of Light. If we've lived in opposition to the natural and moral laws of the universe Ahura Mazda created, our essence is destined for the Realm of Darkness and Separation. Zarathustra didn't believe the Realm of Light and the Realm of Darkness and Separation are actual physical places but instead that they're eternal states of either oneness with or separation from Ahura Mazda.

Zarathustra's concept of the end of the world is thought to be the first recorded doomsday prophecy in history, dated at around 500 BC. The final days, according to Zoroastrian scripture Zand-i Vohuman Yasht, would commence "at the end of the tenth hundredth winter . . . The sun is more unseen . . . The year, month and day are shorter . . . The earth is more barren, and the crop will not yield the seed ... Men become more deceitful and more given to vile practices. They have no gratitude."

There will be a final great battle between good and evil. Good will triumph, and Ahura Mazda will purify the earth with molten metal and a divine, cleansing fire. (Zoroastrians don't consider fire itself to be sacred, but it's intensely important to their religion as a symbol of Ahura Mazda's power, in much the same way the crucifix is intensely important to Christians.) Ahura Mazda will then begin His judgment of every soul on earth. Consistent with Zarathustra's belief that Ahura Mazda is ultimately a compassionate deity who created good but not evil, even those deemed to be evil, or sinners, are not banished to an eternity of damnation but instead face three days of punishment, after which they're forgiven and resurrected. All suffering on Earth will end, and there will be perfection throughout the world once Ahura Mazda's great cleansing has taken place.

There are thought to be approximately three million Zoroastrians currently practicing this beautiful faith throughout the world.

Pentecostalism

In 1901, at a prayer meeting at the Bethel Bible College in Topeka, Kansas, a woman named Agnes Ozman began spontaneously speaking in tongues, or languages not known to the speaker. The Reverend Charles Fox Parham, who was leading the prayer meeting, interpreted that phenomenon as biblical evidence of the Baptism of the Holy Spirit, based on Acts 2:1–5:

When the day of Pentecost had come, they were all together in one place, and suddenly a sound came from heaven like the rush

*of a mighty wind, and it filled all the house where they were sit-
ting. And there appeared to them tongues as of fire, distributed
and resting on each one of them. And they were all filled with
the Holy Spirit and began to speak in other tongues, as the Spirit
gave them utterance.*

The Reverend Parham also cited Acts 2:38–39 as one of the foundations of his beliefs:

*And Peter said to them, "Repent, and be baptized every one of
you in the name of Jesus Christ for the forgiveness of your sins;
and you shall receive the gift of the Holy Spirit. For the promise
is to you and to your children and to all that are far off, every
one whom the Lord our God calls to him."*

The Reverend Parham moved on from Topeka to undertake a
revival meeting ministry and continue his teaching. One of his students in Houston, Texas, was an African American named William
J. Seymour, who was allowed to sit outside the segregated room to
listen to the Reverend Parham.

William Seymour relocated to Los Angeles and, on April 12,
1906, claimed that he'd been filled with and overwhelmed by the
Holy Ghost. A small group of followers who'd met Mr. Seymour at
the home of a gentleman named Edward Lee, rented an abandoned
church on Azusa Street and organized themselves as the Apostolic
Faith Church. The vast majority of today's traditional Pentecostal
denominations credit William Seymour and his Azusa Street Revival as the birthplace of their church.

The Old Testament Pentecost originated after the Israelites'
exodus from Egypt, when it was also called the Feast of Harvest. It

was observed fifty days after the cutting of the first grain offering after the Passover—hence the origin of the word *pentecost*, which in Greek means to "fifty count." The New Testament Pentecost occurred fifty days after the Crucifixion of Jesus Christ.

Some Pentecostals believe that speaking in tongues is the sign of the baptism of the Holy Spirit but isn't a requisite of salvation. Others emphasize the need to repent and be baptized in Jesus's name and then receive the Holy Spirit. All Pentecostals believe, though, that salvation isn't possible without receiving the Holy Spirit.

The work of the Holy Spirit is an essential foundation of the Pentecostal faith. It's not an uncommon Christian belief that the Holy Spirit is within everyone who's been saved. But Pentecostals, unlike most traditional Christian denominations, also believe that the Holy Spirit is more deeply entrenched within those who've experienced baptism, bringing them to a closer relationship with God and empowering them for His service. The Holy Spirit can also "sanctify," which is an act of grace in which the effects of past sins are neutralized and the human tendency toward temptation is eliminated. According to the Pentecostal faith, salvation is only available to those who are genuinely repentant for their sins and worship Jesus as their savior, and Pentecostals believe in the Bible as the ultimate, divine, infallible authority.

Interpreting the Bible literally, the Pentecostal faith keeps a vigilant watch for signs of the impending end of the world as prophesied in the book of Revelation, and they feel that the twenty-first century is filled with those signs. They cite, for example, the international movement to give each citizen of each country a national identification card that will hold all of their personal data, and a technology called RFID (radio frequency identification) in which a microchip containing Social Security numbers, medical records, etc., would be implanted under every citizen's skin. These developments, they believe, might easily be the pre-apocalyptic warnings contained in Revelation 13:16–17:

> *And he causeth all, both small and great, rich and poor, free and*
> *bond, to receive a mark in their right hand, or in their foreheads;*
> *and that no man might buy or sell, save he that had the mark.*

Other signs Pentecostals point to in today's world that were biblically prophesied as the nearing of the end of days include Putin's power in Russia, the growing tension between Syria and Israel, international terrorism, Iran's nuclear program, the declining value of the U.S. dollar, the growth of China's economic and military power, and the conspicuous changes in global weather.

In other words, as far as many Pentecostals are concerned, we don't need to worry that the end-times are coming—they're already here.

The Baptist Church

While some believe that the Baptist Church originated in seventeenth-century England as a result of the Puritan-Separatist movement in the Church of England, many others believe that it was, in essence, founded by Jesus and that it has existed in perpetuity ever since. Their source for the perpetuity belief is Jesus's proclamation in Matthew 16:18:

*And on this rock I will build my church, and the powers of death
shall not prevail against it.*

But whatever its origins, there are general beliefs that form the
foundation of the Baptist Church and most of its denominations,
among which are that:

+ the Bible was written by men with God's inspiration and that
  it reveals the principles that should guide all human beliefs
  and conduct;
+ there is only one true God, the Creator and Ruler of heaven
  and earth; and that the trinity is created by God the Father,
  Jesus Christ the Son, and the Holy Ghost;
+ humankind was created in perfection but fell from grace voluntarily by committing the Original Sin in the Garden of
  Eden;
+ Jesus was born of Mary, who was a virgin;
+ Jesus died for our sins, was resurrected, and is enthroned beside His Father in heaven;
+ the Bible makes salvation available to everyone if they'll be
  born again through genuine repentance and faith, which are
  both sacred duties and inseparable graces;
+ Christian baptism is the immersion in water of a believer
  and that it is a prerequisite to full membership in the
  church;
+ the Four Freedoms put into words by Baptist historian Wal-
  ter B. Shurden are to be honored: soul freedom (meaning that
  the soul is capable of making its own decisions regarding
  faith); church freedom (there should be no outside interfer-

ence in the practices of local churches); Bible freedom (with the help of the most reliable resources available, each individual is entitled to their own interpretation of the Bible); and religious freedom (each person is free to choose their own religion, or their own lack of one).

In 1833, the Reverend John Newton Brown drew up a document called the New Hampshire Confession of Faith, based on which Baptists could organize a missionary society. There have been some revisions during the 175 years since the Confession of Faith was originally written, but it's still widely accepted, and it concludes with a clear, concise statement of Baptist beliefs about the end of days:

We believe that the end of the world is approaching; that at the last day Christ will descend from heaven, and raise the dead from the grave to final retribution; that a solemn separation will then take place; that the wicked will be adjudged to endless punishment, and the righteous to endless joy; and that this judgment will fix forever the final state of men in heaven or hell, or principles of righteousness.

Jainism

The religion of Jainism, with a current worldwide membership thought to exceed twelve million, originated in ancient India, probably around the sixth century BC. Its roots are still being traced to this day as India's oldest writings continue to be discovered and translated, but it's a commonly held belief that Jainism was one of the driving forces behind the inception of Buddhism. Unlike Buddhism, though, it has no single founder, and its doctrines, or truths, evolved and were revealed by a series of "tirthankars," or teachers. Possibly the last and most devout of those teachers was Vardhamana Mahavira, born in 599 BC. He is sometimes credited with starting Jainism, but historians find it far more likely that the religion had already been in existence for centuries when Mahavira came along and devoted his life to spreading the word.

Jains believe that all living beings, both human and nonhuman, have eternal souls, and that all souls are equal. They consider killing another human being, no matter what the circumstance, to be an act of unspeakable horror, and they require that every person who practices Jainism, from the monks and the nuns to the general membership, be strictly vegetarian.

Their emphasis on the concept of karma, on responsibility and consequence for their actions, is intensely important to the Jains' faith. Karma may or may not manifest itself in the same lifetime as the action that created it, but there's no escaping it, and sowing what we reap includes physical, verbal, and mental acts.

Jainism teaches that energies, called *tapas*, are created by the interaction of the living with the nonliving, and these energies are the engine that drives the constant cycle of birth, death, and rebirth. Jains call that cycle samsara. The ultimate goal in Jainism is to lead a life of such exemplary discipline that they can transcend samsara, and the unavoidable hardship and sorrow of it, and live in the blissful perfection of *moksha*, the Jains' word for nirvana, or heaven.

There is a "three-jewel" path leading to *moksha*: right belief, right knowledge, and right conduct. Included in those jewels are five essential laws and abstinences:

- nonviolence, called *ahimsa*
- truthfulness, called *satya*
- chastity, called *brahmacarya* (total celibacy for the Jain monks and nuns, total chastity outside one's marriage for the laity)
- abstinence from stealing, called *asteya*
- abstinence from greed/materialism, called *aparigraha*

Jainism essentially perceives time as a full circle, or two connected half circles or cycles. *Very* basically, picture a clock. The Utsarpinis, or Progressive Time Cycle, would correspond to the hours between 6:00 and 12:00, when humankind evolves from its worst to its best. The closer to 12:00 the cycle progresses, the happier, healthier, stronger, more ethical, and more spiritual we become. Then, from 12:00 back to 6:00, the Avsarpinis, or Regressive Time Cycle, takes over, the inevitable descent from our best to our worst. The whole circle is divided into six Aras, or periods of unequal length. According to Jainism, we're currently in the fifth Ara of the Avsarpini or Regressive phase, a gradual deterioration of human values and spiritualism, with almost twenty millennia to go before the Utsarpini/Progressive phase begins again.

With this cyclical approach to life, it makes complete sense that the Jains believe the universe was uncreated and that it, and the souls (*jivas*) that dwell in it, last for eternity—until and unless they make their way to the heaven of *moksha*. Their view of the end of days, then, would be cause for celebration, since it would involve nothing more and nothing less than the liberation of the soul/*jiva* from the perpetual cycle of birth, death, and rebirth, filled with pain and karmic repercussions, and the ultimate achievement of Jainism: an eternity of bliss in *moksha*.

An illustration of the interaction of the principles of Jainism and its variation on each individual's "end of days" is offered in a refreshingly simple little story:

A man crafts a small wooden boat to take him from one side of a great river to the other. (The man represents *jiva*, or the soul, while the boat represents nonliving things, called *ajiva*.)

He's under way in his journey when the boat begins to leak. (The rushing in of water represents the deluge of karma on the soul, or *asrava*, and the water's accumulation in the boat is the threatening bondage of karma, called *bandha*.) The man promptly plugs the leak and begins bailing the water out of his boat. (The plug represents putting a stop to the onrush of karma, called samvara, and getting rid of the water is the casting aside of karma, known as *nirjara*.)

Successful in his efforts, the man crosses the river and safely reaches his destination, *moksha*, the freedom and bliss of eternal salvation.

CHAPTER FIVE

The Prophets Speak on the End of Days

If there's any one thing that postbiblical prophets have in common beyond the obvious gift of prophecy, it's the fact that they have virtually nothing in common. There's no such thing as a typical prophet, no apparent group God singles out to be recipients of this particular talent, except perhaps a willingness to share their visions with the general public. This chapter, which covers only a tiny cross section of significant "doomsday prophets," includes three Russians—a flamboyant seer, a "mad monk," and a physician; two British authors; a genius mathematician and scientist; and a modest Kentucky photographer. They all have established track records when it comes to the accuracy of their prophecies, and I specifically selected them because I happen to find them particularly fascinating. But you'll notice that even among this small, select group, there's no consensus on the when, how, or even if of the end of days.

Edgar Cayce

There are few psychics/prophets/clairvoyants who have fascinated me more, and whose body of work I've found more compelling, than Edgar Cayce. His life began in 1877. He was a Kentucky farm boy whose formal education ended with grammar school. And by the time of his death in 1945, he'd gained unsolicited worldwide renown as "The Sleeping Prophet," accomplishing healings, spiritual and metaphysical dictations, and prophecies while in a deep, self-induced, trancelike sleep, none of which he was able to recall when he was awake.

His gifts of prophecy and clairvoyance appeared without warning. Cayce was in his early twenties, making a modest living as a photographer, when an illness caused him to lose his voice. After a year of unsuccessful medical treatments, he took a friend's advice to be treated by a hypnotist.

At his first session with a local hypnotist, Cayce suggested that, rather than the hypnotist going to the effort of inducing sleep, it would be more efficient if he put himself to sleep, which he'd discovered years earlier he was able to do with ease. Once he was in a deep trance, Cayce astonished his friend and the hypnotist by launching into a precise description and diagnosis of the condition that had taken his voice away. The grammar school graduate, who was as uninterested in reading as he was in formal education, displayed the anatomical expertise of a skilled physician as he spelled out a list of complex physiological instructions for the hypnotist to give him while he was under. The hypnotist did as he was told, following Cayce's script of suggestions about vocal cords relaxing and arteries opening to restore oxygen and blood to specific paralyzed muscles. And Cayce awoke from that session with his voice fully restored.

Word spread quickly about Edgar Cayce's gift for diagnosing and curing illnesses while he "slept," and he immediately began receiving letters and personal visits from clients throughout the country wanting his help with illnesses of their own. His initial reaction was to decline their requests—he was uneducated, he argued, and inadequate to be given such awesome responsibility. And the fact that when he was awake he had no memory of the expertise he demonstrated when he was in a trance made it even more impossible to believe that his cures were worth relying on. But the one thing he couldn't argue with was that he'd somehow managed to cure himself, with a hypnotist's help, when the medical community had failed for more than a year. So finally he came to the conclusion that if he indeed had been given this gift, and if he could use it to be of help to suffering people, it would be reprehensible of him not to at least try.

Cayce's career of giving "physical" readings continued throughout his life. His wife, Gertrude, would give him the only information he allowed for each reading: the subject's name, address, and their exact location at the agreed-upon time of the reading. Cayce would ease himself into a trance and signal that he was ready to begin with the words, "Yes, we have the body." Gertrude would read questions to him from the subject's letter, and his secretary, Gladys Davis, would sit nearby, recording the reading in shorthand.

One day in 1923, Edgar Cayce, who was still continuing his photography career at that time, happened to meet a printer named Arthur Lammers in the course of his work. Lammers was mesmerized by the world of metaphysics and by Cayce's gift, and he asked for a reading unlike any Cayce had done before: a reading in which, while Cayce was under, Lammers would ask him questions about life, death, the afterlife, the nature of the soul, the future, anything that occurred to him along those spiritually oriented lines, to see what Cayce's "sleeping" mind would answer.

That was the inception of more than two thousand sessions that came to be called "life readings," in which Cayce discussed the metaphysical aspects of his clients' lives and of life in general. The philosophies he offered with profound expertise and depth were completely contrary to his conservative Protestant upbringing, but finally, through these readings, he arrived at an inescapable belief in reincarnation and an awareness that his answers were coming not from him but *through* him. He was sure he was being given information from the subconscious minds of his subjects, and from the Akashic Records—the collective, infinite memories and histories of every thought, moment, word, and event in the eternity of the universe.

In his lifetime Edgar Cayce accomplished more than fourteen thousand readings, and transcripts of those readings have provided the foundation of more than three hundred books about his work. Inevitably, many of those readings involved the future of humankind, of this planet, and of an eventual Apocalypse.

Cayce predicted a series of natural disasters, wars, economic catastrophes, and great civil unrest, all of which will pave the way for the kingdom of God to rule the earth, with sacred peace and enlightenment thriving throughout humanity. Essential to the prophecies about cataclysmic events was Cayce's belief that these events could be avoided if humankind would only change its ways. Prophecies, he believed, have the potential to be enormously useful if people will respond to them as warnings rather than messages of inevitable, irreversible futility.

Edgar Cayce's visions for the future and for the Second Coming include:

+ Predicted in the late 1920s: A shift in the earth's poles around the year 2000, due to changes in the earth's surface. (NASA confirms that in 1998, as polar ice caps melted, ocean currents began flowing toward the equator, which contributed to a continuing change in our planet's magnetic field.)

+ "If there are greater activities in Vesuvius or Pelee (volcanoes) than the southern coast of California and the areas between Salt Lake and the southern portions of Nevada, we may expect, within the three months following same, inundation by the earthquakes. But these are to be more in the Southern than the Northern hemisphere."

+ "Land will appear in the Atlantic (the lost continent of Atlantis) and the Pacific (the lost continent of Lemuria). And what is the coast line now of many a land will be the bed of the ocean. Even many battle fields of the present will be ocean, will be the seas, the bays, the lands over which The New World Order will carry on their trade as one with another."

+ "The earth will be broken up in the western portion of America."

+ "The greater portion of Japan must go into the sea."

+ "Portions of the now east coast of New York, or New York City itself, will in the main disappear. There will be another generation, though, here; while the southern portions of Carolina, Georgia—these will disappear."

+ "Strifes will arise through the period. Watch for them near the Davis Strait (between Greenland and Canada) in the attempts there for the keeping of the life line to land open. Watch for them in Libya and in Egypt, in Ankara and in Syria, through the straits above those areas above Australia, in the Indian Ocean and the Persian Gulf."

+ "As has been promised through the prophets and the sages, the time [of the day of the Lord] has been and is being fulfilled in this day and generation. The Lord, then, will come, 'even as ye have seen Him go' (Acts 1:11), when those who are His have made the way clear, passable for Him to come. He shall come as ye have seen Him go, in the body He occupied in Galilee. The body He formed, that was crucified on the cross. Read His promises in that ye have written of His words, 'He shall rule for a thousand years. Then shall Satan be loosed again for a season.' (Revelation 20:6-7)"

+ And in the wake of a whole procession of dramatic changes in the earth, some of which we've mentioned here, as we prepare for the Second Coming of Christ, "A new order of conditions is to arise; there must be a purging in high places as well as low; and there must be the greater consideration of the individual, so that each soul is being his brother's keeper. Then certain circumstances will arise in the political, the economic, and a whole relationship to which a leveling will occur, or a greater comprehension of the need for it . . . This America of ours, hardly a new Atlantis, will have another thousand years of peace, another Millennium . . . And then the deeds, the prayers of the faithful, will glorify the Father as peace and love will reign for those who love the Lord."

Sir Isaac Newton

The father of modern physics, the discoverer of the theory of gravitation and the theory of optics and probably the greatest mathematical mind in history, Isaac Newton was born on Christmas Day, 1642, in Woolsthorpe, Lincolnshire, England. His father died three months before Isaac's birth, and when Isaac was three his mother left him with his grandmother while she moved away to live with her new husband. She returned eight years later, after which Isaac was sent away to grammar school. While there, he lived with the local apothecary in Grantham, where his fascination with chemicals, and with science in general, took root.

At seventeen he came home to follow in his late father's footsteps as a farmer. He couldn't have been more of a failure at farming, so instead he made his way to Cambridge, where his genius for mathematics and the sciences became apparent. In fact, his mentor at Cambridge, Isaac Barrow, resigned the prestigious Lucasian professorship so that Isaac Newton could have it instead. (Currently, the Lucasian professorship is held by Stephen Hawking.)

Sir Isaac Newton went on, very famously, to invent everything from the reflecting telescope to calculus, and to permanently change the world's view of everything from astronomy to physics to gravity to motion to mechanics to optics. His book, the *Principia Mathematica*, is still considered to be the world's greatest scientific work, and it was published only after his friend Edmond Halley happened to learn that Newton had written part one and put it in a drawer ten years earlier.

While he was busily applying his genius to virtually every earthly academic pursuit, he also began applying it to theology, chronology, and the Bible, for which he developed a lifelong passion. He was convinced that Christianity had strayed from the teachings of Jesus and that the Bible is to be read as literal truth. And he became especially fascinated with the end of days as depicted both in Revelation and in the book of Daniel, commonly considered to be the Revelation of the Old Testament. His only book about the Bible, published six years after his death in 1727, was *Observations Upon the Prophecies of Daniel and the Apocalypse of St. John*, in which he said:

> The prophecies of Daniel and John should not be understood till the time of the end: but that some should prophesy out of it in an afflicted and mournful state for a long time, and that but darkly, so as to convert but few. But in the very end, the Prophecy should be so far interpreted so as to convince many. Then saith Daniel, many shall run to and fro, and knowledge shall be increased . . . If the general preaching of the Gospel be approaching, it is for us and our posterity that these words mainly belong: In the time of the end the wise shall understand, but none of the wicked shall understand. Blessed is he that readeth, and they that hear the words of this Prophecy, and keep those things that are written therein.

In 1704, Sir Isaac Newton wrote several letters regarding the Apocalypse; his mathematical conclusion about when the end of times would come, based on calculations found in unspecified passages in the book of Daniel; and his prediction that the Second Coming of Christ would follow worldwide epidemics and wars, and that it would preceded a thousand-year reign on Earth by the saints themselves. These letters, carefully preserved and collected over these three centuries, came into the possession of the Israel National Library in 1969.

And in February of 2003 Sir Isaac Newton's official calculation regarding the end of the world, scribbled on a scrap of paper, was revealed to the public for the first time.

The year, according to Newton, will be 2060.

He added:

It may end later, but I see no reason for its ending sooner . . . This I mention not to assert when the time of the end shall be, but to put a stop to the rash conjectures of fanciful men who are frequently predicting the time of the end, and by doing so bring the sacred prophecies into discredit as often as their predictions fail.

So there you have it. 2060. The date of the end of time, calculated from biblical information by the most brilliant mathematician the world has ever known, to do with as you will.

Madame Helena Blavatsky

Madame Helena Blavatsky was a fascinating woman—fearless adventurer, ardent student of the paranormal, sought-after clairvoyant of dubious authenticity, cofounder of the Theosophical Society for the study of spiritualism and the occult sciences, and author of a book, *The Secret Doctrine*, that confirmed her skills as a very gifted prophet. Some of her most outspoken critics dismissed her as a complete fraud, while Albert Einstein kept a copy of *The Secret Doctrine* on his desk.

She was born in Russia in 1831. Her father was a soldier, and her mother was a successful novelist. A hint of her peculiar relationship with the truth can be found in the fact that throughout her life she claimed that her mother died when Helena was an infant, even though she was actually twelve years old at the time of her mother's death.

Helena was seventeen when she escaped a loveless three-month marriage to a Russian general named Nicephore Blavatsky, who was more than twice her age. She spent the next ten years traveling. The specifics of those ten years vary from one account to the next and will never be reliably unraveled. But Helena's version included two years of study with the lama in Tibet, where admittance was not easily granted in the 1800s, particularly to women.

She finally returned to Russia and to her husband, on the condition that she be required to spend only a minimal amount of time with him. She began holding seances in her grandfather's home, quickly attracting a cross section of Russian intellectuals who were becoming increasingly intrigued by the paranormal, and by Madame Helena Blavatsky.

Her appeal obviously wasn't limited to her skills as a clairvoyant, since over the next few years she was romantically involved with an Estonian spiritualist and a married opera singer while still living with her husband. She gave birth to a son, Yuri, who was deformed at birth, and none of her lovers claimed paternity. His death at the age of five devastated her and, she once wrote, destroyed her belief in the Russian Orthodox God. She held on to some of her faith, though, as evidenced in a subsequent statement that "there were moments when I believed deeply . . . that the blood of Christ had redeemed me."

Money and clients for her occult pursuits were diminishing, so Helena decided to travel again, this time to Odessa, to Egypt, and to Paris, where she heard about the spiritualist movement that was gaining momentum in the United States. Sure that this was the new beginning she'd been searching for, she boarded a steamship for New York City, arriving in July of 1873 with little more than a dime to her name.

She struggled for more than a year, barely making ends meet with occasional séances and her job at a sweatshop. But then, in October of 1974, her life changed dramatically when she traveled to a remote farm in Vermont for the sole purpose of introducing herself to Colonel Henry Steel Olcott. Colonel Olcott was writing a series of research articles on a pair of brothers who were conducting séances at the farm, and Helena decided he was someone she wanted and needed to meet.

She stayed at the farm for ten days, conducting séances with the Eddy brothers and making a very positive impression on Colonel Olcott. He wrote several articles about her and was delighted when she offered to translate them for publication in Russia. Thanks to those articles and word of mouth, Madame Helena Blavatsky's fame began to spread throughout and beyond New York. Of far more significance, her relationship with Colonel Olcott blossomed into the founding of the Theosophical Society in 1875, an organization that emphasizes cultural understanding between Eastern and Western philosophies, religions, and sciences and that continues to thrive today.

Adding more controversy to an already controversial life, she began claiming the appearance of a parade of manifested spirits during séances. An infamous photograph was taken of Madame Blavatsky seated in front of three of these manifested spirits, whom she called her Ascended Masters: her personal master, El Myora; Saint Germain, draped in an ermine cloak; and her teacher, Kuthumi, through whom she claimed to have channeled much of her written work, including *The Secret Doctrine*.

With or without the help of Ascended Master Kuthumi, Helena Blavatsky wrote *The Secret Doctrine* in 1888, and there's no denying the accuracy of many of the prophecies recorded in that book. For example:

> *Between 1888 and 1897 there will be a large rent made in the Veil of Nature, and materialistic science will receive a death blow.*

"Materialistic science" referred to scientists' view at the time that the world was composed of nothing more than its material, visible, and tangible elements. That shortsighted view changed forever when, in 1895, Wilhelm Roentgen discovered X-rays, exposing a whole new universe of realities beyond the naked eye, and, in 1896, when Antoine Becquerel discovered radioactivity.

The Secret Doctrine also included facts about the realities of energy that were contrary to the beliefs of the majority of scientists in the 1800s but came about after Helena Blavatsky committed them to paper in 1888. To name a few, she announced that:

+ atoms could be divided. Eleven years later, in 1897, Sir J. J. Thomson discovered the electron.
+ atoms are perpetually in motion. Twelve years later, in 1900, Max Planck's work laid the foundation for the quantum theory of physics.

✦ matter and energy can be converted. Seventeen years later, in 1905, Albert Einstein unveiled the theory of relativity.

Her prophecies inevitably extended to the earth and its geographical and spiritual future. She believed strongly, for example, that the lost continents of Atlantis and Lemuria would reemerge, and added:

> The elevated ridge in the Atlantic basin, 9000 feet in height, which runs from a point near the British Islands, first slopes towards South America, then shifts almost at right angles to proceed in a south-easterly line toward the African coast . . . This ridge is a remnant of an Atlantic continent . . . Could it be traced further, it would establish the reality of a submarine horseshoe junction with a former continent in the Indian Ocean . . . An impenetrable veil of secrecy was thrown over the occult and religious mysteries taught [there], after the submersion of the last remnant of the Atlantean race, some 12,000 years ago.

In March of 1996, *Discover* magazine published satellite photographs of the areas she described more than a century earlier. *Discover* explained the photographs as follows:

> The Midatlantic Ridge snakes down the center of that ocean off Greenland to the latitude of Cape Horn . . . Under South Africa, the Southwest Indian Ridge shoots into the Indian Ocean like a fizzling rocket, or perhaps like the trail of some giant and cartoonish deep-sea mole.

Years earlier, in 1954, the *Geological Society of America Bulletin* reported on an exploration of the summit of this same Mid-Atlantic Ridge:

> *The state of lithification of the limestone suggests that it may have been lithified under subaerial [i.e., above water, on land surface] conditions, and that the sea mount [summit] may have been an island within the past 12,000 years.*

Expanding her prophecies to other parts of the world, Helena Blavatsky also wrote in *The Secret Doctrine*:

> *England is on the eve of such or another catastrophe; France, nearing such a point of her cycle, and Europe in general threatened with, or rather, on the eve of a cataclysm. A world destruction as happened to Atlantis will occur. Instead of Atlantis, all of England and parts of the northwest European coast will sink into the sea. In contrast, the sunken Azores region, the Isle of Poseidonis will again be raised from the sea. [The Isle of Poseidonis is thought to be an island approximately the size of Ireland that is a remnant of Atlantis.]*

As cataclysmic as some of Madame Blavatsky's geological predictions were, her prophecy for the ultimate nonphysical future of our planet was optimistic:

> *We are at the close of the cycle of 5000 years of the present Aryan Kali Yuga or dark age. This will be succeeded by an age of light. Even now under our very eyes, the new Race or Races are pre-*

paring to be formed, and that is in America that the transformation will take place, and has already silently commenced. This Race will be altered in mentality and will move toward a more perfect spiritual existence.

H. G. Wells

A discussion about what lies ahead for us and our planet would seem incomplete without acknowledging a prolific author and social activist who came to be known as The Man Who Invented Tomorrow.

Herbert George Wells was born in Bromley, Kent, England, on September 21, 1866. His parents were hardworking blue-collar people, which purely by chance provided Wells with a wealth of access to his childhood passion: books. His mother was a housekeeper at an estate near the Wells home, and he went with her at every opportunity to sneak into the mansion's vast library and read until his mother had finished her work.

Out of family necessity, the young Herbert George's school years were interrupted by a job as a draper's apprentice. When he returned to school he focused his studies on the sciences, received his bachelor's degree, and taught school until, in 1893, he began writing full time.

In the meantime, Wells was launching what can politely be described as a colorful personal life. In 1891, the year after he graduated from college, he married his cousin Isabel. To support both his wife and his parents, he worked two jobs and was rewarded with a case of tuberculosis. He then left Isabel for one of his students, a young woman named Amy Catherine Robbins, whom he married in 1895 and with whom he had the only two legitimate children of the seven he ultimately fathered.

Fortunately for the literary world, Wells also channeled his passion into his first book, *The Time Machine*, the story of a man returning from a trip to the year 802701. It's a fascinating combination of parody and dark science fiction. But the technical principles and details of the time machine itself exposed Wells's unanticipated foresights into nonfiction science and physics — *The Time Machine*, for example, alluded to a time-space continuum years before Einstein published his theory on that same subject.

As his literary success grew, with such science fiction groundbreakers as *The War of the Worlds* and *The Island of Dr. Moreau*, his reputation as a conflicted, outspoken, and often radical social commentator grew as well. He championed the lower classes and so passionately believed in a fair and equal community of humankind that he joined a London socialist organization called the Fabian Society. But he and its leaders, particularly author George Bernard Shaw, quarreled constantly, and Wells used his contentious relationship with the Fabian Society as the basis for his novel *The New Machiavelli*.

H. G. Wells was also a passionate believer that, no matter how bleak it might seem because of man's inhumanity to man, the future was still very much worth fighting for. That basic theme inspired a prolific array of nonfiction work, including *The Outline of History*, which was the twentieth century's second-bestseller. His articulate insights led to his membership on the Research Committee for the League of Nations; meetings with Lenin, Stalin, and Franklin Roosevelt; and a candidacy for the British Parliament.

By the time of his death on August 13, 1946, H. G. Wells had written more than a hundred books, only about half of them fictional, and he had predicted all of the following on paper, years before each of them became a reality:

+ the atomic bomb
+ England's entering the Second World War in 1940
+ the London Blitz
+ the military vehicle we know as the tank
+ the military use of airplanes
+ superhighways
+ computers
+ urban overcrowding
+ uranium bombs
+ VCRs
+ television sets, on which news would be broadcast

H. G. Wells was subject to depression, darkness, and pessimism. The epitaph he wrote for himself read, "God damn you all, I told you so." Which frankly makes his view of the world's potential for endless longevity all the more surprising and touching: he genuinely believed that if humankind would transcend its self-destructive behavior, he envisioned an indestructible world of peace, cooperation, and freedom from habitual hatreds, bigotry, and class-consciousness by the middle of the twenty-first century. Whether or not this planet survives, and we humans survive on it, in other words, is completely our choice and our responsibility.

Grigori Rasputin

I said at the beginning of this chapter that there's no such thing as a typical prophet and that God endows the gift of prophecy to a wide variety of people. Grigori Rasputin is a perfect example of that wide variety.

He was born in 1872 in the small Siberian village of Pokrovskoye. His parents, both peasants, were devoutly religious, and Grigori's father, Efim, read the Bible to his family every night, a practice that influenced Rasputin throughout his life.

He was prone to depression as a child, particularly when, at the age of eight, he lost his older brother to pneumonia. By his mid-teens he'd already gained a reputation as what we'd now call a juvenile delinquent—he drank heavily, he was wildly reckless, and he found the young girls of Pokrovskoye as irresistible as they found him.

He also gained a childhood reputation as a psychic. The story goes that one night he was lying in bed when he overheard his father and a group of houseguests talking about the theft of a horse and theorizing about possible suspects. Grigori walked into the room, identified one of the men as the horse thief, and went back to bed. The group chuckled at the little boy's accusation and went on with their evening. But later, two of the guests followed the accused man home and were shocked to find the stolen horse hidden in an outbuilding.

Rasputin's marriage at nineteen did nothing to calm him down or put an end to his drinking, and there's a certain irony in the fact that he was accused, but not convicted, of stealing horses. He was sentenced to banishment from Pokrovskoye, but he convinced the court to allow him an alternative to banishment—he suggested he take his father's place on a pilgrimage to the Verkhoturye Monastery more than two hundred miles away. The court agreed, and Rasputin gladly accepted what he thought was a comparative slap on the wrist.

He was preparing to leave for the monastery when his wife lost their first son. He had no choice but to proceed with his journey, but it was a long sad lonely trek. Shortly after he arrived at Verkhoturye, Rasputin had the honor of meeting a devout, widely respected recluse named Makary, who told him that the tragic death of his son was a divine message to return to Pokrovskoye and devote his life to God.

Rasputin did exactly that, almost shocking the village with his newfound piety. He stopped drinking, and he spent hours and hours of every day in prayer. As luck would have it, though, his pilgrimage to the Verkhoturye Monastery had also exposed him to a relatively obscure Russian Orthodox sect, called Skoptsy, with an approach to their faith that was more compatible with Rasputin's nature: they believed that sin was an essential element in the connection between humankind and God. Without sin there could be no confession. Without confession there could be no forgiveness. And without forgiveness there could be no God-given cleansing of the soul. It made perfect, convenient sense to Rasputin, and he became a Skoptsy monk, sinning his way through widespread travels as an impressive, well-educated, well-spoken, and intensely charismatic religious teacher.

Rasputin was so impressive, in fact, that in 1903, when he made his first visit to St. Petersburg, he quickly began attracting the upper-class residents. His exhaustive knowledge of the scriptures, his facile talent as a storyteller, and his darkly mysterious charisma combined with rumors of his supernatural powers—which by now were said to include both psychic abilities and the gift of healing—made him irresistible to St. Petersburg society. It was on his return trip to the city in 1905 that he was invited to the home of Grand Duke Peter Nikolaievich and Grand Duchess Militsa, who regarded him as a devout man whom God had blessed with great unearthly powers. Rasputin was given the perfect opportunity to confirm their belief in him when they led him to their beloved dog, who was very ill and had been given only a few months to live. He knelt beside the dog and began to pray, and by all accounts the dog slowly but surely regained its health. The dog lived for years after Rasputin's healing, and Rasputin's reputation as a truly gifted man of God was etched in stone.

The grand duke and duchess eagerly introduced Rasputin to their friends Tsar Nicholas II and Tsarina Alexandra. Even though he didn't demonstrate any of his supernatural powers in their first few meetings, Rasputin made a significant impact on the tsar and tsarina—such a significant impact, in fact, that the tsar began referring to Rasputin as "the holy man." His impact on the tsarina was undoubtedly amplified by the fact that her previous advisor, Dr. Phillipe, had assured her when he left that "Your Majesty will some day have another friend like me who will speak to you of God." Alexandra was quick to assume that Rasputin was that friend she'd been looking for.

In 1905 Nicholas and Alexandra, after having been blessed with four daughters, ecstatically welcomed a son and heir to the throne, Tsarevich Alexei Nikolaievich. His birth was celebrated by all of Russia, while the tsar and tsarina kept the heartbreaking secret they'd learned shortly after Alexei was born: he was afflicted with hemophilia, which made him a fragile sickly child who could never ascend to the Russian throne if he were considered to be physically unfit.

Rasputin was summoned by Nicholas and Alexandra several times during Alexei's childhood, and he was undeniably remarkable at easing Alexei's discomfort. Possibly the most renowned event in the relationship between Rasputin and this frail little boy was recorded by his older sister, Olga:

The poor child lay in pain, dark patches under his eyes and his little body all distorted, and the [injured] leg terribly swollen. The doctors were just useless . . . more frightened than any of us . . . [Alexandra] sent a message to Rasputin in St. Petersburg. He reached the palace about midnight . . . Early in the morning [Alexandra] called me to go Alexei's room. I just could not believe my eyes. The little boy was not just alive, but well. He was sitting up in bed, the fever gone, the eyes clear and bright, not a sign of any swelling in the leg. Later I learned that Rasputin had not even touched the child but merely stood at the foot of the bed and prayed.

Needless to say, that "miracle" secured Rasputin's status with the royal family. Nicholas and Alexandra embraced him gratefully and wholeheartedly and, some would say, blindly. Rasputin, celebrated as he was, had never abandoned his devout belief that sin was the only true path to God. And now, with his own bedroom in the palace, he practiced that belief with the added bonuses of an expensive wardrobe and his virtual pick of the local females, whom he "purified" on a very regular basis. Even Nicholas and Alexandra's daughters weren't off-limits in his eyes—while no one has ever suggested that there was any actual sexual contact between Rasputin and the tsarevnas, he was found in their rooms frequently enough that their governess strongly suggested to Alexandra that he be permanently barred from the girls' bedroom. It speaks volumes about the extent of his influence over Alexandra that, rather than heeding the governess's advice, she defended Rasputin's right to move freely throughout the palace without restrictions.

Predictably, Rasputin's influence over Nicholas and Alexandra was beginning to alarm an increasing number of people, from the Russian Orthodox Church to the grand duke and duchess who'd introduced Rasputin to the royal family. The church conducted an investigation that resulted in devastating evidence against him from countless women, including the attempted rape of a nun. The tsar and tsarina were confronted with a long list of Rasputin's crimes, both proven and alleged, and they tragically refused to listen. Alexandra in particular took the position that the rising tide against Rasputin was the result of nothing but cruel jealousy and resentment "because we love him."

World War I was raging, and in 1915 Nicholas traveled to take command of the troops on the eastern front. Whether or not this was Rasputin's idea is a matter of debate, but there's no doubt about the effect of Nicholas's decision: his absence left Tsarina Alexandra as the sole ruler of Russia, which essentially left Rasputin in a position of great power and influence over her and, as a result, the entire country. Among his first priorities was the removal of his detractors from positions of significance within the government, replacing them with his proven loyalists. To this day it's a widely held belief that Rasputin, and Alexandra's almost slavish reliance on his advice, was directly responsible for the loss of confidence in the imperial government.

It was decided by a growing number of Rasputin's enemies, both outside and within the government, that he had to be eliminated. He wasn't about to step aside, nor was the tsarina about to allow it. And so, on the night of December 16, 1916, Rasputin was invited to the home of Prince Felix Yussupov for the ostensible purpose of meeting Yussupov's wife, Irina. The evening proved to be an odd testament to Rasputin's power. He unwittingly ate his share of cakes laced with poison and drank his share of alcohol laced with poison. To Yussupov's and his fellow conspirators' irritation, neither had the slightest affect on Rasputin, so Yussupov resorted to shooting him in the back. Rasputin fell to the floor. Yussupov bent over him to make sure he was dead, at which moment Rasputin leaped up and attacked Yussupov.

Yussupov managed to escape Rasputin and shoot four more bullets at him, one of those shots hitting Rasputin in the head. For good measure, Yussupov then proceeded to beat Rasputin with a club until there was no more movement or sound coming from him. Yussupov and his fellow conspirators wrapped Rasputin's body in a curtain and threw it into the Neva River—incredibly, the death was listed as a drowning, since water in Rasputin's lungs established that he was still breathing when he was dropped into the dark river.

It was later discovered that in December of 1916 Rasputin wrote a letter to Tsarina Alexandra predicting that he would be murdered before the first of January, 1917. He then added:

If I am killed by common assassins then you have nothing to fear. But if I am murdered by nobles, and if they shed my blood, their hands will remain soiled. Brothers will kill brothers and there will be no nobles in the country.

The remainder of the letter clarified Rasputin's prophecy: if he was murdered by the poor, the royal family would prosper. But if he was killed at the hands of princes, the tsarina and her entire family would be assassinated in less than two years.

A year and a half after the death of Rasputin at the hands of princes, Nicholas, Alexandra, and their children were executed by Bolshevik guards on July 16, 1918.

It is no surprise that the controversy surrounding the life of Rasputin, who came to be known as the "mad monk," continues to this day. There are those who believe that despite his fairly despicable personal behavior, he was a genuinely gifted healer and psychic, a prophetic adviser to Tsarina Alexandra who indisputably saved Alexei's life. Others argue just as passionately that Rasputin was a con artist and fraud who used his charisma and talent for hypnosis to endear himself to the most powerful family in Russia and create the illusion of healing in a sick, highly suggestible young boy.

Wherever the truth lies, many of his prophecies have survived since the middle of the First World War, including this one involving his vision of the coming Apocalypse:

Mankind is going in the direction of the catastrophe. The less able ones will be guiding the car. This will happen in Russia, in France, in Italy and in other places. The humanity will be squashed by the lunatics' roar. The wisdom will be chained. The ignorant and the prepotent will dictate the laws to the wise and to the humble person. So, most of the humanity will believe in the powerful ones and no more in God. The punishment of God will arrive late, but it will be tremendous. And it will arrive before our century ends. Then, finally the wisdom will be free from the chains and the man will return entirely to God, as the baby who goes to his mother. In this way, mankind will arrive on the terrestrial paradise.

Sir Arthur Conan Doyle

He created the character of Sherlock Holmes, about whom he wrote four novels and fifty-six short stories. He was a successful physician who served in a medical unit in South Africa. He was knighted by King Edward VII for an article he wrote entitled "The War in South Africa: Its Cause and Conduct," in which he defended England's handling of the Boer War. He became a renowned writer and public speaker on spiritualism and the afterlife. And he committed to paper in 1930 a list of prophecies that history showed to be remarkably accurate.

His name was Arthur Conan Doyle, and he was born to devoutly Catholic parents in Edinburgh, Scotland, on May 22, 1859. His early career as a physician led him to his wife, Louise, whose brother Jack he treated for terminal cerebral meningitis. Jack's illness and death drew Arthur and Louise into a deeply devoted, respectful marriage that resulted in the birth of two children, at a time when Arthur was making the transition from successful physician to brilliantly gifted author.

The first Sherlock Holmes story was published in 1887. In 1893, Louise was diagnosed with tuberculosis. Arthur moved the family to the healthier climate of Hindshead, Surrey, England, in 1897, and it was there that he met the love of his life, a woman named Jean Leckie. For almost ten years, Arthur Conan Doyle and Jean Leckie somehow managed to carry on an affair that was both passionate and platonic, and Arthur never violated his oath that Louise was never to know about Jean and was never ever to be hurt.

Louise died in 1906, and for quite some time Arthur sank into health problems and depression, struggling with the guilt of a decade of secret keeping and withholding from a wife who'd devoted her life to him. But the love between him and Jean survived, and they were married in the fall of 1907.

In 1881, Arthur Conan Doyle happened to attend a lecture on spiritualism—rather remarkable under the circumstances, since his childhood Catholicism had dissipated into agnosticism by then. Something clearly moved his soul at that lecture, though, and didn't let go. He began writing articles for spiritualist publications. He attended séances. He volunteered to be hypnotized at a lecture on mesmerism (the study of animal magnetism, in vogue at that time). And finally, in 1893, he joined the British Society for Psychical Research, an organization that, among other things, investigated alleged hauntings and similar paranormal phenomena.

By 1920, Sir Arthur Conan Doyle was one of England's and America's foremost writers and public speakers on the subjects of spiritualism and the afterlife. It was a courageous undertaking on his part, because he accurately assumed it would compromise his lifetime of credibility. But his spiritual convictions were so strong and so deep in him that he willingly paid that price without equivocation or apologies until the day he died of heart failure on July 7, 1930.

A man as open-minded, diverse, and spiritually available as Arthur Conan Doyle was a perfect channel for prophecies. Some of them came from his Spirit Guide Phineas, and some of them were based on material he'd gleaned from mediums throughout England and the United States. All of them were contained in a letter he wrote shortly before his death, almost an open letter to humankind out of heartfelt concern, intended not to frighten but simply to encourage vigilance and preparation.

In 1930, Arthur Conan Doyle predicted that:

+ a period of natural convulsions will take place during which a large portion of the human race will perish; earthquakes of great severity and enormous tidal waves would seem to be the agent.

+ war will appear only in the early stages and will appear to be a signal for the crisis to follow; the crisis will come in an instant.

+ the destruction and dislocation of civilized life will be beyond belief.

+ there will be a short period of chaos followed by some reconstruction; the total period of upheavals will be roughly three years.

+ the chief centers of disturbance will be the Eastern Mediterranean basin, where not less than five countries will entirely disappear.

+ in the Atlantic there will be a rise of land which will be a cause of those waves which will bring about great disasters upon the Americas, the Irish and Western European shores, involving all of the low-lying British coasts.

+ further great upheavals would occur in the southern Pacific and in the Japanese region.

+ *mankind can be saved by returning to its spiritual values.*

Nostradamus

Michel de Nostredame, aka Nostradamus, was born in St. Remy de Provence, France, in 1503. More than five hundred years later his prophecies are still being exhaustively studied, debated, praised, and decried, and the man himself is the subject of both great admiration as a prophet and equally great disdain as a fraud.

I will never claim to be an expert on the subject of Nostradamus, but I do know that in his early years he was a brilliant physician and alchemist. He worked tirelessly to heal countless victims of a plague that swept through France not long after he received his degree in medicine from the University of Montpellier, and the herbal medications he created were so effective in curing the incurable that he was accused of being a heretic—a deadly charge at the time. No less than the Pope himself declared the charges unfounded after hearing of Nostradamus's undeniable success against the plague. Nostradamus was known for his lifelong generosity toward the poor.

Nostradamus spent four years writing his first book of prophecies, called the Centuries, but was reluctant to publish it for fear of the cruel religious persecution prevalent against "seers and soothsayers" of that era. Finally, though, he felt too strongly that his book might be of use to society to keep it hidden, and he published it in 1555 at his own very real peril. Last but not least, Nostradamus took no personal credit for his prophecies but instead acknowledged God as their author and as the One from whom he received his gift. As he wrote in the preface of his first book of prophecies, which he dedicated to his son:

> Thy late arrival, my son, has made me bestow much time, through nightly vigils, to leave you in writing a memorial to refer to . . . that might serve for the common profit of mankind, out of what the Divine Being has permitted me to learn from the revolution of the stars.

So whether or not his prophecies were or are considered accurate, it's hard to imagine that a man of his kindness, faith, humility, and selflessness would deliberately perpetrate a fraud.

Tragically, the same plague Nostradamus fought against so successfully killed his wife and two children, and he spent the next several years as a traveling physician. It was during these long, lonely years that he began actively studying and experimenting with the occult, for which he held a lifelong fascination. It was also on one of his routine journeys between France and Italy that he had what is considered to be his first prophetic experience.

He was on a narrow footpath in Italy when he came upon a small group of Franciscan monks. Nostradamus was of Jewish lineage, but his family had converted to Christianity, and he was raised in the Catholic faith. So, like any respectful Catholic, he began stepping aside to let the monks pass. But suddenly he focused on one of them and, overcome with awe, he fell to his knees and genuflected at the feet of Father Felice Peretti, a swineherd before he entered the monastery.

When the astonished monk asked what on earth Nostradamus was doing, he replied, "I must yield myself and bow before his Holiness."

Nineteen years after the death of Nostradamus, that monk, Father Peretti, became Pope Sixtus V.

When Nostradamus's travels ended, he remarried, this time to a wealthy widow with whom he had six children. They settled in Salon, France, and it was there that he began his prophetic writings.

His works had a very distinctive structure. He wrote in four-line verses, or quatrains. Then he organized the quatrains into what he called Centuries—one hundred quatrains per Century, although since he wrote a total of 942 quatrains in his lifetime, there was one Century that contained only forty-two quatrains.

As for his style, it can only be described as obscure. It was full of Greek and Latin and anagrams and odd, complicated plays on words. One school of thought is that his writings were deliberately vague so that they would be too hard to interpret for anyone to claim he was inaccurate. The truth is actually a distant relative of that theory: Nostradamus knew that he faced possible persecution, including torture or death, if he clearly revealed himself as a prophet. But if his works were obscure and confusing enough, no one could make an ironclad case against him for being a heretic seer in league with the devil. So the fact that debates continue to this day about the "real" interpretation of the Nostradamus quatrains is a testament to his ability to protect himself and the integrity of his prophecies.

It was one of Nostradamus's less obscure quatrains that put him in great favor with the French royal family and elevated his status during his lifetime. The quatrain reads:

> *The young lion will overcome the older one*
> *On the field of combat in single battle.*
> *He will pierce his eyes through a golden cage*
> *Two wounds made one, then he dies a cruel death.*

A few short years after Nostradamus wrote those words, France's King Henry II was killed during a jousting tournament when his opponent's lance slipped through the "golden" face mask of the king's helmet, piercing his eye. King Henry's wife, Catherine d' Medici, knew of Nostradamus's prophecy about her husband, and after his death she regularly used Nostradamus as her personal consultant.

The prophecies of Nostradamus have been translated, dissected, analyzed, and interpreted by countless people in countless books, articles, and films. I can't possibly do them justice here. But for the purpose of our discussion of the Apocalypse, there are several quatrains that lend themselves perfectly.

Nostradamus predicted that on the long road to the end of days, the world would see a rise to power of three antichrists who would terrorize and sadistically brutalize anyone who offered them less than blind, slavish loyalty.

His description of the first of these antichrists reads:

> *An Emperor shall be born near Italy*
> *Who shall cost the Empire dear.*
> *They shall say, with what people he keeps company,*
> *He shall be found less a Prince than a butcher.*
> *From a simple soldier he will rise to the Empire*
> *From the short robe he will attain the long.*
> *Great swarms of bees shall arise.*

And, in a separate quatrain:

> *The captive prince, conquered, is sent to Elba;*
> *He will sail across the Gulf of Genoa to Marseilles.*
> *By a great effort of the foreign forces he is overcome,*
> *Though he escaped the fire, his bees yield blood by the*
> *barrel.*

The identity of Nostradamus's first Antichrist seems indisputable to his countless students and fans: Napoleon Bonaparte, the emperor of France from 1799 to 1814, was born in 1769 on the island of Corsica, fifty miles from the coast of Italy. No one would disagree with the description of him as a "butcher" throughout his reign. And, for good measure, his imperial crest was the symbol of the beehive. Napoleon was exiled to the island of Elba but escaped for one hundred days. After a defeat at Waterloo he relinquished all power and was exiled to the tiny island of St. Helena.

The second Antichrist was described by Nostradamus as a "great enemy of the human race" and a master manipulator:

> *Out of the deepest part of the west of Europe,*
> *From poor people a young child shall be born,*
> *Who with his tongue shall seduce many people.*
> *His fame shall increase in the Eastern Kingdom.*
> *He shall come to tyrannize the land.*
> *He shall raise up a hatred that had long been dormant.*
> *The child of Germany observes no law.*
> *Cries, and tears, fire, blood and battle.*

In a separate quatrain Nostradamus adds:

> *A captain of Germany shall come to yield himself by false*
> *   hope,*
> *So that his revolt shall cause great bloodshed.*
> *Beasts wild with hunger will cross the rivers*
> *The greater part of the battlefield will be against Hister.*

It's no surprise that this is widely believed to be Nostradamus's prophecy of the rise of Adolf Hitler, who was born in Austria in 1889 to a poor family. References like "tyrannized" and "raised up a hatred" and "observed no law" and "seducing many people with his tongue" are understatements to describe the psychopathic, sadistic, inhuman monster that "child of Germany" proved to be.

However, critics of Nostradamus's works are quick to point out that "Hister," rather than being an uncanny reference to Hitler that was just one letter off, happened to be the name of the lower Danube River during Nostradamus's time. This is one of countless quatrains in which the debate over the "true interpretation" isn't likely to end.

As for the third Antichrist, Nostradamus was again both very descriptive and subject to exhaustive debate:

> *Out of the country of Greater Arabia*
> *Shall be born a strong master of Muhammad . . .*
> *He will enter Europe wearing a blue turban.*
> *He will be the terror of mankind . . .*

> *From the sky will come the great King of Terror.*
> *He will bring back to life the King of the Mongols;*
> *Before and after war reigns.*

> *The sky will burn at forty-five degrees.*
> *Fire approaches the great new city.*
> *By fire he will destroy their city,*
> *A cold and cruel heart,*
> *Blood will pour,*
> *Mercy to none.*

Before September 11, 2001, it was widely accepted that the "great new city" was a reference to New York City, with the words "the sky will burn at forty-five degrees" referring to New York's location near forty-five degrees latitude. After September 11, 2001, the "obvious" reference in Nostradamus's prophecy was to the World Trade Center, consumed in flames, burning so high in the air before the towers collapsed that the flames were at a forty-five-degree angle to the horizon.

Which brings up an important point about Nostradamus and virtually every other prophet in history: their prophecies have to be put in the context of the times in which they were said or written. For example, one of Nostradamus's most widely quoted quatrains in discussions about his doomsday prophecies reads:

> In the Year 1999 and seven months
> The Great King of Terror will come from the sky.
> He will bring back Ghengis Khan
> Before and after War rules happily.

Obviously, Nostradamus scholars are still having a field day interpreting who or what the "Great King of Terror" was, especially those who believe it was an "obvious" reference to a fourth Antichrist, or a precursor to the Antichrist, as John the Baptist was to Jesus. To the skeptics who say, "You see? No such thing happened in 1999," the believers reply, "How do you know he just hasn't revealed himself yet?"

As for "the Year 1999 and seven months," many Nostradamus scholars point out that that date shouldn't be taken too literally. Nostradamus lived in an age when people believed strongly in a correlation between world-altering events and the turn of the millennia. (And let's face it, after the hysteria of the transition to the year 2000, we haven't exactly outgrown that belief ourselves.) So it's possible that Nostradamus saw a vague date in the distant future for that particular prophecy and, because the prophecy involved an event of great global enormity, he assumed that it would happen in close proximity to the dawn of a new millennium.

There are a number of quatrains that are thought to be Nostradamus's prophecies leading to the end of the world. To quote just a few:

> *After a great misery for mankind an even greater approaches.*
> *The great cycle of the centuries is renewed.*
> *It will rain blood, milk, famine, war and disease.*
> *In the sky will be seen a fire, dragging a tail of sparks.*

> *The Sun in 20 degrees Taurus*
> *There will be a great earthquake; the great theater full up will be ruined.*
> *Darkness and trouble in the air, on the sky and land,*
> *When the infidel calls upon God and the Saints.*

> *Saturn joined with Scorpio transiting toward Sagittarius,*
> *At its highest ascendant,*
> *Pest, famine, death through military hand,*
> *The century as well as the Age approaches its renewal.*

> *At a latitude of forty-eight degrees*
> *At the end of Cancer there is a very great drought.*
> *Fish in the sea, river and lake boiled hectic,*
> *[Southern France] in distress from fire in the sky.*

In the year when Saturn and Mars are equally fiery,
The air is very dry, a long comet.
From hidden fires a great place burns with heat,
Little rain, hot wind, wars and raids.

The great mountain, 4247 feet in circumference,
After peace, war, famine, and flooding
Will spread far, drowning great countries
Even antiquities and their mighty foundations.

You will see, sooner and later, great changes made,
Extreme horrors and vengeances,
For as the moon is thus led by its angel,
The heavens draw near to the reckoning.

And finally, the quatrain that may give comfort to anyone who's wondering if they should start putting their affairs in order before the end of days arrives:

Twenty years the reign of the moon shall pass.
After seven thousand years another similar monarchie
*   shall tenure.*
When the sun shall take hold of its remaining days,
Then my prophecy shall be finished.

Nostradamus calculated that human history began in 3203 BC. Add seven thousand years to that date and you arrive at the conclusion that Nostradamus predicted this planet will come to an end in the year AD 3797.

The last prophecy of Nostradamus is found in the following quatrain:

> *On returning from an embassy, the King's gift safely*
> *stored*
> *No more will I labour for I will have gone to God*
> *By my close relatives, friends and blood brothers,*
> *I shall be found dead, near my bed and the bench.*

On the night before his death, Nostradamus, who'd just returned from a trip to an embassy, called for a priest to give him last rites. The priest commented that Nostradamus seemed perfectly healthy to him. But Nostradamus assured him, "You will not see me alive at sunrise."

The next morning, on July 2, 1566, Nostradamus's family found him dead, lying between the bed and his bedside bench.

Contemporary Prophets Weigh In

In 1970, born-again fundamentalist Hal Lindsey published a book called *The Late Great Planet Earth*. Among his predictions in that book (all based on his interpretation of the Bible, particularly the books of Daniel and Revelation) were that Christ would physically return to Earth no later than 1988; that the United States would not be a significant geopolitical power by the time of the apocalyptic tribulations; and that there would be a ten-member United States of Europe that would evolve into a "Revived Roman Empire" ruled by the Antichrist.

The timing of the book's publication undoubtedly contributed to its immediate success and fueled a renewed belief in the imminent end of days. The world's memory was still fresh of the 1967 Six-Day War, the armed conflict between Israel and the Arab states of Egypt, Jordan, and Syria. In six days, Israel conquered the Sinai Peninsula, Gaza Strip, West Bank, and Golan Heights, which became collectively known as the Occupied Territories. Just as sales of the Bible skyrocketed after the terrorist attack on the World Trade Center on September 11, 2001, the Six-Day War heightened the urgency of that search for the truth about when this planet's story will end. But *The Late Great Planet Earth* is still in print, has sold more than thirty-five million copies and has been published in more than fifty-four languages, so it's not as if its popularity is just a passing whim.

Obviously the 1988 prediction was inaccurate, but Lindsey continues to believe that the apostle John, credited with writing the book of Revelation, was an actual "eyewitness to events of the twentieth and twenty-first centuries." On a 1997 television appearance on Fox News, he said, "The prophet [John] who wrote the book of the Revelation says, 'I looked, I saw and heard.' A first-century man was propelled up to the end of the twentieth century and he actually saw a war of technical marvel . . . An intercontinental ballistic missile warhead reentering the earth's atmosphere; poison water, radioactivity, every city on earth virtually destroyed."

I've read the book of Revelation more times than I can begin to count, and I reread it when I heard that declaration. I know Revelation is rumored to be a series of "encoded symbols," but I can't find even a hint of what Hal Lindsey was referring to. Of course, to be fair, Lindsey's position is that only a "Christian guided by the Spirit of God" can accurately interpret the symbols in Revelation, so apparently the presumption is that those of us who have a whole different take on Revelation are simply misguided.

And then there are the Left Behind books, written by Baptist preachers Tim LaHaye and Jerry Jenkins. This series about the Second Coming of Christ has sold over sixty-five million copies, and the essential message is that the physical return of Jesus is quickly approaching. Their view is that the earth's demise is quickly approaching too.

According to LaHaye, "We have more reason to believe that ours may be the terminal generation than any generation since Jesus founded His church two thousand years ago."

The Left Behind series takes the position that what will cause the end of civilization is a worldwide conspiracy of secret societies and liberal groups whose purpose is to destroy "every vestige of Christianity." Coconspirators include the ACLU, the NAACP, Planned Parenthood, the National Organization for Women, major television networks, magazines, and newspapers, the U.S. State Department, the Carnegie Foundation, the Rockefeller Foundation, the Ford Foundation, the United Nations, Harvard, Yale, two thousand other colleges and universities, and, last but not least, the "left wing of the Democratic Party." If these united organizations and societies have their way, according to LaHaye and Jenkins, they will "turn America into an amoral, humanist country, ripe for merger into a one-world socialist state."

Sadly, nothing in the Left Behind series suggests that there's any point in attending to the people and environment of our planet, seemingly because a literal interpretation of the Bible doesn't propose any such altruism as the end of days approaches.

Is it me, or does that seem completely contrary to what Jesus had in mind?

There's Arnold Murray of Arkansas' Shepherd's Chapel, who predicted in the mid-1970s that the Antichrist would appear before 1981 and that the war of Armageddon would start in June of 1985;

And Pat Robertson, who saw the world ending in the autumn of 1982;

And Moses David of a group called the Children of God, with his prediction that the real battle of Armageddon would result in a defeat of both Israel and the United States by Russia in 1986, after which a global Communist dictatorship would be established and Christ would return to earth in 1993;

And Edgar C. Whisenant, who, in 1988, published a book called *88 Reasons Why the Rapture Could Be in 1988*;

And Baptist minister Peter Ruckman, whose analysis of the Bible resulted in his certainty that the Rapture would happen sometime around 1990.

The list goes on and on, and on and on, proving, if nothing else, that the passionate pursuit of the "truth" about the end of days is likely to continue until the end of days itself.

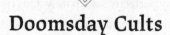

CHAPTER SIX

Doomsday Cults

I can't say it often enough throughout this book: preparing for a disaster, including the eventual end of the world, is fine. Probably even smart. Living your life cowering in terror over it, and/or losing everything your soul truly knows about God and His love for you, is tragic. It's the difference between building a bomb shelter for the worst eventuality and then going on about your business, or building a bomb shelter and hiding in it for the rest of your life. That's not a life, not what God has in mind for any of us. And yet, in a way, the isolation and fear on which doomsday cults thrive are not unlike a life of cowering in a bomb shelter braced for a cataclysm that's probably a century away. I can honestly say I would rather face Armageddon any day than experience the nightmare of the stories in this chapter, each one of which can be directly traced to a clever narcissistic sociopath preying on society's innate fear of the end of the world and leading their victims to a fate far, far worse than doomsday will ever be.

One of the most disquieting things about the populations of doomsday cults is that they come from every walk of life, every level of intelligence and financial status, every culture and race and every faith. We don't have the luxury of saying, "That could never happen to me or my perfectly sane family and friends." The truth is, yes, it could, unless we educate ourselves about these destructive cults, who joins them, and who creates them. Knowledge really is power. And there's another aspect of doomsday cults that's imperative to bear in mind: compassion dictates that we never dismiss the victims of cults as simply a bunch of insane weirdos who deserved what happened to them. There's no such thing as a life that doesn't matter, especially when in most cases the only thing these victims did wrong was to run into a charismatic sociopath who happened to say all the right things when they were at their most vulnerable.

Countless books have been written about cults, and there are many highly qualified experts on this subject. I would never claim to be one of them. But I've done my share of study, particularly about doomsday cults, and my share of working with victims of these cults and their equally victimized and devastated families and friends. So between a lot of reading and a lot of personal experiences throughout my seventy-one years, I've learned enough to make some informed observations.

Doomsday cult members are often intensely devout believers in God, Jesus, the Bible, and the concept of Armageddon preceded by the arrival of a Christ-like messiah. They tend to be inherently honest and well-intentioned, making it much more difficult for them to imagine that the charismatic, equally devout biblical expert who's trying to recruit them is actually a deceptive, manipulative sociopath who uses God, Jesus, and the scriptures as nothing but props and lures. They're typically searching for a place where they will feel they truly belong, where they get a sense of being an active, important part of something that matters. In some cases their lives have just gone through a major upheaval—maybe the loss of a job, a failed marriage, or the death of a significant other. In other cases, their lives have become mundane, unfulfilling, and, in their opinion, meaningless. Every bit as significantly, many of them have been taught to be blindly obedient to their religion whether it makes sense to them or not, while just as many who are more freethinking have found some inconsistencies and/or leaps of logic in their church's philosophies. Almost unanimously, though, they believe themselves to be sinners, too flawed to deserve redemption, particularly when the end of the world comes and only the truly worthy will be saved.

And then, if they're truly unlucky, along comes someone whose charisma, seeming self-assuredness, and outspoken passion for God draw them like moths to a flame. This man doesn't just "talk the talk," he "walks the walk," with plans to create a society separate from the cruel, self-centered, sinful, uncaring, pointless, Godless world, a society where God is actively worshipped, in word and deed, every day, not just on Sundays. Everyone will be of equal importance in this new society (except, of course, its leader), hard at work for the common good, belonging, and absolving their past sins through their new pious devotion to God's will, translated through this charismatically devout man who has made their faith feel exhilarating again. That prophet they've been yearning for? He is that prophet, and he'll prove it. But he's not just a prophet. He's the messiah their religion has been promising, the one they've been watching for, whose very appearance is a sign that the end is near and whose path is the one way to salvation when Armageddon comes. To doubt him or disobey him is to doubt or disobey God

Himself, never a good idea but a particularly bad idea on the threshold of doomsday. As for families and loved ones who aren't enlightened enough to understand or believe, the only defense against their hypocritical skepticism is complete separation. After all, if those heretics were as committed to the recruits' happiness and well-being as they claim, why were the recruits' lives so empty, meaningless, and devoid of the true Light until now?

In a life that has reached a point where it's filled with nothing but questions, in other words, what's more potentially appealing than a strong, God-centered voice saying, "I've got the answers you're looking for. Come with me."

And the leaders, like most sociopaths, know how to attract exactly the followers they're after: the trusting rather than the skeptical; the generous rather than the selfish; the group-oriented rather than the loner; the hardworking rather than the lazy; and certainly those with an eagerness to believe in something far bigger and greater and more sacred than themselves rather than those who are satisfied with their lives and their beliefs.

Once the aspiring cult leader has the attention of potential recruits, he'll usually fall into variations on a pattern of behavior that would be almost laughably predictable if it weren't so destructive:

- He'll claim that his personal theology is in unique possession of the truth, unlike traditional religions that are full of contradictions and hypocrisy.
- He'll also make claims that can't possibly be proven or disproven—that he's routinely receiving special orders and insights from God; that he's a reincarnated messiah or prophet; that God has assigned this mission specifically to him; and most certainly that he and he alone can guide his most faithful

followers safely into God's arms when the inevitable Apocalypse comes, while the sinful nonbelievers on Earth perish.

+ As a "test of devotion," he'll insist on either tithing from the group or the "donation" of his followers' earthly possessions and holdings. (And what more efficient way to hold people in subtle captivity than to strip them of their resources?)

+ He'll typically have a list of admirable, irresistible group goals on hand that includes such humanitarian pursuits as feeding the poor, volunteering in missions and shelters, gathering clothing for the needy, etc. (It's likely not to occur to the group until later that all their efforts are directed inward, not outward toward society in general.)

+ As quickly as possible he'll gather his recruits into some form of communal living situation, separate from their families and loved ones, explaining that only by committing their lives to God (and himself) twenty-four hours a day, seven days a week can they prove their intention to be cleansed of the sins of society and embrace the pure, divine enlightenment that will see them through the end of the world. (And what better way to control people's minds than to isolate them from everyone who can offer alternative points of view?)

+ Slowly but surely he'll begin dictating every detail of the lives of his followers once they're assembled and under his watchful eye. He'll typically start with a stupefying schedule of "Bible studies," which are really his own self-serving interpretations of carefully selected passages, none of them subject to questions or debate. (The control will gradually extend and expand, under threat of God's/the leader's disapproval and/or banishment, so that eventually the group will be too intimidated to make even the simplest decisions on their own.)

+ An effective "us against them" mentality will be reinforced with monotonous regularity, so that any interference from such "outsiders" as families, friends, law enforcement, the tax man, or any other governmental agency will be viewed as potentially fatal persecution from the godless heathens who are trying to destroy the messiah's work on Earth. And what more dire, terrifying threat for defecting from "us" to "them" than the messiah's promise of eternal damnation when the end of times descends?

The good news is, there are some telltale signs of a dangerous doomsday cult leader that make even the most skilled, charismatic liars among them relatively conspicuous if you listen closely, pay attention, and *think*:

+ Any "prophet/messiah" who claims to have a closer relationship with God than you do is a liar.
+ Any "prophet/messiah" who claims you need him or her in order to communicate with God is a liar.
+ Any "prophet/messiah" who claims that only he or she knows the truth of what God has in store for you, for your future, or for humankind is a liar.
+ Any "prophet/messiah" who claims it is God's will that you cause harm to yourself or to any other living being is a liar.
+ Any "prophet/messiah" who claims to be infallible is a liar.
+ Any "prophet/messiah" who claims that all those who criti-

cize him or disagree with him are evil and doomed to God's eternal wrath is a liar.

+ Any "prophet/messiah" who demands isolation from those who have consistently loved, supported, and been honest with you, and who jeopardizes your financial security is a liar.

+ Any "prophet/messiah" who insists that no one cares about or understands you as much as they do is a liar.

+ Any "prophet/messiah" who believes he or she is exempt from the laws of God and society, and is entitled to divine immunity from consequences, is a liar.

+ Any "prophet/messiah" whose power is based on fear, abuse, and threats is a liar.

+ Any "prophet/messiah" who claims to be your sole source of salvation when the Apocalypse happens is a liar.

Heaven's Gate

Heaven's Gate was a doomsday cult founded by Marshall Applewhite and Bonnie Nettles, who adopted a variety of nicknames over the years, including The Two, Bo, Do (rhymes with Bo), Peep, and Ti. Marshall and Bonnie declared themselves extraterrestrials who traveled here from the Kingdom of Heaven, a story they clearly preferred to the documented fact that they met in a psychiatric hospital where he was a patient and she was a nurse.

Heaven's Gate actually evolved from a 1975 organization called the Human Individual Metamorphosis, whose members left their loved ones, careers, and earthly possessions behind to gather in a desert in Colorado awaiting a UFO that never came. The Human Individual Metamorphosis evolved into Total Overcomers Anonymous, formed by Do after Bonnie's death from cancer in 1985 and united in Do's apocalyptic belief that the earth's population was about to be "recycled." That group evolved into Heaven's Gate when Do relocated them to San Diego in the mid-1990s.

Do taught his followers that our souls are separate, superior entities that temporarily take up residence in our bodies and that our souls' separation from our bodies is the final act of metamorphosis. His soul, by the way, had once resided in the human body we know as Jesus Christ after traveling here in a spaceship two thousand years ago. The extraterrestrial beings who travel throughout the universe in those spaceships are on a mission to elevate humanity's level of knowledge, which is why Do referred to extraterrestrials as the "level above human."

The purpose of Heaven's Gate's members was to prepare themselves to enter the Kingdom of Heaven, believing as they did that they were separate from and superior to the evil forces that control Earth. Once their preparation was complete, they believed, they'd be transported to the kingdom by committing suicide as a group, liberating their souls from their earthly bodies. Their souls, after a brief period of sleep, would ultimately be absorbed by a "level above human" who was waiting for them on board a spaceship that, according to Do, was hidden behind Comet Hale-Bopp that was passing close to Earth in 1997.

Do was clearly warning the rest of us that the end of life on our planet was imminent in a videotaped message in which he said, "You can follow us, but you cannot stay here and follow us. You would have to follow quickly by also leaving this world before the conclusion of our leaving this atmosphere in preparation for its re-cycling."

On March 22, 1997, shortly after that videotape was made, thirty-nine members of Heaven's Gate, including Do, lay down on mattresses in their immaculate San Diego house and killed them-selves with a mixture of phenobarbital and vodka. The eighteen men and twenty-one women ranged in age from twenty-six to seventy-two. They were dressed in identical black Mandarin-collared shirts, black pants, and Nike shoes. The suicides took place in three shifts over a period of three days—fifteen on the first day, fifteen on the second day, and nine on the third—so that those left behind could cover the bodies with purple shrouds bearing the words *Heaven's Gate*.

All of the deceased were also found with their identification in their pockets, as well as a five-dollar bill and three quarters. An as-tute columnist for the *San Francisco Chronicle* subsequently un-earthed a quote from Mark Twain that seems as if it must be more than just an unfortunate coincidence: "The fare to get to heaven on the tail of a comet was $5.75."

A suicide note from the group read, "By the time you read this, we suspect that the human bodies we were wearing have been found . . . We came from the Level Above Human in distant space and we have now exited the bodies that we were wearing for our earthly task, to return to the world from whence we came—task completed."

"Task completed," tragically and needlessly, to escape the "im-minent recycling of life on Earth" that proved to be nothing more than the manipulative rhetoric of a man who clearly thought the purpose of having power was to abuse it.

Jim Jones and the Peoples Temple

Two decades before the Heaven's Gate tragedy was the horror of the Peoples Temple, a doomsday cult founded by a well-educated former mainstream Christian named James Warren Jones.

Initially ordained in the Disciples of Christ Church, Jim Jones originally founded the Peoples Temple in 1955 as a mission in Indianapolis devoted to helping those who were living in poverty and with catastrophic illness. He began his ministry preaching the Holy Bible, love, and equality to his large interracial congregation. He also began claiming the ability to cure cancer and heart disease, which understandably prompted the first of many unwelcome governmental investigations into Jim Jones, his organizations, and his practices.

The more powerful Jim Jones became in the eyes of his followers, the more he rejected the Bible as a pack of lies and taught that he himself was the messiah, the Second Coming of Christ. Only he, he claimed, stood between his congregation and the imminent destruction of the world in a nuclear holocaust. He and his devoted, multiracial Peoples Temple membership, being on the side of enlightened righteousness in an otherwise evil society, would be the sole survivors of this nuclear extermination, thanks to an anticipatory mass suicide and simultaneous resurrection, and they would create a new Eden. It was probably no coincidence that in 1965, right around the time the government started its first investigation of Jim Jones, he moved the Peoples Temple to Northern California—more specifically, to Ukiah, which *Esquire* magazine listed as one of nine U.S. cities that could survive a nuclear attack.

As the Peoples Temple expanded into San Francisco and Los Angeles, the gospel according to Jim Jones became more and more communistic and anti-Christian, and his dangerously manic behavior increased in direct proportion to his addiction to prescription drugs, primarily phenobarbital. At the same time, defectors from the church began reporting Jim Jones's and the Peoples Temple's human rights practices and potential income tax abuses to the government and the news media. By 1977, the pressure from such close scrutiny inspired Jones to lead about a thousand of his most devoted Peoples Temple members to relocate to a 4,000-acre agricultural project on land they'd leased from the government of Guyana in 1974.

Jonestown, as the project came to be called, was anticipated as a communal "promised land." Instead it involved brutally difficult work and a sparse, regimented existence in the middle of the steamy South American jungle, thousands of miles from everyone and everything familiar. Jim Jones's health and sanity suffered dramatically from the relocation, so that sudden rages and hours of delusional ranting over the Jonestown loudspeakers long into the night weren't uncommon.

Finally a man named Tim Stoen, a member of the upper echelon of the Peoples Temple organization and Jim Jones's closest advisor, defected from the group, returned to the United States and formed a group of his own. It was called the Concerned Relatives, and its purpose was to liberate loved ones from the "concentration camp" of Jonestown and the grip of Jim Jones and the Peoples Temple. The Concerned Relatives' efforts were so effective that in November of 1978, members of the media joined California Congressman Leo Ryan on a fact-finding trip to Guyana.

The residents of Jonestown put on a great display of communal harmony to welcome Congressman Ryan and his companions on their arrival, and Jim Jones assured the visitors that, contrary to the

Concerned Relatives' reports, all members of the Peoples Temple were free to leave the organization and Guyana any time they liked. That claim lost all credibility the next day when one of the reporters received a note from a Jonestown resident asking for help in escaping. A total of sixteen Peoples Temple escapees left for the airstrip with the Ryan party that morning. As they emerged from the truck to board the two planes that were waiting there for them, they were ambushed by a handful of Jim Jones's gunmen. Congressman Ryan, an escaped resident of Jonestown, and three members of the media were killed. The rest of the group suffered severe injuries.

That horror was only the beginning of the unspeakable Jonestown tragedy on November 18, 1978. Jim Jones was well aware that international law enforcement would demand justice for the murders and attempted murders he'd ordered at the airstrip. He also knew that the Peoples Temple could never survive the inevitable impending media scrutiny. And so he gathered the residents of Jonestown in the community center and announced that the time had come for the mass exodus from this evil world they'd prepared for as part of their commitment to him, their messiah, their Second Coming of Christ—in other words, he ordered the "revolutionary suicide" of every member of the Peoples Temple, from the elderly to the helpless children and infants. Most drank Kool-Aid spiked with cyanide and various tranquilizers. Jim Jones took a far easier way out, with a self-inflicted gunshot wound to his head. In the end, solely on his orders, more than nine hundred residents of Jonestown and five people at the nearby Guyana airstrip lost their lives that day. It's hard to imagine that the nuclear holocaust he warned against with such fervor would have been worse than the cruel deaths the membership of the Peoples Temple suffered at the hands of the man to whom they literally entrusted their lives.

The Branch Davidians

In the early nineteenth century, a man named William Miller founded a group called the Millerites. Among other things, the Millerites predicted that the end of the world, heralded by the Second Coming of Jesus Christ, would occur on October 22, 1844.

When that date came and went fairly uneventfully, October 22, 1844, came to be known to the Millerites, understandably, as the Great Disappointment.

The Millerites picked several more end-of-the-world dates, all based on their interpretation of certain biblical passages. When those dates proved to be as meaningless as had October 22, 1844, the membership of the Millerites declined significantly. Several members, though, persisted in their basic belief in an imminent, ultimate battle between good and evil and in the Second Coming of Christ. In 1863 they formed the Seventh-day Adventists, most definitely a church as opposed to a cult, and still thriving, with a current membership of more than twelve million worldwide.

In 1919, a man named Victor Houteff joined the Seventh-day Adventist Church. But ten years later, after finding what he perceived to be several flaws in the church and its doctrines, he left to form his own sect, the Davidian Seventh-day Adventists, which ultimately evolved into the Branch Davidians. It was in 1935 that Houteff bought land for his Davidian Adventists outside of Waco, Texas, and named the settlement the Mount Carmel Center.

One day in 1981, a twenty-two-year-old dyslexic high school dropout and failed rock star named Vernon Howell joined the Branch Davidians in Waco. By 1990, he'd staged a heavily armed takeover of the Mount Carmel Center, become leader of the Branch Davidians, and changed his name to David Koresh. As he explained to his congregates, "David" came from his being the reigning ruler of the biblical House of David, and "Koresh" was the Hebrew form of the name Cyrus, the king of Persia who freed the Jewish prisoners in Babylon so they could return to Israel.

David Koresh taught that he was the messiah, the Second Coming the Branch Davidians had been anticipating since their inception, God's messenger who would personally trigger the apocalypse and then guide his followers safely to salvation. In his tediously repetitive marathon Bible studies, he instilled belief that he would be leading his flock into violent battle with the U.S. government that would mark the end of the world and his followers' passage to eternal lives. No one within the Branch Davidians was allowed contact with anyone on the "outside," since those "outsiders" were evil and bound to lead them away from the righteousness embodied by no one but David Koresh.

He had twenty "wives" within the cult, who he promised would have the honor of bearing his "soldiers." Conveniently, he ordered that all the Branch Davidian men take a vow of celibacy. His youngest "wife" was the ten-year-old daughter of a devout Koresh follower. And in case any of Koresh's younger wives or other children in the Mount Carmel Center chose to disobey or misbehave, a wooden paddle was always nearby for beatings as severe as "the messiah" demanded. David Koresh accepted and achieved nothing less than total devotion and absolute, unquestioning obedience from his flock.

That fact became tragically apparent during a fifty-one-day standoff, the horrifying realization of David Koresh's vision of a violent battle with the U.S. government that would mark the end of his followers' world. The government had indeed been watching Koresh, the Branch Davidians, and the suspicious activities at the

Mount Carmel Center, and on February 28, 1993, literally dozens of agents from the Bureau of Alcohol, Tobacco and Firearms arrived with a warrant to search the compound for illegal weapons. After an initial gun battle in which four ATF agents and six Branch Davidians were killed, David Koresh allowed a handful of ATF agents into the compound just long enough to remove their dead comrades.

And then the standoff began. ATF heavy artillery aimed squarely at the compound and probably just as much heavy artillery aimed right back at the ATF. The best of the best FBI negotiators were brought in to keep up a dialogue with David Koresh on the direct phone line the ATF had arranged. The negotiators' top priority was to secure the freedom of the forty-six children who'd been living as innocent hostages behind the distant center walls. It was finally agreed that David Koresh would broadcast a series of two-minute sermons on the radio and that he would release two children for each sermon. That agreement led to the release of twenty-one children in the first five days.

After a standoff that lasted a total of fifty-one days, the government agencies that had assembled near Waco at the Branch Davidian compound arrived at the horribly flawed conclusion that in the end, if they forcefully attacked, the majority of adults holed up within the center would make their escape to save the children still left inside. Completely miscalculating the control David Koresh had over his followers, and their belief that death would lead them and their children to the eternal glory their messiah had promised, the agents advanced on the compound with a full battalion of tanks and tear gas.

Within minutes, the Mount Carmel Center was engulfed in flames. Approximately fifty adults and twenty-five children died in the fire.

Among the casualties was David Koresh.

And perhaps as a testament to David Koresh's final, maniacal insistence on total control over his own and his followers' destiny, the catastrophic fire that consumed the compound, according to FBI wiretaps, appeared to have been set. So in a way, he was absolutely prophetic—he predicted the end of the world and then played his part in seeing to it for all those people who trusted him, and all those innocent children who had no choice about it at all. Somehow I think the Branch Davidians expected more and better from their long-awaited messiah.

The Unification Church: Sun Myung Moon

Legend has it that one day in 1936, on a Korean mountainside, Jesus Christ appeared to a sixteen-year-old boy and gave him the news that he'd been chosen by God to establish the Kingdom of Heaven on Earth. That boy, Sun Myung Moon, proclaimed himself the messiah, the Second Coming, and/or the Lord of the Second Advent, and, in 1954, established what was officially called the Holy Spirit Association for the Unification of World Christianity, commonly known as the Unification Church. Half a century later, its membership purportedly numbers in the tens of thousands in one hundred countries around the world.

By 1957 the Reverend Moon (a self-ordained title) had written a 536-page manifesto called Divine Principle, which he claimed was directly communicated to him by Jesus Christ. Moonies, as his followers are called, believe the Divine Principle to be the third testament of the Bible and follow its authority with unflinching loyalty. And predictably, anyone who questions Moon's status as the messiah or doubts the credibility of the Divine Principle is in league with the Devil, doing Satan's handiwork.

Among the basics of Moon's teachings:

+ Adam and Eve were initially created to have a platonic relationship until they reached perfection. Only then would they be worthy of marriage and childbearing for the purpose of establishing God's kingdom on Earth. But because of Eve's sexual sin—sex with the devil, i.e., the spiritual fall from grace—followed by sex with Adam, i.e., the physical fall from grace, God's intention for them to be the "true parents" of humankind was never realized.

+ Because of Eve's sexual relationship with Satan, all sin committed by unredeemed humans is not a moral choice but is instead the result of genetics—we're all sinners as descendants of Eve and Satan, in other words, until and unless we achieve salvation. And what do you know, Sun Myung Moon is the only possible source of salvation. Salvation via Moon could happen for women by being "cleansed" by him, which meant having sexual intercourse with him. It could happen for men through "blood cleansing," or having sexual intercourse with a woman who'd been "cleansed" by Moon. It could happen through a marriage personally orchestrated and blessed by Moon. And/or it could happen by absolute submission to Sun Myung Moon's omnipotence—willingness to allow Moon to select a mate, to hand over all earthly assets to the church, to encourage their children to think of Moon and his wife as their "true parents," and so on.

+ Jesus Christ, according to Divine Principle/Sun Myung Moon, was not the son of God or the result of a virgin birth.

Jesus's intended purpose was to father perfect children through an approved marriage, but he was crucified before he could accomplish that purpose. Rather than symbolizing redemption for Christians, the cross is actually a symbol of failure, and Jesus never experienced a physical resurrection. The Second Coming that God promised isn't a reference to Jesus at all, it's a reference to a "third Adam" who will satisfy God's long-awaited plan of providing physical salvation through marriage from which genetically sin-free children would be born. Moon's Divine Principle unmistakably implies that Moon himself is that "third Adam."

+ The true Trinity is composed of God, the "third Adam," and his bride, and God's kingdom on Earth can be realized only through the marriages Moon and his wife personally arrange or approve. Members of the Unification Church are the only "True Family," with the glorified title of "True Parents" being reserved for no one but Moon, aka the third Adam, and his exalted wife. (The fact that Moon divorced his first three wives doesn't seem to diminish the Moonies' enthusiasm for the True Parents concept, which certainly implies that one third of the church's Trinity is interchangeable.)

+ Salvation is complete only when both physical and spiritual redemption have taken place. Physical redemption requires total obedience to Sun Myung Moon, the third Adam, while spiritual redemption requires fund-raising, enlisting new church members, and other means of expanding Moon's power. But God will not forgive until and unless there has been some payment for the sins that have been committed by us flawed humans. (Moon has twelve children, by the way, and since they were fathered by the third Adam and have therefore been genetically purified, they're considered by Moonies to be without sin.)

✦ The commonly prophesied end of the world actually refers to the end of evil on Earth . . . which coincidentally can be achieved only through the auspices of Sun Myung Moon.

Moon summed up his beliefs about himself, to which he requires Moonies to adhere unequivocally, in the following way:

There have been saints, prophets, many religious leaders in past human history. Master here [referring to himself] is more than any of those people and greater than Jesus himself . . . I am the Alpha and Omega, the beginning and the end.

Which makes his recurring legal problems seem more than a little ironic. He's been convicted and spent time in prison over the years for such varied crimes as perjury, fraud, bigotry, and tax evasion. And yet his holdings include major shares in about three hundred U.S. corporations and foundations, from publishing companies to newspapers to toy, clothing, and jewelry manufacturers.

The "Reverend" Sun Myung Moon promised that the messiah would be revealed, not in the clouds as the Bible predicts but here on earth, by the year 2000. That messiah was not to be Jesus Christ, who failed in his mission a couple of millennia ago. Instead it was to have been a man born in 1920 in Korea—as Moon was—and God was to punish all who failed to recognize and embrace that messiah.

All these years later, the validity of Sun Myung Moon as the world's savior is still eluding me and many of you as well, I'm sure. And so far that seems to be okay with God. Have you noticed?

Jeffrey Lundgren

I almost hate to give this man the dignity of having his name mentioned in print. But since he's been executed and is no longer around to bask in a little more publicity, I do think he's useful as a comparatively tiny example of how a "doomsday prophet" can destroy the lives of perfectly intelligent, well-meaning people.

Jeffrey Lundgren was born in Independence, Missouri, in 1950 to parents who were active in a Mormon splinter group called the Reorganized Church of Latter-day Saints. His father was a strict disciplinarian with a passion for firearms, a passion he eagerly shared with his son. His mother, by all accounts, was a rigid, fairly distant woman.

Jeffrey was a rather chubby, unattractive, inexplicably arrogant boy without a shred of talent for sports or other activities that traditionally inspire admiration among schoolmates. What he did have an uncanny talent for was memorizing and reciting endless biblical passages, and he learned very early in life that the appearance of an unusual closeness to God—even if it was utterly insincere and acquired only by rote—was an easy way to establish his popularity and self-proclaimed superiority.

He was attending Central Missouri State University when he met and began dating a fellow RLDS student named Alice Keeler. Alice was a shy loner who'd grown up with a father who was often depressed and violent toward her and her siblings when using his vast array of multiple sclerosis medications, and a mother who worked long hard hours to support the family. An RLDS leader had once told her that she would meet and marry a prophet of true greatness, so when she began dating and became pregnant by Jeffrey

Lundgren, she assumed he must be that prophet of true greatness and became his slavishly obedient wife.

After four years in the navy, Lundgren was unsuccessful at any number of jobs because of his arrogance and irresponsibility. He was also an abusive husband and serial philanderer, while Alice stood by her man, bore his four children, and continued clinging to her marriage, assuming there could be nothing but hell to pay for walking out on an RLDS prophet of true greatness.

In the meantime, Jeffrey was becoming disenchanted with the RLDS and decided to form his own sect, essentially a splinter group of this Mormon splinter group. He proclaimed himself the one whose divine mission it was to unearth the truth in the Holy Bible, and his childhood talent of reciting endless biblical passages worked just as effectively to attract followers when he was an arrogant, abusive, philandering, flat-broke father of four. Those followers were classic examples of perfectly decent, earnest, devout people who simply bought into the very skilled act of a very skilled fraud. One of them in later years said that when Jeffrey Lundgren came along, he felt for the first time as if he'd found a family where he belonged and where he was wanted. Another made this simple, tragic statement: "I felt like everything I'd ever done, I'd failed at. Jeffrey made me feel as if finally I could do something right, and something important, by following him and doing God's work."

His growing flock began donating money to support Jeffrey and his family, but he quickly grew dissatisfied with the modest donations and announced that according to orders from the Bible itself, it was time for him and his family to move to Kirtland, Ohio, where God would be endowing him with his true messianic power.

Kirtland, Ohio, wasn't a random destination for Jeffrey Lundgren. Based on a "revelation from God," Joseph Smith, founder of the Mormon Church, had a huge, magnificent temple built there in 1836, and Jeffrey and Alice Lundgren quickly secured jobs as tour guides at the temple when they moved to Kirtland in 1984. It didn't take long for Jeffrey to become dissatisfied with his meager tour guide salary, and he began dipping into the temple's donations and profits to the tune of what's estimated to be from $25,000 to $30,000.

Jeffrey's job as an RLDS guide gave him access to visitors from around the country, and during tours he would teach and preach his own unorthodox, messianic, self-absorbed version of the scriptures. His proclamations of himself as a prophet and the reincarnated Christ, along with an arrogance that the vulnerable and naive translated as spiritual superiority, began inspiring followers to move to Kirtland to learn at the feet of this charismatic man who promised them salvation from the impending Armageddon.

Before long the RLDS officials became aware of Jeffrey's shocking variations on the teachings of the church and confronted him. In response, Jeffrey withdrew his church membership and quit his job. Undoubtedly with the help of stolen church funds, not to mention the increasing number of followers who began handing over their paychecks and other worldly possessions to their new great prophet and messiah, Jeffrey moved his family and his faithful flock to a rented farm in the countryside near Kirtland.

It was at the farm that Jeffrey started wearing military fatigues on a regular basis, including during interminable Bible studies. He accumulated a large arsenal, carried a loaded gun at all times, and interspersed prayer sessions with marksmanship and combat training. He became the sole arbiter of what constituted a sin, which could include anything from withholding a paycheck from him to sitting in the wrong chair at communal dinners. He became the group's sole recipient of God's commands, and its sole salvation in the impending war of Armageddon. The final days of this planet were imminent, he warned relentlessly. Without him there was no hope of meeting God and being endowed with eternal life.

Among Jeffrey's future plans for his spiritual, Godly group was the seizing of the RLDS temple that had banished him. To earn their place on his promised journey to see God Himself, his followers were required not only to overtake the temple but also to promise to kill anyone and everyone who got in their way. The arsenal grew, the combat training intensified, and the endless Bible recitations droned on.

It was February of 1988 when one of the devotees, Kevin Currie, finally caught on that Jeffrey Lundgren wasn't a messiah or a prophet, he was simply a dangerous, cruel, sociopathic, megalomaniacal thug who used his knowledge of the Bible and his followers' terror of doomsday, and of him, to achieve complete domination. Currie escaped the farm and fled to Buffalo, New York, fearing Jeffrey's retribution every step of the way. He contacted the FBI about Jeffrey, his arsenal, the relentless combat training among his blindly obedient followers, and his plan to seize the RLDS temple. Not completely convinced the report wasn't a prank, the FBI faxed the information to Kirtland Police Chief Dennis Yarborough. Chief Yarborough took the report seriously and initiated an investigation into Jeffrey Lundgren and his family and followers at the relatively isolated farm.

Unbeknownst to Kevin Currie, the FBI, or the Kirtland police, Jeffrey, thanks to yet another vision, had significantly revised the means by which his flock could earn their place on the journey to see God, and prove their dedication and total obedience to their messiah, Jeffrey Lundgren. Rather than overtaking the RLDS temple, they should focus on a goal much closer to home—they should sacrifice (read "execute") a family that had been getting on Jeffrey's nerves ever since they had arrived at the farm. Dennis Avery wasn't living up to Jeffrey's idea of a true man and head of the household, often deferring to his wife and letting her make some of the few decisions Jeffrey left to them. Dennis also questioned Jeffrey occasionally during Bible classes, which was an act of heresy. Cheryl Avery, Dennis's wife, was headstrong and clearly didn't understand or respect the appropriately subservient, dutiful role of a woman in the household and the group in general. And the Averys' three daughters, aged fifteen, thirteen, and six, were just plain unruly and disobedient. Add them all up and it was obvious—God would never grant the group forgiveness if they knowingly allowed sin to exist among them, and without God's forgiveness, there would be no eternity for them. But if the group sent the most egregious sinners in the compound, the Averys, to arrive at the "judgment bar" before the rest of them arrived, God would take out his wrath on the Avery family and spare the followers of their great prophet and messiah, Jeffrey Lundgren.

And so it was that on April 17, 1989, while Alice Lundgren disappeared for a few hours with the youngest children of the group, the Avery family was led one by one to the barn near the main house under a variety of pretexts and executed by the men and women of this devout group and their divine savior, Jeffrey Lundgren. Dennis Avery was the first to be killed. Six-year-old Karen Avery was the last. Their bodies were placed in a pre-dug pit and covered with lime and dirt, with nothing but a few trash bags to mark their mass grave.

"It had to be done," Jeffrey reflected afterward. "It was commanded by God."

It can only be described as tragic irony that the morning after the murders, the Kirtland police and the FBI arrived at the farm. They knew nothing about the execution of the Avery family that had taken place the night before, so they had no reason to ask about it. Instead, they were there to follow up on rumors that weapons were being amassed and that a takeover of the Mormon temple was being plotted. They found nothing of any specific relevance to those rumors—they could give the farm only a cursory glance since they had no probable cause for a search warrant—and none of Lundgren's followers volunteered information that could have led law enforcement to the five bodies that had been buried in the barn the night before. Alice Lundgren used the excuse much later that "they [law enforcement] weren't asking the right questions." But neither she nor anyone else in the group had helped by coaching the police and the FBI on what those right questions were. Another Lundgren follower, a meek-looking woman in her forties, explained her silence, and her participation in the Avery murders, with the chillingly simple statement, "I was a sinner, and I knew I could be next."

That same day, the day after the murders and the day the law showed up unexpectedly at the farm, Jeffrey Lundgren divided his followers into small groups and ordered them to leave the farm at intervals during the night. They were to travel to a specific location in Pennsylvania, where he and his family would meet them and give them further instructions. A Kirtland police officer drove past the farm a few days later and found it chilling that the Lundgren camp seemed to have abandoned the property awfully suddenly.

The Lundgren group settled temporarily in Tucker County, West Virginia, where Jeffrey claimed that God would lead him to the Sword of Laban, referred to in the Book of Mormon as a symbol of divine authority and kingship. From there it was off to a barn near Chilhowee, Missouri (without the Sword of Laban, which had somehow eluded Jeffrey's grasp), where after a cold winter week Jeffrey disbanded the group, ordering the men to get jobs so that they'd have money to give to Jeffrey when they reconvened in the spring.

Throughout his time in West Virginia and the move back to Missouri, Jeffrey had become even more violent, paranoid, and megalomaniacal than ever. Foxholes, twenty-four-hour-a-day guards, and even an antiaircraft machine gun to shoot down law enforcement helicopters were among the new staples of the group. The married men were ordered to willingly offer their wives to Jeffrey on his whim so that they could be "cleansed with his seed." Jeffrey knew and thrived on the fact that his followers were now too terrified of him to disobey him, and he reminded them on a regular basis that the same thing could happen to any one of them that had happened to the Averys if he chose. And if constant fear of his wrath wasn't frightening enough, he also reminded them over and over and over again that the end of the planet Earth was right around the corner, and only he held the key to their survival and to God's willingness to welcome them into His kingdom.

There was yet another fear holding the group's devotion to Jeffrey Lundgren together, a psychological angle that's not uncommon among cult members. Those who were beginning to have doubts about their messiah's sanctity as a prophet and son of God had to face the fact that if Jeffrey Lundgren was a fraud and a liar, then they had participated in killing five innocent people, three of them children, for reasons having nothing whatsoever to do with God or His will. Their basic ability to live with themselves and what they'd done was dependent on believing in Lundgren's authenticity.

When the group temporarily disbanded, Jeffrey took Alice, their son Damon and the younger children, and loyal devotee Danny Kraft to the warmth of San Diego, California, where he and Alice had lived for a short time after Jeffrey's tour of duty in the navy.

A few of the group, in the meantime, seized the opportunity to escape Jeffrey Lundgren once and for all, finally abandoning their hope that he wasn't simply a cruel, murdering madman. Among them was a man named Keith Johnson, whose conscience about the Avery murders was eating him alive. And so on December 31, 1989, Keith poured his heart out to Kansas City law enforcement about the murders and everything else he knew about Jeffrey Lundgren. He even drew them a map to the exact location of the Avery family's grave. That map and a written report of Keith's story triggered a series of events that led to Chief Yarborough and several of his deputies in the Kirtland, Missouri, police department to arrive at and search the still-abandoned farm on January 3, 1990. Following Keith Johnson's map, they found the gravesite of the Avery family fairly quickly, and the tragic news of the murdered family buried in a barn quickly captured the attention of the local and national media. Warrants were issued for Jeffrey and Alice Lundgren, their nineteen-year-old son Damon, and ten of Jeffrey's followers, some of whom turned themselves in the moment they saw the televised reports that the Averys had been found.

On January 7, 1990, Jeffrey Lundgren, his wife, Alice, and their son, Damon, were arrested in their motel room in California. Law enforcement also seized the arsenal of weapons and ammunition the "messiah and great prophet" had assembled. The Lundgren family, after some predictable legal wrangling, were extradited back to Missouri, where they were reunited with their old devotees in jail, awaiting a series of trials.

Alice and Damon Lundgren were each sentenced to five life terms.

Nine of Jeffrey's followers were given a lesser variety of sentences. Larry Johnson, the informant/hero who'd bravely stepped forward to law enforcement, was given immunity for his testimony.

Despite a stupefying four-hour plea for mercy to the jury that included the claim, "It's not a figment of my imagination that I can in fact talk to God, that I can hear his voice. I am a prophet of God. I am even more than a prophet," Jeffrey Lundgren was sentenced to death. As the date of his execution approached, he tried to convince the courts that he was too obese and diabetic to be executed without a "cruel and unusual" amount of pain. The courts didn't agree, and on Tuesday, October 24, 2006, Jeffrey Lundgren, messiah and great prophet or murderer-liar-philanderer-thief-abuser-narcissist-sociopath, depending on whom you talk to, was executed—his own personal doomsday, I guess, but undoubtedly not what his devoted followers had in mind when he assured them that the end of the world was right around the corner.

The Manson Family

It is common, tragic knowledge that Charles Manson and his "family" of devout followers committed some of the most infamous murders in the history of American crime. At Manson's command, and under his absolute control, five young people viciously slaughtered seven total strangers in two separate upscale neighborhoods in the Los Angeles area in 1969. The exhaustive publicity of the Manson Family, its brutality, its journey through the court system, and, above all, its diminutive, wild-eyed leader, Charles Manson, has left the indelible memory in most people's minds of the insanity of a band of "drug-crazed hippies." And there's no doubt about it, these killers were drug-crazed, by their own admissions, and they looked and lived like many hippies of the late 1960s, in a communal, unstructured environment.

What often gets lost in the historic infamy of the Manson Family is the fact that, at its core, it was a doomsday cult, with Charles Manson as its messiah. And it's as clear an example as we'll ever find of the fact that the Bible can be twisted, turned, and stood on its head depending on the mind and motivations of whoever's reading it.

In other words, we really don't have the luxury of believing that if we're not drug-crazed hippies, we're immune to persuasive doomsday "saviors" with off-center, self-serving interpretations of the book of Revelation. Whether Charles Manson actually believed his complicated view of the Apocalypse or whether he simply used it when he discovered it was an effective manipulation device is anybody's guess. But then, let's face it, the same issue could easily be raised about Marshall Applewhite, Jim Jones, David Koresh, Sun Myung Moon, Jeffrey Lundgren, and every other doomsday cult leader who's systematically destroyed the lives of a lot of trusting, vulnerable, unfulfilled, God-fearing people.

Charles Manson was born in Cincinnati, Ohio, on November 12, 1934. His mother was sixteen years old. The identity of his father was never clearly established, and whoever he was, Manson claims never to have met him. Manson's last name came from his mother's brief marriage to an older man named William Manson.

Manson had what can best be described as an unstable child-hood. For the most part he was raised by his grandmother and/or his aunt while his mother was either in prison for armed robbery or simply not around for days and weeks at a time. He was twelve years old when he began bouncing back and forth between boys' homes and jail—he committed his first armed robbery when he was thirteen and was in and out of prisons and reformatories until he was nineteen. He was evaluated by any number of prison counselors and too few psychiatrists, all of whom found him disturbed and disturbing. At the same time, one of them commented that Manson possessed "certain facile techniques for dealing with people. These . . . consist of a good sense of humor and an ability to ingratiate himself." In fact, he enthusiastically took a Dale Carnegie course on "how to win friends and influence people" during his teenage years, and even though he didn't finish, he apparently picked up some effective pointers.

He also seems to have picked up some effective pointers for attracting "the family" in the future when he began his first real career in Los Angeles, as a pimp. (He traveled to Los Angeles in 1955 in a car he stole in Ohio.) Then came more prison time, for a variety of federal offenses, during which he dabbled in Scientology, the Bible, and Buddhism long enough to adopt some jargon from all three, and he became obsessed with songwriting, playing the guitar, and, most significantly, the Beatles.

It was after those stints in prison that Charles Manson began accumulating followers, the vast majority of whom were in their late teens to early twenties and, for a variety of reasons, in search of a sense of belonging and being part of something that mattered. Or, as one of the Family members put it, "traveling around the country looking for God." He started in the Haight-Ashbury section of San Francisco, one of the most famous gathering places for the hippie movement of the late 1960s, and returned to Los Angeles with the first female members of the Family.

Between his guitar playing, songwriting, female entourage, and developing philosophy about the approaching Armageddon, Manson temporarily attracted the curiosity of Beach Boys drummer Dennis Wilson and record producer Terry Melcher, the son of actress Doris Day, who was living with actress Candice Bergen at 10050 Cielo Drive, a small street near Benedict Canyon, which cuts through the Hollywood Hills. One night, Charles Manson happened to be a passenger when Dennis Wilson drove Terry Melcher home to Cielo Drive and dropped him off at the gate. The Cielo Drive house was subsequently leased to director Roman Polanski and his beautiful actress wife, Sharon Tate.

There are strong theories that it was Terry Melcher's ultimate rejection of Charles Manson and his music that inspired Manson to choose 10050 Cielo Drive as the target for six savage murders committed at his command on August 9, 1969—of Steven Parent, age eighteen; Sharon Tate, twenty-six, actress; Sharon's unborn son; Abigail Folger, twenty-five, Folgers Coffee heiress; Voytek Frykowski, thirty-two, boyfriend of Abigail Folger; and Jay Sebring, thirty-five, renowned hairstylist. Less than twenty-four hours later, several miles away in the Los Feliz area of Los Angeles, two more murders took place on Manson's orders—Leno LaBianca, forty-four, owner of a successful chain of supermarkets, and his wife, Rosemary, thirty-eight, owner of a dress shop, were viciously killed in their own home. All the dead were Caucasian.

The word *pig* had been written in blood at both locations, and at the LaBianca house the word *healter-skelter* [sic] was scrawled in blood on the refrigerator door. And contrary to the initial impressions of the Los Angeles police, the murders were far from motiveless, and the words *pig* and (properly spelled) *helter-skelter* were partial keys to unraveling the twisted tragic mystery of yet another doomsday cult.

At its simplest, Manson's prophecy of and role in the Apocalypse went like this (and it was undoubtedly even more convincing when told with mind-numbing repetition to a bunch of lost, vulnerable young people with an endless supply of recreational drugs in their systems):

+ While Charles Manson apparently never made any specific claim of being the reincarnated Christ, he spoke often of having once lived two thousand years ago, a lifetime that ended with his death on the cross. He also regaled the Family on countless occasions with his "vision" during a psychedelic mushroom trip: the bed he was lying on became a cross; he could feel the nails in his feet and see Mary Magdalene weeping below him; and when he surrendered to death he could see through the eyes of all humanity at the same time. Many Family members later admitted that they truly believed Charles Manson was Jesus, returned to earth as a sign promised in the Bible that the end of the world was coming.

+ The biblical book of Revelation, 9:15, reads, "So the four angels were released, who had been ready for the hour, the day, the month and the year, to kill a third of mankind." The four angels, Manson was sure, were the Beatles. This belief was reinforced by an earlier reference (Revelation 9:3) to "locusts," obviously synonymous with "Beatles" in Manson's interpretation, especially as they're described in verses 7 and 8: "their faces were like human faces, their hair like women's hair . . . they had scales like iron breastplates [the Beatles' guitars] . . . they have tails like scorpions [the guitars' electrical cords]." The first verse of Revelation 9 refers to a "fifth angel . . . and he was given the key of the shaft of the bottomless pit," who's later referred to in verse 11: "They [the locusts] have as king over them the angel of the bottomless pit." Needless to say, that fifth angel of the bottomless pit, that "fifth Beatle," was Charles Manson.

✦ As a result, Manson convinced himself and the Family that the Beatles were sending him messages through their songs. To name just a couple: George Harrison's "Piggies," recorded on the Beatles' *White Album*, was a commentary on materialism, society's upper class, and greed. Obviously, to Manson, it was an edict to select materialistic, upper-class victims to murder, and to leave the word *pig* in the victims' blood as a kind of souvenir/explanation. And then there was the song "Helter Skelter," also on the *White Album*, which contains the lyrics, "When I get to the bottom I go back to the top of the slide/Where I stop and I turn and I go for a ride/'Til I get to the bottom and I see you again." To the Beatles it was undoubtedly a harmless reference to an amusement park slide. To Manson it was a description of the Family emerging from the bottomless pit to reclaim the world after the great war of Armageddon.

✦ Another Beatles song from the *White Album* begins, "Blackbird singing in the dead of night/Take these broken wings and learn to fly/All your life you were only waiting for this moment to arise." Manson's interpretation: in the war of Armageddon the blacks were going to rise up against the whites and destroy them. (See the above reference to Revelation 9:15 about killing a third of mankind. A third of mankind, Manson said, was the Caucasian race.) The Beatles were telling the blacks that the time had come for the war to begin. Unfortunately, the blacks weren't moving quickly enough for Manson's taste, so he commanded the Family to begin the slaughter of Caucasians and "pigs," as brutally and violently as possible. The blacks would obviously be blamed, the whites would rise up in outrage, and Armageddon, the war between the blacks and the whites, would begin. The whites, in fear and outrage, would head to the ghettos to retaliate, but the blacks would ultimately triumph. They would begin rebuilding from the vast destruction this war of wars had caused, but they would find themselves unskilled at governing this new Caucasian-free planet. So naturally, they would turn to Manson and his Family, who'd been living in the "bottomless pit" (located in the California desert, according to Charlie). By that time, the Family would number 144,000 (referred to in Revelation 7) and would reclaim a world that was now rid of the unenlightened, i.e., those who didn't listen to the warnings and the teachings of the angel of the bottomless pit, the reincarnated Christ, Charles Manson.

Charles Manson and those members of his Family who had the misfortune to follow his orders in pursuit of their own salvation—

Susan Atkins, Charles "Tex" Watson, Lynette Fromme, Leslie Van Houten, and Patricia Krenwinkel—are serving life sentences for the Tate/LaBianca murders.

If you read the stories in this chapter as nothing more than cautionary tales, they will have served their purpose. But it's my hope that, beyond that, they'll demonstrate the tragic danger of letting fear and one charismatic, manipulative, power-driven voice turn doomsday from an eventual possibility to a self-fulfilled prophecy. One more time: anytime someone tells you they've received a message that even hints at harming any living creature, including yourself, you can count on it beyond all doubt that the message, if there really was one at all, did *not* come from God. And if they claim that they hold the key to the only true interpretation of the Bible, ask them right up front to clarify their position on the fifth commandment, which very clearly reads, "Thou shalt not kill."

CHAPTER SEVEN

The End of Days Through My Eyes

For the coming of the Son of Man will be just like the days of Noah. For as in those days which were before the flood they were eating and drinking, they were marrying and giving in marriage, until the day that Noah entered the ark, and they did not understand until the flood came and took them all away; so shall the coming of the Son of Man be.

Matthew 24:37–39

I've been asked hundreds if not thousands of times when I see this world coming to an end. It's interesting that rarely does anyone ask *how* I see it ending. The question is simply when, as if the only real issue is whether or not it's time to start packing, or stop bothering to pay our bills, or to cancel our magazine subscriptions. And I suppose that's why, while I consider the end of days to be an endlessly intriguing subject, I avoid discussing it at length during television and personal appearances: I refuse to indulge the idea that the end of days is something we should obsess about and panic about and throw ourselves around the room about. I don't believe it's possible to live the lives we came here to live while being perpetually braced to die.

We've discussed in previous chapters the many different years in which the world will "definitely" end, from the first century after Christ's Crucifixion to the many predictions of the Millerites, the Mayan calendar's projection of 2012, Sir Isaac Newton's precisely calculated 2060, Nostradamus's prophecy of AD 3797, et al. We've talked about the tragic consequences of letting fear of the end lead to homicidal and suicidal panic orchestrated by sociopathic frauds. If nothing else, I hope the message has come through loud and clear that there have been far too many wasted lives, and too much wasted anxiety, over an event I believe we're actually going to create for ourselves.

An Overview of the End of Days

As a psychic, I can see clearly through the end of this century. Beyond that, nothing. It's as if sometime during the year 2100, the lights go out—not for the planet, but for us humans, who will have succeeded in making Earth uninhabitable in the next ninety-two years or so.

And it's true, the earth itself won't be destroyed at the end of days. There's not a meteor shower out there with our name on it, the earth isn't going to explode from a catastrophically overheated core, and it's not going to drift out of its orbit too far from the sun to sustain life. From ancient civilizations to today's experts, we've been warned over and over and over again: if we don't take care of this sacred home we've been given, it won't be able to provide us with shelter, food, and comfort any longer, just as surely as a house we abuse and neglect will be condemned as unfit for human habitation sooner or later.

The Next Ninety-two Years

It's going to be an interesting century, that's for sure, full of soaring highs and crushing lows, brilliant advances and inevitable steps backward, turbulent chaos and almost unprecedented peace as the countdown to the end of days proceeds.

Before I begin a breakdown of what lies ahead in the first forty-two years and the last fifty years of this century, I do want to offer a word of caution to US present and future presidential candidates. Sometime between 2008 and 2020 I see a sitting president dying in office of a heart attack. The vice president who assumes the presidency will stun the world by announcing his intention to declare war on North Korea in light of his accurate belief that they actually are in possession of weapons of mass destruction. His efforts to rally congressional and international support for this declaration of war will be resoundingly unsuccessful and the source of enormous alarm, and he'll be assassinated before his term ends.

On a more positive note, before the end of 2010, to the chagrin of countless pharmaceutical companies, the common cold will be a thing of the past. I don't know the specifics, but the cure will involve heat (duh). There's a small self-contained cubicle that will become a common fixture in most clinics and doctors' offices. At the first hint of a cold, patients will step into this cubicle for five or six minutes, where a combination of its precisely elevated temperature, an antibiotic vapor, and their own body heat will destroy the rhinitis germ that causes most colds, many allergies, and a variety of asthma-related illnesses. Speaking not just as a psychic but also as a victim of my share of colds every year, let me just assure medical and scientific researchers and pharmaceutical companies around the world that there's a massive fortune to be made for whoever invents, perfects, and secures the patent on this cubicle.

And now, with those two special alerts out of the way, here are the broad strokes of the upcoming ninety-two years as I see them now. But never underestimate our power to influence the future, for better or worse, so don't even think about taking these forecasts as an excuse to sit back, put your feet up, and stop trying. For most of us, this is our last visit to Earth. Let's not set ourselves up for an eternity of wishing we'd made more of a difference while we were here.

2010–2050

The twenty-first century is going to usher in the arrival of an extraordinary flood of highly advanced spirits from the Other Side. In the next chapter we'll discuss why that's true. For now, it's worth mentioning because of the great strides we have to look forward to in the areas of childbirth and infant care. The timing is no coincidence. We're preparing for those highly advanced spirits by seeing to it that we give them the best start on earth we can possibly offer.

By 2010 we're going to see some brilliant leaps forward in the field of diagnosing deficiencies and illnesses in the fetus, thanks to vastly improved ultrasound and amniocentesis. Fetal surgeries will be so precise that they'll be able to correct those deficiencies and illnesses as well as many birth defects and genetic challenges. There will also be fetal injections to guarantee nutritional balances and healthy immune systems before our future children are even born.

Inspired by our ancestors' routine practice of accepting the help of gravity during childbirth, 2010 will also see the reemergence of birthing chambers, for the benefit of both mothers and newborns. These birthing chambers will involve a pulley system allowing the mother to give birth while suspended from strong padded over-hanging straps. The baby drops down, as gravity always intended, into soft sterile pillows that are waiting in the hands of the doctors, nurses, and/or midwives in attendance. The walls of the small circular birthing chambers will act as screens on which calming imagery of the mother's choosing will be projected. Gentle music and the sound of quiet waves will accompany the imagery. Lights will be dimmed, and aromatherapy will be put to subtle use. The experience will be more reverent than clinical, a far less jarring transition for the infant from the Other Side to Earth and a far more considerate event for the mother.

Immediately after the child is born, a routine series of blood tests will reveal any protein and chemical imbalances that will by then be known to cause a whole array of psychological disorders, so that everything from depression to potential schizophrenia will be addressed at birth. Cells will also be painlessly harvested from inside the infant's cheek, to serve two purposes. The first, over the objections of the civil rights organizations, will be to register the child's DNA in what will eventually be an international databank of every person on Earth. The benefits to the immediate tracking of lost, missing, abandoned, and exploited children, an equally quick resolution of paternity issues and crime solving will far outweigh any privacy concerns. DNA "fingerprints" will be discreetly imprinted on identification, school and hospital records, Social Security cards, drivers' licenses, credit cards, etc., that can be scanned for authenticity as easily as bar codes are scanned now, and identity theft will eventually become an archaic crime.

The second purpose in harvesting and preserving infants' cells at birth has to do with the brilliant advancements in cloning we can look forward to by around 2025. Having a few cells on hand will make it possible to clone a new organ to replace one that has failed, so that the agonizing wait for organ donors and the obscene practice of selling organs on the black market will be distant memories.

Last but not least on the subject of childbirth, sometime around 2010, hospitals will begin saving and carefully preserving placentas, for a great cause—it will be discovered in the next few years that a protein complex or nutrient of some kind in the placenta can slow the progress of Alzheimer's disease.

By the way, in case it hasn't become apparent already, the late 2007 breakthrough in which skin cells are being programmed to mimic embryonic stem cells is every bit as much of a miracle as it seems, if not more so. Not only will it lead to a thrilling explosion of cures for previously incurable illnesses, strokes, and paralysis, but by 2012 it will also result in the ability to exchange old body parts for compatible new ones, from spinal cords to limbs to burned or cancerous skin.

There's no way to narrow this down to a specific year, but please be aware that as the century progresses, there will be increasing numbers of infertile women and men whose sperm counts are too low to produce children. Countless biological theories will be pursued, but none of them will solve the mystery. Instead, the very simple explanation can be found on the Other Side: as the end of days closes in, fewer and fewer spirits will choose to reincarnate and be around when life on Earth ceases to exist. The fewer the spirits wanting to come here, the fewer the fetuses they'll need to occupy. And the fewer the fetuses required, the fewer the pregnancies. What's interesting, and comforting, is that along with the diminished number of successful pregnancies, couples will find themselves less and less interested in having children. Their conscious minds may not understand why that is, but their spirit minds will be well aware that they charted themselves to be here at this extraordinary time when spirits choosing to be born on Earth will become scarce and the population at the end of days will be dramatically diminished.

Here's the good news: during the first fifty years of the twenty-first century, we're going to see the end of some of the most insidious diseases and afflictions of our time.

Cancer will be destroyed by injecting highly addictive drugs specifically into the nuclei of cancerous cells, which will ultimately result in the cancerous cells consuming and eradicating themselves to satisfy their addiction. I once thought this form of treatment would be in use by at least a handful of exceptional oncologists, if only on an experimental basis, no later than 2006. I don't see it happening now until about 2010.

Also in 2010, diabetes will be significantly reduced and ultimately cured through brilliant advancements in the use of proteins.

Microchips implanted in the base of the brain will restore healthy signals between the brain, the muscular system, and the neurological system, putting an end to paralysis and Parkinson's disease no later than 2012.

In about 2013 or 2014, muscular dystrophy, multiple sclerosis (MS), and ALS (Lou Gehrig's disease) will be defeated through some highly specialized use of the human growth hormone.

The year 2014 will see the introduction of a safe, healthy pill or capsule that will replace gastric bypass and lapband surgeries, and anorexia and bulimia will be eliminated by a newly discovered medication that targets the pituitary gland.

In 2015 there will be virtually no invasive surgery. Instead, laser surgery, which of course is already being used with great success, will be brilliantly enhanced by a computerized sensor that will be able to pinpoint, analyze, and take appropriate medical action on the area in question.

Blindness will become a thing of the past by 2020 at the latest without a reliance on organ transplants when a tiny digital device is discovered that, when implanted in the frontal lobes of the brain, will create or reactivate normal, healthy communication between the brain and the eyes.

No later than 2020, thanks to the development of a synthetic material that perfectly duplicates the human eardrum, we'll see a virtual end to deafness.

One of the twenty-first century's most significant medical breakthroughs will be the perfection of synthetic blood in about 2025. It will be universal in type, enhanced with nutritional and immune system supplements and easily manufactured so that there will always be a safe, healthy, plentiful blood supply for transfusions.

The really dire bad news for health won't make its appearance until late in the second half of the century, which we'll discuss several pages from now. The only really alarming developments in the first half will be far outweighed by the advancements I've just described, but they're worth mentioning:

+ A bacterial infection resembling the "flesh-eating disease" of several years ago will arrive in 2010, transmitted to humans by almost microscopic mites undetectably imported on exotic birds. Known medications and antibiotics will be completely ineffective against this funguslike, extremely contagious disease, and its victims will be quarantined until it's discovered that the bacteria can be destroyed through some combination of electrical currents and extreme heat.

+ In around 2020 a severe pneumonia-like illness will spread throughout the globe, attacking the lungs and the bronchial tubes and resisting all known treatments. Almost more baffling than the illness itself will be the fact that it will suddenly vanish as quickly as it arrived, attack again ten years later, and then disappear completely.

Strides in mental health in the first half of this century will be extraordinary, virtually eliminating the majority of the disorders that plague society today. And if we want to create a more productive, more successful, more peaceful, better-educated world in which crime is an anomaly rather than the norm, we should solve the mysteries of ADHD, OCD, depression, bipolarism, and schizophrenia and we'll be well on our way.

Earlier we discussed the fact that newborn infants will be tested and treated for chemical imbalances that might lead to future psychological problems. That will be true for children, adolescents, and adults as well. No later than the end of 2009, there will be very precise formulas describing which imbalances will cause which problems, and which treatments will be most effective in solving them. We'll see an end to the liberal, often careless prescribing of Ritalin and antidepressants with no blood tests at all to indicate whether those medications are even appropriate. Instead, links will be discovered between specific psychological disorders and specific protein deficiencies, so that when those deficiences are pinpointed and addressed with precision, the disorders will permanently disappear.

By 2013 we're going to see an amazing development in the treatment of mental illness. There will be a device, used exclusively by highly trained psychiatrists and neurologists, that will employ electromagnetic impulses to treat and often cure these brain malfunctions. This device will glide slowly and smoothly across the surface of the skull, much like an MRI, both horizontally and vertically. As it moves, it will detect any abnormalities in the brain, the cerebrospinal fluid that surrounds the brain, blood circulation in and around the brain, and neurological and chemical activity within each hemisphere of the brain and between the two hemispheres, the individual lobes, etc.

Details of the scan, with diagnostic readouts, will be monitored by the psychiatric or neurological administrator. When the device senses a disturbance—slow or blocked circulation, for example, or "misfiring" or dormant neurotransmitters—it emits a series of electromagnetic impulses of varying intensity with pinpoint precision to stimulate the problem area, no matter how microscopic and otherwise undetectable it might be. These treatments on a monthly basis, combined with appropriate medications, will contribute as dramatically to the world of mental health as DNA has contributed to the world of law enforcement, essentially "curing" everything from bipolar disorder and depression to ADHD, OCD, post-traumatic stress syndrome and chronic anxiety.

As for schizophrenia and severe cases of epilepsy, those will be successfully treated in 2014 by a microchip implanted in the brain that will essentially "override" the system when it detects that any kind of malfunction, misfire, or shutdown is about to happen. This tiny microchip will perform the same function for the brain that the pacemaker performs for the heart, and with equally brilliant success.

We have a very substantial drop in the crime rate to look forward to in the next fifty years. One reason for this is the influx of advanced spirits that will be arriving from Home as the century progresses, as we'll explain in depth in the next chapter. The other reason is the advancements in law enforcement and forensics that will absolutely thrill every loyal *CSI* fan.

Probably the most dramatic headline is the fact that by 2025 at the latest, law enforcement will have new and expanded databases at their disposal that will make it almost not worth the trouble to commit crimes.

SCAN (I have no idea what the letters in that acronym stand for) will be a massive international database of DNA collected from newborn infants and volunteers from the general population. It will be perpetually interactive with the currently existing CODIS (the Combined DNA Index System), which is focused on DNA gathered from criminals and crime scenes. The SCAN database will link each person's DNA to such vital personal information as their medical records and their emergency contacts. If it did nothing else but eliminate the all-too-common tragedy of unidentified murder and other fatality victims, SCAN would be more than worth the forfeiture of privacy. But its ability to instantly identify lost, missing, abandoned, and stolen children will make it a Godsend.

The SCAN DNA database will actually be fully operational no later than 2015, as will the expanded capabilities of today's Automated Fingerprint Identification System, or AFIS. Added to the tens of millions of fingerprints currently stored and accessible to law enforcement will be full handprints, palm prints, footprints (as singular as fingerprints, it turns out), and prints of the sides of our hands, left behind when we write and almost unavoidably rest the side of our hands on the writing surface. The side-of-the-hand print is unique enough, and will be recognized enough as a valuable forensics tool, that its inclusion in the AFIS database will solve an internationally renowned kidnapping by the end of 2009.

In development at the end of 2008 and in full use by worldwide law enforcement no later than 2014 will be a database of the utterly unique "fingerprints" that are somehow imbedded in the iris of the human eye. The day will come when tiny iris-scanning devices are installed at every ATM machine, cash register, public building, and airport as a standard, doubly effective security measure. Let's say, for example, that someone manages to steal your ATM card and pin number. The ATM machine will refuse to dispense cash when the iris scanner is able to tell in less than a second that it has an impostor on its hands. But almost as satisfying, at that instant both a silent alarm and the database will be alerted, and the police will know the identity of the would-be thief within moments of the attempted theft.

Most complex and most groundbreaking of the databases in our future, though, will be the voice database that will be perfected and in full international use by 2025. This database will be so highly sensitive that it will be able to detect every tiny detail of pitch, tone, rhythm, dialect, and countless other variables that will someday make each voice on Earth as distinctive as a fingerprint, no matter how many filters, synthesizers, and other voice-altering devices are used.

Now, imagine the combined forces of all these databases, as information is immediately transmitted to every airport, train station, bus depot, car rental company, hotel and motel, bank and ATM machine, restaurant and diner and convenience store throughout the world when a criminal is on the run, a child is abducted, or a missing-persons case is filed. Database receivers will be as common in public buildings and businesses as surveillance cameras are today, and law enforcement will instantly be alerted when a fingerprint, palm print, hand/side-of-the-hand print, iris "print" or voice "print" is recognized by the receiver.

Added to this series of coordinated global efforts will be an international version of John Walsh's *America's Most Wanted*, which will air seven days a week, twenty-four hours a day on its own non-profit satellite channel, broadcasting information on every fugitive and every missing person and child to an audience of countless millions in every corner of the world, with corresponding tip lines and Web sites. While the entire global law enforcement community will be instrumental in initiating and producing this brilliantly successful effort, it will have its real roots in the halls of Scotland Yard.

No later than 2014, satellites will be able to detect crimes and send alerts to law enforcement of the specific location where their help is needed. And in case there are no eye witnesses on the scene, or eyewitness accounts of the crime are inconsistent, as they often are, satellites in orbit for no other purpose will be able to instantly transmit detailed digital footage of a crime scene, the ultimate in discreet surveillance cameras.

In the next chapter we'll discuss the extraordinary spiritual unity this planet will experience before the end of days. The seeds of that unity, and of a true global awareness of the God center in each of us, will be planted in the next twenty years or less, accompanied by some dramatic changes in the world of organized religion.

Pope Benedict will be the last elected Pope. His reign will be succeeded by a new Catholic practice of selecting a college of cardinals, essentially a triumvirate of popes who will collectively share papal responsibilities.

Between 2015 and 2018, a union of Protestant faiths will be organized, finally acting on the fact that there really is strength in numbers, to tackle such worldwide problems as hunger, poverty, homelessness, and the need for universal medical care.

By around 2025 the strength-in-numbers approach will be successful enough to inspire a voluntary coalition of all religions that care to participate. This powerful coalition will be unified by its yearning for more depth and substance in its connection to its Creator, and by its willingness to abandon traditional counter-productive bureaucracy and countless committees and instead take an active, hands-on approach to feeding, clothing, housing, curing, and spiritually nurturing those who need God's heart at work through His children *for* His children.

This 2025 global interfaith coalition will result in the worldwide construction of Healing Centers—compounds of four pyramid-shaped buildings staffed entirely by volunteers and generously equipped with donated supplies, offering around-the-clock food, clothing, shelter, basic personal hygiene and laundry facilities, medical care, crisis counseling, legal aid, and anything and everything else the populations of surrounding communities can't provide for themselves.

Of particular significance to the massive spiritual awakening later in this century will be the Healing Centers' Dedication Schools, which will offer, among other things, extensive courses in world religions and will require the completion of each of those courses prior to graduation.

By 2040, thanks in large part to these Healing Centers and efforts inspired by them, we're going to see a great unity of global faiths, based on an educated awareness that their similarities far outnumber their differences, and on the conspicuous impact their combined humanitarian efforts are having on this earth. And as we'll discover in the second half of the century, this unity of faith is only the beginning of a worldwide spiritual transformation.

The year 2020 will mark the end of the U.S. presidency and the executive branch of the government. Let's just say the American public will finally be fed up by then and leave it at that.

The legislative branch will essentially absorb the responsibilities of the executive branch, with a streamlined body of elected representatives, an equal number from each state, forming the new legislature, which will be known simply as the Senate. The "party" system of Democrats, Republicans, Independents, et al., will uncomplicate itself into Liberals and Conservatives, who will debate and vote on each proposed bill and law in nationally televised sessions.

Requirements for Senate candidates will be stringent and continuously monitored. For example, senators will be prohibited from having any past or present salaried position with any company that has ever had or might ever have a professional or contractual connection to federal, state, or local government, and each senator must submit to random drug and alcohol testing throughout his or her term.

The long-term effects of this reorganized government and closely examined body of lawmakers will be a return of legislative accountability and public trust, and state governments will follow suit no later than 2024 by becoming smaller mirror images of the national Senate.

Among the laws that will be enacted during the Senate's first six-year term will be:

- ✦ the flat tax
- ✦ tax bonuses for those with careers in the arts, education, law enforcement, and public service
- ✦ national observance of all major holidays celebrated by all major religions, as well as a Day of Remembrance for Holocaust survivors, victims, and their descendants
- ✦ "neutering" of all male and female pedophiles proved guilty by irrefutable evidence as a mandated part of their prison sentence
- ✦ a public health system
- ✦ driving under the influence of drugs or alcohol, even on the

first offense, will result in mandated inpatient rehab and detox, and the immediate seizure and auctioning of the vehicle
to defray the rehab and detox expenses

As for a couple of other topics of national interest:

By 2020 America will see the end of IRAs, mutual funds,
pension, and retirement plans, and yes, it's true, the stock market.

And hard as it may be to believe at this moment, by the mid-
2020s the global image of the United States will be significantly re-
habilitated. What's fascinating is that we'll accomplish this by shifting
the vast majority of our humanitarian focus back on our own problems and their solutions. The United States will evolve into a nation
that inspires rather than invades and be admired all the more for it.

I think it was in about 1972 that I announced on a San Francisco
television show called *People Are Talking*, "We're starting into a
polar tilt." I was as surprised by the announcement as the hosts of
the show were, especially since I had no idea what a polar tilt was,
and rarely has my office been as flooded with calls questioning my
sanity as it was after that telecast.

It turns out that a polar tilt is a shift in the angle at which the
earth tilts on its axis, toward or away from the sun, causing all sorts
of changes in ocean currents and weather in general. Out of curiosity, my staff and I did a little research and discovered that a nine-
teenth-century Scottish scientist named James Croll wrote in 1875
about the climate changes caused by the tilt of the earth's axis, and
Edgar Cayce commented on the polar tilt as well.

That having been said, the polar tilt will reach its peak by 2020,
in addition to which:

- In around 2018 worldwide seismic activity will result in a rash of volcanoes and earthquakes. The resulting atmospheric dust will create enough pollution to cause disastrous crop failures in the early 2020s.
- Rains approaching monsoon intensity will hit the eastern seaboard of North and South America in about 2025.
- Between 2025 and 2030 dramatic tidal waves will hit the Far East and Florida. The Florida tsunamis will be the result of an unprecedented swarm of hurricanes.
- In around 2026 a series of powerful tsunamis will crash into Japan. As a result of this major oceanic disturbance, a new land mass will emerge among the Hawaiian Islands.
- The year 2029 will usher in a rash of meteor showers and the unceremonious return to Earth of some of the trash and debris we've abandoned during our space explorations. Fortunately, considerably more damage will be done to our topography and plant life than to our human and animal life.
- Before the year 2050 I absolutely believe that in the wake of major volcanic and subterranean disturbances in the Atlantic and Indian oceans, both Atlantis and Lemuria will rise magnificently from their underwater graves.

Later in this chapter we'll discuss the atmospheric, topographical, and climatic circumstances that will make all the difference in the world, so to speak, in the second half of the century and essentially leave it up to us just how quickly the end of days will come.

No later than 2015 all newly built houses will be solar powered and prefabricated, made of stone or flame-retardant synthetic wood over reinforced steel, with roofs of ceramic tile and solar panels that are both shatterproof and fireproof. Standard in each home will be a sophisticated security system, including steel-core exterior doors and unbreakable windows that can be opened only by the home's central computer, in an emergency triggered by an alarm that simultaneously alerts the fire and police departments, and by the homeowner through a scan of their "eyeprint." The eyeprint will be a configuration of the cornea and iris, as distinctive as a fingerprint, much like we discussed regarding the iris "fingerprint" database. All access points of the house will include a peephole, which the residents and authorized guests will look into so that the central computer can scan the eyeprint and allow entry.

That same central computer can be programmed to play music, turn TVs and other home computers on and off, control appliances and lighting, and completely manage the phone system—making voice-activated calls, blocking calls, selectively answering calls, and providing a crystal-clear, hands-free conversation in any room or rooms of the house.

Building codes for every home, and public building, for that matter, will mandate powerful, well-concealed air purifiers, eliminating virtually all airborne viruses and sources of allergies and asthma attacks.

And another common fixture in most upscale homes by 2015 will be highly functional and incredibly convenient robots. They'll be available to the general public by 2019 and will respond to more than five hundred complicated voice commands, from cooking to cleaning to pet care to reading bedtime stories to helping children with their homework to teaching computer skills.

Last but certainly not least, it will be a very rare private home that by 2040 won't be equipped with a retractable roof to allow the family hovercrafts to come and go as routinely as the family cars currently come and go from our garages.

Protecting ourselves from terrorists and unsafe air will become an increasingly urgent priority as technology advances, with the result that by the late 2020s some of us will be living in domed cities.

The concept of domed cities will be developed by an international collaboration of experts. The first of these cities will appear in the United States. Germany, England, and Japan will follow immediately, with India, the Middle East, and the Far East being the last to participate. Eventually there will be domed cities on every continent, made of a composite of three-ply synthetic glass and plastic that's infinitely more durable than anything in existence today. It will be tinted for UV protection but still high enough and clear enough to be virtually undetectable to the population thriving beneath it, and it will open and close to allow, or deny, air travel. The air will be purified, the temperature will be regulated, and all conditions in general will be scientifically controlled for maximum health.

Ironically, the downside of domed cities will be their desirability. The more ideal they become, the more crowded they'll become, and the more crowded they become, the more stressful they'll become. It will take only a couple of decades for the population of domed cities to be "weeded out" as the wealthy take over and the poor are excluded.

That inequity will be solved to some extent by the appearance of several domed rural regions throughout the world. Communal societies will form there and become very successful organic agricultural centers.

Not until the second half of the century will the novelty and environmental purity of domed living lose much of its appeal, and the general population will venture out into the "real world" again, leaving domed cities much less crowded, much more affordable, and much less in demand.

Of course, as always, our greatest hope for the finest possible quality of life in the coming century, and for any chance of postponing or averting the end of days, is a brilliantly educated generation or two who can succeed in the many areas in which we've either failed or fallen short.

By approximately 2020, the educational system will undergo massive structural changes, and not a moment too soon.

Teachers will be well paid, they'll be subjected to thorough background checks, and they'll be required to hold degrees in child psychology in addition to their teaching credentials, since children's educational and emotional needs will be considered to be of equal importance.

Higher salaries for teachers will attract more teachers, and in 2020 there will never be more than fifteen Primary school students per teacher in any classroom.

Primary school children will study the usual reading, writing, spelling, math, and social studies, as well as nutrition, basic ethics, an art or music course, a foreign language course, and an active, hands-on course in ecology. No child will leave junior school without knowing how to read and write, and chronic tardiness, absences, or incomplete homework assignments will be considered the fault of the parents, not the children, resulting in a combination of fines and requisite parenting classes.

Senior schools will involve students linked by laptop to assigned teachers at education centers throughout each state. Teachers and students can instantly access each other with the push of a button, making truancy a breeze to detect and the overseeing of each student's work far more individualized than it is now. Tests in each subject will be given every three months, locally, administered by "live" graduate students in the teaching curriculum.

As for higher education, every student will have instant cyberspace access to the application process at every college and university around the world, just as every college and university will have the instant cyberspace ability to recruit students from around the world. It will become the norm for university students to attend schools overseas, and as this century progresses it will be higher education that's the primary force, along with the great coalition of religions we discussed earlier, behind the eventual formation of a true global community.

From 2050 to the End of Days and Beyond

There will be human life on Earth again, millions and millions of years from now, when this planet has had the opportunity to cleanse itself of our presence here. And the rest of that thought is: *unless every one of us does everything we can, every single day, to save the earth.*

This earth, this home away from Home, is God's creation, not ours. It was here before we were, and it will outlast us if we don't get over this arrogant idea that we're entitled to live here.

Sometimes you'd think that we're all a bunch of teenagers, left unsupervised in the house while our parents are away. Given enough time and freedom, there won't be a house left worth living in, and, I promise, the same is true of our treatment of this planet.

We need to focus on the biggest possible picture to get a perspective on the facts that will determine our success or failure in the second half of this century, and whether or not it will culminate in the end of our days on Earth. Appearances can be deceiving, after all. For example, from our point of view, it can seem very much as if our planet is the center of the universe, with the sun, moon, stars, and distant galaxies revolving around us. But the truth is, we're just one of eight planets—many of them much larger than we are—that revolve around the sun; there are countless other suns in the cosmos providing heat, light, and life to their own solar systems; and there are far more solar systems in far more galaxies than our most brilliant astronomers have begun to imagine yet.

Similarly, convenient and comforting as it can be to look out our windows and assume that if everything looks fine, everything must *be* fine, we're doing ourselves a great disservice to ignore the problems we've created and that we must solve if life on Earth is going to continue into the next century.

For example, because we humans can get very busy being smug about our superiority and dominion on Earth, and our indestructability no matter how we abuse this planet, I think it's worth paying at least a moment's thought to an issue brought up in a fascinating article called "How Will the World End?" written by Herbert C. Fyfe for *Pearson's Magazine* in July of 1900. In that article Mr. Fyfe points out:

Countless ages ago in the world's past history there was a time when huge monsters, both on land and sea, were common. These reigned supreme for a time, only to succumb at length and disappear. Many species even within our own time have become extinct; can man then always hope to have the preeminence?

"When once a type is gone," said the late Mr. J. F. Nesbit, "Nature never renews it. So infinite are her resources that no pattern, no number of patterns, matters. And it may be that man, a late arrival, is destined to a far shorter use of the earth than the cockroach or the lobster."

Not over flattering to human vanity, but nevertheless true! . . .

The fact is, we know little about the origin of diseases, and why at certain seasons certain epidemics arise. The bacillus of plague, of influenza, of cholera, of typhoid, or any other disease propagated by germs, finds that the climatic or atmospheric conditions are favourable, and promptly proceeds to multiply, and, once it had a free run, it could destroy the entire human race in a month.

We might try to take comfort in the fact that this article was written more than a century ago, but it's worth asking ourselves how much has changed on the points Mr. Fyfe is raising. We humans still absolutely believe we're the most superior species on this planet, and I guess if "most superior" means "most destructive," a case can be made. But isn't it silly, really, that while we're busy driving other species to extinction, we've overlooked the distinct possibility that we're driving ourselves to extinction at the same time, with the same careless neglect and demolition of the very planet we rely on for survival? What has given us the impression that we're not every bit as vulnerable, if not more so, as every other earthly species, especially when we look at the long list of fatal human diseases we can't seem to conquer? And if correcting that misguided impression helps us to wake up and start paying serious attention to the well-being of this earth, then so much the better and God bless Mr. Fyfe.

Global Warming

I'm telling you this as a psychic, as a concerned citizen of the world, as an extensive traveler who's personally seen 60-million-year-old glaciers melting off the Alaskan coast, and as a grandmother whose greatest wish is that my grandchildren's grandchildren will be born on a planet in which they can thrive: global warming—the gradual, alarming increase in temperatures during the last century—is a potentially fatal threat to Earth. That's a fact no matter how you feel about Al Gore, and no matter whether you're a tree-hugging hippie or a right-wing conservative. And if we don't take it seriously and do something about it today, it will become one of the primary factors in creating an uninhabitable world ninety-two years from now.

I can tell you with psychic certainty that the landscape of this planet at the end of days will be the same continents we have now, each of them severely diminished by flooding. Two-thirds of the earth is currently covered by water. By the end of this century, water will cover three-quarters of the planet as ice caps, glaciers, and snow from the highest mountains continue to melt. Most of the melting ice will flow into the oceans, drowning coastal cities and driving the population toward the middle of the continents. What doesn't melt into the seas will seep into the earth, to its red-hot core, creating steam and pressure, which will in turn cause a rash of catastrophic volcanoes around the world. Mount Lassen, Mount St. Helen's, and Mount Etna will be among the first to erupt, but even the dormant Mount Fuji will come to life again no later than 2085, decimating much of Japan.

Contributing to the atmospheric violence of the last three decades of this century will be an array of weather extremes that will make our current climate look ordinary. Hurricanes and monsoons will more than double in frequency and intensity. The average heat and cold record temperatures throughout the world will be a minimum of ten degrees hotter than they are now. Tornadoes will become destructive year-round threats, rather than seasonal, throughout the central North and South American continents and in areas of Europe and Africa once thought to be topographically immune from them. And where flooding isn't prevalent, drought will be, so that it will become virtually impossible to find a healthy, profitable place to live, let alone a safe one.

Yes, all thanks to global warming. So how dare any of us ignore it or trivialize it, when it's literally the difference between life and death for humankind.

A major contributor to global warming is the infamous "greenhouse effect," a term we've heard so often that I'm not sure we even pay attention to it anymore. And believe me, we need to. I certainly don't pretend to have a background in science or the slightest bit of expertise, but as I understand it, the greenhouse effect is caused by atmospheric gases, particularly carbon dioxide, methane, and ozone. (At ground level, ozone is a polluting form of oxygen.) They retain and reflect the sun's energy back to Earth to keep us warm. If it weren't for the basic greenhouse effect, this planet would probably be nothing but solid ice.

The danger we're increasingly creating is really an *enhanced* greenhouse effect, in which too much carbon dioxide, methane, and ozone are filling the air, so that too much energy from the sun is being retained and reflected back to Earth, with the result that we keep on getting warmer and warmer. So a key to the solution to global warming is the reduction of the amount of carbon dioxide, methane, and ozone we're allowing to be released into the atmosphere, through the burning of fossil fuels like coal and oil, for example. And eliminating vast areas of trees and other foliage dramatically compounds the problem, since plants take in carbon dioxide and give off oxygen—helping to reduce carbon dioxide from the air without our having to lift a finger, in other words, and further rewarding us with oxygen, without which we cannot survive.

Ozone as a pollutant at ground level is obviously not to be confused with the essential ozone layer, which forms a thin shield in the upper atmosphere that protects life on Earth from the sun's ultraviolet rays. As far back as the 1980s, scientists began gathering evidence that the ozone layer was being depleted, exposing us to potential radiation and the related possibility of skin cancer, eye damage, and harm to the immune system. NASA has even begun monitoring holes in the ozone layer—commonly called holes but actually specific areas of extreme thinning or depletion.

And in this case the primary culprit is CFC—a man-made gas called chlorofluorocarbon—which for decades was popularly used in spray cans and refrigerators. In the year 2000, 120 countries around the world agreed to phase out the use of CFC. Sadly, while the ozone layer is capable of repairing itself if no further harm is inflicted on it to exacerbate the damage, the healing process is guaranteed to be very slow. Chlorine, which is one of the components of chlorofluorocarbon, has amazing durability in the atmosphere, and it just takes one atom of chlorine to destroy one hundred thousand molecules of ozone.

Add all of this up and we've got a planet that's slowly being warmed to the point of cataclysmic flooding and violent weather events because of extreme levels of greenhouse gases and an ozone layer too diminished to dilute the sun's radiation and harmful effects on those greenhouse gases. Rather than preserving and enhancing our global forests, we're clearing them out to create toilet paper and housing developments, eliminating some of our greatest silent allies in providing oxygen and cleansing the air of excess carbon dioxide. And every one of those interacting elements that's leading the earth to potential uninhabitability is caused by us. Tragically, we've become a cancer here, sending species after species of animals into extinction and apparently forgetting that we humans are every bit as vulnerable to extinction as any other species on Earth.

I've heard the same "Go Green" public service announcements you have, and seen the same bumper stickers. But too often there's no follow-up explanation about what "going green" means or exactly why it makes a difference. I also hate to admit it, but I tend to have an aversion to activist slogans like "Go Green." Unfairly, I'm sure, it makes me feel excluded unless I have time to pick up a sign and head to Washington (and God bless every one of you who demonstrates for important causes), and it also implies that all of us know what it is we're supposed to do about it. I didn't know, but I've made it my business to find out so that I really can do something about it, and so that I can share the information with you.

I'm not advocating these suggestions because they're just plain nice, planet-friendly things to do. I'm advocating them, and implementing them myself, because it actually is up to us to either resign ourselves to the end of life on Earth at the end of this century or see to it that we have many more centuries to enjoy and appreciate this beautiful home away from Home.

And yes, it truly is this simple:

- Use only recycled paper. Why? Because it saves the atmosphere about five pounds of carbon dioxide per ream of paper.
- Set your thermostat just two degrees warmer in the summer than you're accustomed to and two degrees cooler in the winter. Why? Because those tiny adjustments will keep approximately two thousand pounds of carbon dioxide per year.
- Don't run your dishwasher until it's completely full. Why? Because it will save the atmosphere about one hundred pounds of carbon dioxide per year.
- Pick the three lamps you use most in your house and change the bulbs to easily accessible compact fluorescent bulbs. Why? Because you'll eliminate an extra three hundred pounds of carbon dioxide from the atmosphere every year.
- Adjust the heat on your water heater to a maximum of 120 degrees, and have it insulated. Why? Because it saves 1,550 pounds of carbon dioxide from the air every year.
- Reduce the duration of your showers by two to three minutes. Why? Because 350 pounds of carbon dioxide will be saved every year thanks to less water needing to be heated.
- Check your tires every month to make sure they're properly inflated. Why? Because it will save 250 pounds of carbon dioxide per year.

+ Change your heating and air-conditioning filters, or clean them, as often as recommended. Why? Because it will keep the units from having to work harder than they're designed to work to keep you comfortable, as well as keeping an extra 350 pounds of carbon dioxide out of the atmosphere per year.

+ Turn your computer off rather than letting it "sleep," and unplug electronics when you're not using them. Why? Because it will save a minimum of twelve hundred pounds of carbon dioxide per year.

+ Take care of the simple chore of caulking and weather-stripping your exterior doors and windows. Why? Because not only will you be more comfortable all year long, but you'll also eliminate seventeen hundred pounds of carbon dioxide per year.

+ Plant a tree, or have one planted by an organization like Tree-People, in honor of a lost loved one. Why? Because you'll be adding more oxygen to the atmosphere and saving an amazing two thousand pounds of carbon dioxide.

Those simple adjustments alone add up to a saving of nine thousand five hundred pounds of carbon dioxide per person per year. If you need a little more motivation to be convinced, they'll also save you money.

And a few more suggestions for today or the near future, since they're not necessarily as simple (or affordable) as the above list:

+ As you replace old appliances, buy new ones that bear an Energy Saving Recommended logo, designed to save both carbon dioxide emissions and money.

- Making sure the walls and ceilings of your home are well-insulated can save a minimum of two thousand pounds of carbon dioxide, not to mention plenty of expense, every year.
- Changing single-pane windows to double-pane windows conserves energy, saves a fortune in power bills, and eliminates an amazing ten thousand pounds of carbon dioxide.
- Switching from your current showerhead to a low-flow showerhead will save approximately 350 pounds of carbon dioxide.
- When it's time for a new car, remember that a hybrid will save almost seventeen thousand pounds of carbon dioxide per year. Even a more fuel-efficient car will save thousands and thousands of pounds of carbon dioxide and hundreds of pounds of expense at the same time.

By the way, since the paper industry is the third-largest contributor to global warming factors, seek out toilet paper, facial tissues, and paper towels and coffee filters that are made from recycled paper; recycle magazines, newspapers, and paper grocery bags; give your dry cleaner a garment bag to use for your dry cleaning to encourage them to get rid of all that annoying extra paper and plastic, and never drop off dry cleaning without returning those equally annoying wire hangers.

And on the subject of "annoying," I'm sure it would horrify all of us to see how many landfills are piled with Styrofoam cups, since about twenty-five billion of them are thrown away every year. Plastic bags from the market are a little more recycleable than Styrofoam but not much. Paper or glass cups and mugs make drinks taste better than Styrofoam does, don't you think? As for all the debris left over from trips to the store, washable canvas shopping bags eliminate that so conveniently.

Again, I wouldn't carry on for quite so long on this subject if it weren't literally a matter of life and death, of whether or not we'll ever live on this earth again once we've gone Home. We caused these problems, and it's our job to clean them up. And while we're at it, let's pray every single day that it's not already too late.

Our Health at the End of Days

We obviously can't be healthy in an atmosphere that isn't. So when I say that illness is what's going to ultimately end our lives on Earth, please understand that I'm not really making a distinction between the fatal diseases in our future and the disastrous environment we're in the process of creating.

I can't stress enough that when the end of times comes, these disease-related deaths will be amazingly easy and peaceful. Spirituality will be so commonly understood by then that people will know exactly what perfect joy awaits them on the Other Side that they'll essentially just "step out of their bodies" and into the tunnel, fearless and full of hope. I can't help but be fondly reminded of three of my ministers who went Home in the last year and a half. Each of them, when they passed a few months apart, was found in bed, lying peacefully on their backs with their hands folded on their chests. Their deaths were clearly as graceful, confident, and God-centered as could be. And with only the most rare exceptions—the result of what will by then be an almost unheard-of act of violence—that's what death will be like for everyone at the end of times.

Ironically, in the first half of this century, we're going to see the majority of today's most devastating diseases eradicated. Cancer, leukemia, diabetes, muscular dystrophy, multiple sclerosis, ALS, Alzheimer's disease, heart disease—all of those will be so long gone by 2050 that they'll seem almost archaic. And yet the medical world will be caught completely off guard when, in about 2075 or 2080, there will be a sudden worldwide spread of diseases that seem almost archaic to us today, particularly polio and smallpox. We've become complacent and stopped vaccinating against those two disastrous illnesses in the US, and some combination of that complacency and the unhealthy atmosphere we've created will give them the perfect opportunity to reappear.

The environment will take its toll on our immune systems, there's no doubt about it. It's karmic, really, the earth's way of paying us back for all the abuse and neglect—still another reason we've got to start treasuring and nurturing this planet if we ever expect it to do the same for us again. There will be dramatic increases in fibromyalgia, chronic fatigue syndrome, sterility and infertility, and countless, virtually untraceable allergies. It's probably also a form of payback that we'll be more vulnerable than ever to diseases carried by unhealthy animals, from currently unheard-of bird flus and variations of Lyme disease to a deadly relative of West Nile virus that will arrive via insects from South America.

These illnesses and plagues will hit hard and very suddenly, much more quickly than scientists and researchers can keep up with them, let alone conquer them. And that, sadly, along with a toxic atmosphere and having nowhere to live that's not disastrously flooded and weather challenged, is what will bring us to the end of our lives on Earth.

The End of Days Through My Eyes

Not a nuclear holocaust—when all is said and done, no world leader will be insane enough to actually push that legendary red button.

Not a collision with some monster asteroid or meteor shower, a fatal, haphazard whim of the cosmos.

Just our own self-created, self-fulfilled prophecy of the end of days.

> *This is the way the world ends.*
> *This is the way the world ends.*
> *This is the way the world ends.*
> *Not with a bang, but a whimper.*

—T. S. Eliot

CHAPTER EIGHT

Humankind at the End of Days

I don't think it's productive to have any discussion about the end of our time on Earth that doesn't explain the full context of what will happen to us before, during, and after. Without that, the subject of the end of days is nothing but sensationalism, a series of threatening, fear-inducing headlines that offer no hope and no reminder that we were living busy, productive, joyful lives before we came here, and we'll go right on with those same lives when our days on this planet are over.

It's simply a fact that as this century progresses, humankind will become more and more spiritually oriented. I'm seeing it already, every single day, in readings, lectures, and television appearances. Clients whose questions even five years ago were primarily focused on Mr. or Ms. Right, finances, career concerns, and health problems are now almost exclusively wanting to know about their spiritual goals—specifically, whether or not they're on track in fulfilling those goals and whether or not they're accomplishing the life purposes they set up for themselves.

This increasing global growth in spirituality as a priority is no accident and no coincidence. God didn't create a whimsical, haphazard universe in which it's a roll of the dice what might happen next. There's an eternal order, a divine plan that guides our spirits like an inescapable safety net, even when we're too self-involved to believe that it's there and that it will never, ever let us fall. God's plan for us has existed since time began, and it will go right on existing into infinity. And it's because of that plan that we can count on Earth becoming a far more God-centered place as the countdown to the end of days begins ticking away more loudly.

Preparing to Come Here

Later in this chapter I'll describe the specifics of our arrival back Home and the perfect eternity of our lives there. For now, I want to remind you—and I do mean "remind" you, since your spirit remembers it perfectly—of the process we undertake when we decide to take a temporary break from the Other Side and come here to challenge our souls toward their highest possible advancement.

Life on the Other Side, as you'll read in a while, is idyllic. It's paradise. We're surrounded by endless, exquisite beauty. We live among the angels and the messiahs, loved and loving, perpetually busy and stimulated, in a sanctified atmosphere that's alive with the immediate, tangible presence of God.

It seems almost insane that from time to time we choose to leave Home for yet another incarnation on this harsh, imperfect planet. But as my Spirit Guide Francine always says when I complain to her about some particularly tough challenges I'm going through, "What have you learned when times were good?" Perfection, wonderful as it is, doesn't inspire growth. And God created each of us with our own unique potential and a divine insistence on reaching that potential, no matter what it takes. On the Other Side we can study all we want about every subject that exists, including fear, negativity, temptation, violence, and cruelty. But studying those subjects without experiencing them is like reading every book to be found on driving a car without ever getting behind the wheel. Since fear, negativity, temptation, violence, and cruelty don't exist at Home, we have to come here to confront it, grow from it, and ultimately overcome it, not only for the benefit of humankind but also for the progress toward the highest potential of our souls.

We never arrive on Earth without mapping out specific goals and challenges for ourselves, just as we'd never decide to attend college and then pull out of the driveway without having a clue what school we're headed for, what courses we want to take, or where we'll be living while we're there. Our plans for each new incarnation are meticulously detailed, to guarantee the success of our trip away from Home. We choose our parents. We choose our siblings. We choose our birthplace and the exact time and date of our birth, which means we select every detail of our astrological chart. We choose every aspect of our physical appearance and every physical and mental challenge we'll be facing. We choose our friends, our lovers, our spouses, our children, our bosses, our coworkers, our casual acquaintances, and our pets. We choose all the Dark Entities we'll meet along the way. (More about Dark Entities later in this chapter). We choose every city, neighborhood, and house we'll live in. We choose our preferences, our weaknesses, our flaws, our skills, and our areas of incompetence.

It's a reliable assumption that the more difficult the circumstances a spirit charts for its new incarnation, the more advanced that spirit is in its journey toward perfection. One of the many things that makes my hair stand on end is when I hear some judgmental fool state as if it's true that someone who's mentally or physically challenged is "obviously" being punished for some sin they committed in a past life. Just exactly the opposite is true. The superior courage and wisdom it takes to chart a life involving any form of severe disadvantage is worthy of our greatest admiration and nothing less. It's the definition of an advanced soul.

As this century progresses, more and more of these advanced souls will be incarnating. That's not a guess or an assumption, it's simple logic. We write our charts with full knowledge of the earthly "backdrop" against which we'll be living the life we're mapping out. Civil wars, world wars, the Great Depression, the Holocaust, the World Trade Center tragedy—every one of those events, every event no matter how historic or seemingly trivial, was and is anticipated on the Other Side by those who choose to be here and involved at the time. Again, the more difficult the life a soul charts for itself, the more advanced the soul that composed the chart. Advanced souls have willingly participated in earthly cataclysms since the beginning of life on Earth, and advanced souls will willingly participate at the end.

By definition, then, as we approach the year 2100, we're going to see more and more advanced souls volunteering to incarnate and be here for the end of days (if they choose, which we'll discuss momentarily). And as the population of advanced souls on this planet increases, the spirituality on Earth will become increasingly powerful, almost palpable, a global, inspiring, purifying wave of the divine.

In addition to the growing number of advanced spirits among us, my Spirit Guide Francine tells me that the veil between the dimension of the Other Side and the dimension of Earth is slowly but surely fading away. To understand that, you have to know that the Other Side is only three feet above our ground level. It simply exists on a frequency so much higher than ours on Earth that it's difficult for us to perceive its presence. As this century progresses, the difference between these two frequencies will diminish, with the result that humankind will become increasingly aware of the spirit world of Home—i.e., increasingly at peace with the approaching end of days thanks to more and more reminders of where we came from and where we're joyfully headed.

It's worth noting that, just as I'm meeting more and more people whose spirituality is a top priority, I'm also meeting more and more people who are on their last incarnations on Earth. Remember, we choose when and how often to take these brief "field trips" away from the Other Side, and it's not uncommon for a spirit to choose to come here dozens of times. (I'm on my fifty-second incarnation, for example, and my last, I'm delighted to add.) I'm convinced that some of us are on our last incarnations because we've learned all we feel we need to from the earthly experience, while others of us are simply aware that by the time we'd be considering another "field trip," Earth won't be able to sustain human life any longer. And I can't stress enough, we'll be perfectly content with the sacred bliss of eternity, not on this temporary plane we're just visiting but on the divine dimension of our *real* Home.

Exit Points

I mentioned earlier that the increasingly advanced spirits who choose to incarnate in this century can also choose whether or not they want that incarnation to end with the end of humankind's days on Earth. That's because in the charts we write before we come here we include something called Exit Points.

Exit Points are simply circumstances we prearrange that can result in the end of the incarnation we're about to undertake, if we choose to take advantage of them at the moment they occur. We write five Exit Points into our charts, but we don't necessarily wait until the fifth one to head Home. We might decide on our first one, or our second, third, or fourth, that we've accomplished all we intended on this trip. Nor do we space them out in regular intervals when we plan them. We might arrange for two or three Exit Points in the same year, for example, and our next one another twenty or thirty years later.

Obvious Exit Points include critical illnesses, accidents, near misses, and any other events that could logically be expected to result in death but are "somehow" survived against all odds. Other Exit Points are so subtle that we might not even notice them until and unless we look back on them later. A decision "for no reason" to drive a different route from usual to a frequent destination; "trivial" delays that cause us to miss a plane or be on the road at the time we'd intended; staying home from a social event or an appointment because we suddenly "just don't feel like it" — any number of incidents that seem meaningless at the time could easily be our spirit's memory of an Exit Point that we've decided against taking.

The fact of Exit Points brings up another fascinating point about the end of days: every human being who's alive when the end of days arrives will be here by their own charted design, and will have written "the end of life on Earth" as their fifth Exit Point. Their conscious minds might not be aware of that choice, but their spirit minds will know that their chart is now complete and their purpose for their final trip to this planet has been accomplished.

Extraterrestrials

One of the most dramatic headlines in 2012 will be the discovery of some mysterious debris in a California/Nevada desert. It will be impossible to tell what the original shape of the large, mangled object was, but the alloy it was made of clearly wasn't manufactured from earthly materials. A group of civilians will come across it and, for a refreshing change of pace, will thoroughly document the event and notify the authorities rather than the tabloids. As a result, the government won't have the opportunity to "spin" the debris into nonexistence, nor can those who discovered it be accused of trying to perpetrate a fraud by selling their story.

This discovery will occur in conjunction with a series of untraceable signals that will disrupt satellite transmissions and wireless communications throughout the world. And by the end of 2012 or the beginning of 2013, having finally put two and two together, organized groups of explorers, researchers, government agencies, and other experts will undertake formal worldwide expeditions in search of extraterrestrials.

Of course, extraterrestrials have been here for millions of years and they're here now, calling as little attention to themselves as possible as they contribute to our society through careers that their advanced knowledge make possible. They're among our most brilliant researchers, space engineers, nuclear physicists, teachers, scientists, judges, social reformers—any pursuit that will leave its mark as indelibly as their collaboration with us on the Great Pyramid and Stonehenge all those centuries ago. Two of them are currently valued employees of NASA, and one of them was a Nobel Prize winner. It's preposterous to be afraid of extraterrestrials, as science fiction books and movies have encouraged us to be. Let's face it, they're so far beyond us technologically that they can easily and routinely travel here from Andromeda, the Pleiades, and other galaxies we aren't even aware of yet. But we think they don't have the technology to destroy us in the blink of an eye if that were their purpose for being here?

In about 2018, extraterrestrials will be making our search for them much easier—they'll begin "outing" themselves, safely and sanely and very much in public, to such organizations as the United Nations, Scotland Yard, NASA, and even a Camp David summit. They'll step forward by the thousands and willingly subject themselves to a whole battery of psychological and biological tests, confirming that the origins of their various species are not earthly.

By the early 2020s, we humans will reach an accord with the extraterrestrials in our midst and those still to come. Many of the dramatic advancements in our own space travel will be the direct result of what we've learned from them, from the manned Mars exploration in 2012 and the chartered moon junkets in the late 2030s to the lunar base of the early 2040s that will become a wildly popular tourist destination.

Let's face it, we're not just a part of a global community, we're also a part of a universal community. Why that seems to frighten some people I have no idea. Because we earthly residents are the universal version of the "new kids on the block," we have an infinite wealth of development and spiritual growth to look forward to from our brothers and sisters on other planets when we finally embrace them and start listening.

Of even more importance, residents of other planets are God's creation, His children, just as we are, after all. They have the same journeys of the soul that we do, the same options of reincarnation, and the same sacred bliss to look forward to on the Other Side—not *our* Other Side, but their own. Every inhabited planet throughout the universe has a divine Home of its own, and just think how grateful we might be for that fact when we can no longer live on the earthly home we're in the process of destroying.

I know that some of you who are reading this are feeling a deep, odd twinge of familiarity in your soul, very possibly without having a clue what's causing it. It's not because you're actually aliens from somewhere else in the universe. Aliens know exactly who they are and where they came from. Instead, it's because, probably without a conscious awareness of it, you're a highly advanced spirit called a Mystical Traveler, and Mystical Travelers have a whole different perspective on the earthly end of days.

Mystical Travelers

In all this talk about advanced spirits, I don't want to give the mistaken impression that "advanced" means "more important." In God's eyes, every one of us is of equal importance and value. We are all His children, and He created each of us to be utterly unique, each with our own purpose, dependent on our highest possible level of advancement. For a simple earthly example of the equal importance of various levels of advancement, think of the military. Generals are absolutely highly advanced and essential, but without the armies of soldiers they command, what do you think their odds would be of winning a battle? I promise you, every purpose God bestows is indispensable to His great plan for this infinite, flawless universe, and every spirit is equally cherished. So when I talk about a level of highly advanced souls called Mystical Travelers, I'm not implying that these are souls who've been specially endowed by God or are held in higher esteem than the rest of us.

Mystical Travelers are spirits who, in the course of their soul's journey, have essentially said to God, "Wherever in this universe you need me, I'll willingly go." Their universal mission is to help maintain the divine spiritual connection between God and His children as a thriving, viable, ever-present force. Toward that purpose, they've volunteered to incarnate on any inhabited planet in any galaxy where God needs them. Most Mystical Travelers have experienced many lifetimes on Earth as well as on other planets, and whether or not they become public figures, they quietly touch the lives around them in ways that are almost transcendent in their impact. They seem divinely lit from within, and the rest of us are drawn to them, quite literally like moths to flames. They're uncommonly peaceful, uncommonly empathetic, uncommonly spiritual, and uncommonly graceful in the often difficult work they're here to do on God's behalf. Mother Teresa was a Mystical Traveler. Joan of Arc was a Mystical Traveler. Thirteen-year-old poet, philosopher, and theologian Mattie Stepanek was a Mystical Traveler. There are more among us who may never become famous but who will leave no doubt about their spiritual brilliance for those who will never be the same because of them. And even more of them will gather on Earth as this century progresses, to lend their incomparable hearts, courage, and spirits to God's greatest service while the end of days draws closer.

Then, rather than the eternity of divine perfection on the Other Side that most of us have to look forward to when life on Earth becomes impossible, Mystical Travelers will stop at Home just long enough to chart their next incarnation on any other planet in any other galaxy where God needs them most.

The Dark Side at the End of Days

The Dark Side is that segment of the population who've rejected God and His laws of humanity, integrity, compassion, and non-judgmental love. We'll call them Dark Entities for this discussion, since their polar opposites, those who embrace and revere God and the white light of the Holy Spirit, are called White Entities. And don't let it enter your mind that "dark" and "white" are references to race or skin color. The mere suggestion of any such thing is offensive.

God didn't create the evil negativity that rules the Dark Side. What He did create are spirits endowed with free will. And some spirits used that free will to turn their backs on their Creator and pursue lives unencumbered by adoration of anyone but themselves. Dark Entities are their own gods, too narcissistic to believe in any being superior to them. They might profess a deep, profound belief in God, and they might even be able to recite the entire Bible by heart—if they think it will help gain the trust, allegiance, and adoration of someone they're eager to manipulate and control. They might also be very fond of working Satan and other mythical devils into their monologues (Dark Entities only occasionally tolerate actual give-and-take conversation), but only when they're facing consequences they don't like and they need someone else to blame.

The Dark Side exists in both human and spirit form, just as we White Entities do. In human form, they look exactly like the rest of us. (Don't forget, if it weren't for the choices they've made, they'd *be* the rest of us.) They might be a family member, a lover or spouse, a neighbor, coworker, a boss, a supposed friend. In spirit form, their negative energy can deeply affect everything from mechanical and electrical devices to our mental health without our even realizing what's happening. But whether they're in human form or spirit form, Dark Entities all share the same basic qualities:

- They have no conscience, no sincere remorse, and no sense of responsibility for their actions. They take all the credit and none of the blame for everything that happens around them, and self-justification is their first and only response to criticism.

- In psychiatric terms, they're true sociopaths. They expertly mimic human behavior without ever really feeling it. They can simulate charm, sensitivity, empathy, love, regret, and piety to gain proximity to us. They promptly drop the act once they've won us over, though, having no further use for it and frankly finding it to be too much work. We White Entities, because our emotions and faith are genuine, have trouble imagining that we've been witnessing a performance. So we cling to our trust in them and our loyalty to them, trying desperately to reinspire that wonderful person we're sure is in there because we saw them with our own eyes, unable to grasp that that wonderful person never really existed in the first place.

- As far as the Dark Side is concerned, we White Entities are nothing but a collection of walking mirrors. If their reflection through our eyes is flattering, we're valuable to them. But the minute we catch on that we've been looking at a mask, and they no longer like the way they look in our "mirror," they'll react in one of two ways—they'll get as far away from us as possible, or they'll repeat the award-winning performance that attracted us in the first place in the hope of attracting us again.

+ Dark Entities couldn't care less about the laws of God or the laws of respectable society. They live by their own self-serving rules, which change at their convenience and don't necessarily apply to anyone else around them. They view even their worst behavior as perfectly, invariably acceptable; but they might become outraged if someone else aims that same behavior at them. The result of this seeming inconsistency is that the White Entities close to them are kept constantly off balance, which gives the Dark Entity that much more power.

+ The goal of the Dark Entity isn't to turn a White Entity dark. They know that can't be done. Their goal is to extinguish the White Entity's light, since darkness can't exist where light is present. They don't necessarily try to destroy the White Entity physically. More often they'll simply create as much emotional turbulence, self-doubt, guilt, and depression as possible in as many White Entities they have access to, so that the White Entities lose their self-confidence, strength, and power.

+ Dark Entities rarely enjoy each other's company—with no light to extinguish, no flattering reflection to gaze into, and no control to be gained over someone with the same bag of tricks, there would be no point. Instead, they methodically and deliberately seek us out. And at least once in our lives, we're likely to seek them out too. It has nothing to do with being stupid. It has to do with taking our spiritual responsibilities seriously and believing it's our moral responsibility to reach out to someone we perceive to be lost, in trouble, or misunderstood.

Of course, it's against our humanitarian instincts to turn our back on a child of God who needs us. But when it's the Dark Side we're up against, we're wasting our time. A Dark Entity can't be turned white, any more than a White Entity can be turned dark. We can't appeal to a conscience that doesn't exist; we can't inspire genuine remorse in someone who takes no responsibility for their actions; and we can't ignite sincere love in someone who only loves God Himself on an as-needed basis. I say this as both a spiritual psychic and as a person who's learned the hard way: if there's a Dark Entity in your life, in Jesus's own words, *"Shake off the dust from your feet [and] leave."* (Matthew 10:14)

No discussion of who Dark Entities are would be complete without making it clear who they *aren't*. Not all murderers and other violent criminals are Dark Entities. Not everyone who's ever hurt you is a Dark Entity. Not everyone who's ill-tempered or hard to get along with is a Dark Entity. Not everyone you don't like, or who doesn't like you, is a Dark Entity. There are White Entities I don't like. There are White Entities who don't like me. This isn't about labeling people, or passing judgment, or worst of all, becoming a spiritual snob, which can be just as repelling as the Dark Side itself. It's simply about learning how and why we need to pay close attention to who's in our lives. True, we wrote every one of those people into our charts before we came here. But we wrote in some of them to teach us the wisdom of knowing when to walk away—the one area in which the Dark Side can be of use to us for a change.

They sound like the perfect candidates to be sent straight to hell, especially at the end of days, don't they? You're about to read, though, why I'll never believe that hell is where any of us ends up.

The Left Door

I promise you from the core of my soul that the closest thing to an actual place called "hell" is this earth we're living on, this tough boot camp we voluntarily come to from time to time for progress along the eternal journey of our souls. There is no bottomless pit. There is no fiery abyss of flames and agony. There is no eternal banishment to a place more horrible than we can ever imagine.

That being true—and it is—it's fair to wonder what happens to the Dark Side when their lifetime ends. The answer isn't pretty, but again, they have no one to thank but themselves.

When a Dark Entity dies, their spirit never experiences the tunnel and the sacred light at its end. Instead, they're propelled straight through the Other Side's Left Door, or, as my granddaughter used to call it when she was a little girl, Mean Heaven. Please don't let me create the mistaken impression that when we reach the Other Side we see two doors and have to choose between the left and the right. Only a handful of times have I heard of a near-death survivor being conscious of finding two doors at the end of the tunnel, and there was no danger of their stepping through the wrong one.

The Dark Side has already chosen the Left Door through an unrepentant lifetime of physically, emotionally, and/or spiritually abusing God's children, so no other door is even visible to them when they die. And inside the Left Door is an infinite abyss of godless, joyless, all-consuming nothingness.

The only permanent residents of this abyss are faceless beings in hooded cloaks, who've become the artistic and literary archetype for the persona of Death, aka the Grim Reaper. These beings don't act as dark spirit guides or avenging angels. They function more as a council, overseeing the paths of the spirits who make a brief appearance in their presence.

And the spirit's time in the void behind the Left Door is nothing if not brief. Unlike spirits on the Other Side who can choose when and whether to return to Earth for another incarnation, Dark Entities travel straight from their bodies at death, through the Left Door into the Godless darkness they've chosen, and right back in utero again, on a self-inflicted horseshoe-shaped journey that leaves them as dark at birth as they were at death in their previous life.

Let's take Ted Bundy as a prototype of the Dark Side, since his series of murders are indisputed and by all accounts he didn't experience a moment of even insincere remorse before he was executed. The instant Ted Bundy died, his spirit traveled through the Left Door and entered the womb of some poor unsuspecting woman who is probably wondering where she went wrong as a parent, when the truth is the dark course of her child's life was already determined before it was born. I've said a million times in lectures, and I'll say it again now: do *not* get pregnant immediately after hearing the news that Charles Manson has died, unless you want to be the horribly unlucky recipient of that dark spirit when it horseshoes back to Earth again.

I can't tell you how relieved I was, and how many of my long-standing questions were answered, when I learned the truth about the Dark Side's journey through the Left Door and back into the womb. As a psychic, I can look at most people and see a whole crowd of spirits from the Other Side, from Spirit Guides to departed loved ones to angels. But from time to time I'll notice someone who seems to have no spirits around them at all, who seems isolated from the divine loving support that constantly surrounds most of us. I used to worry that I was developing "blind spots" where some people were concerned, and if that were true I needed to do something about it. Now I know that there's a perfectly good reason why some people don't have a team from the Other Side around them: it's impossible to accumulate a team from a place you've never been. Those solitary people are Dark Entities who, by their own choice, take the Left Door instead, and pay a horrible spiritual price for it too.

I've also found great spiritual comfort in the truth of the journey of the Dark Side. On one hand, I know that the perfect God I believe in could never really be vindictive enough to banish any of His children from His sacred presence for eternity. On the other hand, I couldn't make peace with the idea that Ted Bundy and I, who are what I'll politely call polar opposites on the subject of the sanctity of humanity, could end up in the very same embrace of the Other Side between lifetimes, as if there is no significant difference between my soul and the soul of a serial killer.

Now I know what sends Ted Bundy and other card-carrying members of the Dark Side through the Left Door for countless dark incarnations while most of us make it safely Home to the Other Side: the Dark Side defiantly turns their backs on a God who never did and never will stop loving them, which is the one thing most of us find as spiritually inconceivable as the Dark Side itself.

And to prove that our Creator really does love each of His children eternally and unconditionally, not even Dark Entities are doomed to horseshoe from the Left Door into the womb again forever. The spirits and angels on the Other Side are well aware of these lost spirits, and sooner or later they literally catch them in their quick transit from one dimension to another and bring them Home to be embraced by God and infused with love again by the white light of the Holy Spirit, the only force powerful enough to reunite them with the sanctity of their souls.

The Dark Side at the End of Days

The continuous cycle Dark Entities experience when each incarnation ends—from Earth through the Left Door and right back in utero again—is obviously going to hit a serious snag when life on Earth is no longer possible: how can they horseshoe into an earthly womb when there are no longer any earthly wombs to be found? What will happen to the earth's Dark Side after the end of days?

There is in this universe an infinite, unfathomable force field, a great "uncreated mass" we can't begin to comprehend, a core from which the love and power of God emanate. This uncreated mass is where the rarest, most highly advanced souls from every inhabited planet willingly end their journeys, forfeiting their identities to be literally absorbed into the essence of God's force field. Once a spirit has given itself to that ultimate power, it never regains its previous identity. It doesn't cease to exist, it simply becomes indistinguishable and inseparable from the mass of which it's become a part. For example, picture pouring a cup of water into the Pacific Ocean. That cup of water hasn't ceased to exist, but it can't and won't ever again be separated from the huge body that's consumed it.

So there are those rare, supreme spirits who offer their very identities to God's infinite uncreated mass. And it's into that same ultimate sanctity that Dark Entities will be absorbed at the end of days, in a final, loving, holy embrace of purification by the One who created them and who never let their rejection of Him dissuade Him from adoring them.

Earthbounds at the End of Days

Earthbounds, or ghosts, as many of you know, are spirits who, for a variety of reasons, either see the tunnel that will take them to the Other Side when they die and reject it, or they refuse to acknowledge it at all. This leaves them stranded, outside of their bodies, caught between the lower vibrational level we exist in on Earth and the much higher-frequency vibrational level of Home.

Ghosts are clueless that, in earthly terms, they've died. They're very much alive as far as they're concerned, exactly where they were an hour, a day, or a week ago. Nothing has changed from their perspective except for the sudden, inexplicable fact that no one seems to be able to see or hear them because they've "changed frequencies" without knowing it. People who've experienced hauntings complain about how ornery and irritable ghosts seem to be. Try having everyone around you suddenly start treating you as if you don't exist and see if you don't find it irritating.

While the details vary dramatically from one ghost to the next, the two most common reasons why they inadvertently or deliberately miss the opportunity to go Home boil down to passion (which can be either love or hate) and fear. Some stay behind to care for a child they adore, or to wait for a lover to come home, or to protect their cherished home from intruders. Others stay behind to seek revenge on real or imagined enemies (which never works, by the way, so don't spend one minute worrying about that). Still others are so afraid God will find them undeserving of His loving welcome Home that they remain earthbound rather than face Him.

Fortunately, mostly for them but for us as well, let's face it, there is no such thing as a ghost who's eternally trapped here on Earth. Thanks to an enormous and constantly growing human awareness that will be virtually universal by the last decades of this century, a lot of ghosts are directed to the tunnel and the Other Side by people who recognize them and understand that there's really great compassion in saying, "You're dead. Go Home." But the spirits on the Other Side are far more aware of earthbound souls than we are, and they perform their own constant interventions for as long as it takes until each ghost has celebrated the joyful reunion that's waiting for them on the other end of that tunnel.

I will never forget the indescribable experience of visiting Ground Zero not long after the despicable terrorist attacks on the World Trade Center on September 11, 2001. Among the countless feelings that flooded through me were the surprise, relief, and gratitude that not a single one of the three thousand casualties of that awful tragedy failed to make it quickly and safely Home. Not a single ghost was left behind, confused and lost and frightened, thanks to God's exquisite, perfect, loving grace.

And exactly the same thing will happen at the end of days. Through the grace of God, none of His children will be left behind or cast aside, including the earthbounds who will suddenly see the tunnel, joyfully embrace it, and join the rest of us in continuing our perfect, blissful lives on the Other Side.

The Cosmic Other Side

As long as Earth exists, our Other Side will exist as well.

It's where all our earthly spirits come from when we enter the womb, and it's where we return when we die. It's a very real place, more beautiful than our finite minds can imagine, but our spirit minds remember it and are Homesick for it from the moment we leave until the moment we get back.

It's not far, far away. It's not over the rainbow, or beyond the moon and the stars. As I mentioned earlier, it's right here among us, another dimension superimposed on ours, just three feet above our version of ground level. Its topography is a perfect mirror image of Earth, with one exception: because there's no erosion or pollution on the Other Side, its landscape is an image of the earth from thousands of years ago, when bodies of water were pure blue and mountains and coastlines were perfectly intact. On the Other Side, Atlantis and Lemuria, our lost continents, thrive. So do the world's great architectural, literary, and artistic masterpieces, even if they're crumbling or have long since been destroyed in our harsh world.

The same is true for every other inhabited planet. Their Other Sides are three feet above their ground levels, at a much higher vibrational frequency than that of the planet they surround. Their topographies are identical to their "home" planets, and their great works and structures are impeccably preserved.

Remember, the end of days on Earth will mean that this planet will be unable to sustain life, but the planet itself will remain intact. As long as Earth itself exists, our Other Side will exist. The same is true for every other inhabited planet and their respective Other Sides. And as inhabited planets become more spiritually advanced and less separate from one another—which we have to look forward to in the coming decades—their Other Sides will begin blending with the great, infinite, universal Other Side, especially when their environments will no longer support human life. If the earth were destroyed tomorrow, we and our Other Side would join the spirits whose planets have already completed their natural cycles, who are living the same joyful, sacred lives that wait for us among the stars, where our Home beyond Home called the Cosmic Other Side eternally thrives. To picture its location in the most beautiful possible way, think of the ancient imagery of "The Great Man" in the night sky.

The Great Man's head is the constellation Aries.

His feet are the constellation Pisces.

The rest of His body is outlined by the other ten constellations of the zodiac.

That is the closest we can come to imagining where we can look to find some hint of the Cosmic Other Side.

The Cosmic Other Side is as identical a reflection of the universe as our Other Side is of Earth, and it's populated by incarnated spirits and messiahs from formerly inhabited planets that no longer exist.

All, of course, simply part of God's promise that we are eternally safe and loved, and the lives he gave us are guaranteed to never end.

Leaving Earth, Going Home

I once appeared on *Larry King Live* with the late Mattie Stepanek, the theologian, philosopher, poet, and Mystical Traveler who passed away at the age of thirteen. Mattie, as most of you know, suffered

for much of his life from a tragic inherited disease called dysauto-
nomic mitochondrial myopathy, and he was in a wheelchair when
we met, speaking with the help of a respirator, the most cheerful,
positive, self-assured, God-centered child you can imagine.

Larry King asked, "Mattie, are you afraid of death?"

And Mattie replied, "I'm afraid of dying, but I'm not afraid of
death."

I think there's great universal truth in that statement, I'm just
not sure I've ever heard it put more simply and clearly. As we an-
ticipate the end of days, or just the end of our lives on Earth when-
ever and however they occur, isn't it really the *process* of death that
frightens us, as opposed to death itself?

Ask anyone who's had a near-death experience and they'll all tell
you the same thing: they no longer have any fear of death whatsoever. That was true for Mattie Stepanek, and it's true for me. I had
a near-death experience when I underwent routine surgery at the
age of forty-two. In fact, it's fair to say I had an actual death experience, since the monitor keeping track of my vital signs flatlined for
a few minutes. And I have the advantage of remembering every
moment of it, so I can give you a firsthand account of exactly what
happens when we die:

✦ The legendary tunnel immediately appeared. It didn't come
from "up there somewhere." Instead, it rose up from my
body, seemingly from my own etheric substance. It didn't
lead up toward the sky, it led "across," at maybe a twenty-
degree angle, confirming what my Spirit Guide Francine had
told me a million times—the Other Side really is a paradise
that's right here among us, only three feet above our ground
level.

✦ I had never felt, or been, so completely, thrillingly, vibrantly alive as I was when I moved through the tunnel. I felt free and weightless, relieved to be rid of my body and free from the pull of gravity. I was immediately infused with peace, bliss, and total recall of Home and the truth of eternity. With that recall came a release of all worry about the loved ones I'd left behind. I knew they would be fine as they proceeded living out their charts, and I also knew that in what would seem like the blink of an eye to me, we'd be together again on the Other Side, so there was no sadness, no sense of loss, and no missing them.

✦ The sacred, brilliant white light appeared ahead of me. Everything I'd heard and read about it was true—somehow, it seemed almost alive, pulsating with God's love and His infinite knowledge, and an awareness flooded through me that the light was as familiar to me as my own soul.

✦ The figure of a loved one appeared in the large opening at the end of the tunnel. (In my case it was my cherished Grandma Ada, whom I'd yearned to see again since I was eighteen.) Beyond her I could see a grassy, flower-filled meadow, like the most beautiful meadow on Earth with its colors enriched and magnified a thousand times.

That trip Home for me was obviously interrupted, by Grandma Ada gesturing for me to stop and by a distant voice of a friend by my hospital bed pleading, "Sylvia, don't go, you're so needed." I was deeply depressed for days about finding myself back on Earth, and while I eventually became grateful to have stayed, I can promise you from the core of my soul that death was and is absolutely nothing to fear. It is exactly the return to the all-encompassing love of God's arms that we've all hoped it will be—and that our spirits remember perfectly and look forward to.

Before I describe the utter joy of our actual arrival on the Other Side, I want to clarify my strong beliefs about a couple of the most breathlessly anticipated events of the end of days, urging you as always to study, think, and come to your own conclusions.

The Second Coming and the Rapture

According to Christian literature and legend, two major events involving Jesus Christ will be among the most telling signs that the end of days are at hand: his reappearance on Earth in human form, and his appearance among the clouds to take the faithful to heaven in a phenomenon called the Rapture.

They're both beautiful thoughts, but I don't happen to believe that either of them will happen when the end of days arrives.

I take Jesus at his sacred word when he said, in Matthew 28:20, "And lo, I am with you always, to the very end of time." He didn't say, "I *will be* with you," which implies some future event, but of far more importance, it also implies that there might be some period of time when he's absent from us. That's simply not true. He's been with us every second since his divine Resurrection, he's with us at this moment, he'll be with us when we return to our lives on the Other Side, and he'll be with us throughout our joyful eternity at Home. We can stop waiting for him and watching for him. He's already here, an essential part of our present tense.

Didn't he accomplish everything we could ever want or need or hope for during his one divine incarnation? For what reason would he come again? To prove that he's real, and that he truly is the Son of God? Don't we already know that beyond all doubt? And sadly, isn't it likely that his Second Coming would create the same controversy and skepticism he faced two thousand years ago?

Besides, what more effective way to put every phony "reincarnated messiah" out of business—and believe me, more and more of them will be cropping up as this century progresses—than to say, and mean, "I've stopped looking for Jesus 'out there,' because I have the peace of knowing he's already right here."

Then point to your heart and remember:

And lo, I AM with you always, to the very end of time.

I also believe that the anticipation of the Rapture—Christ embracing the faithful in the sky at the end of days—is actually the anticipation of imagery that was never meant to be taken literally. And I believe that the real Rapture preceding the end of days will be far more thrilling and far, far more sacred.

Remember, part of the Rapture of the book of Revelation is God's judgment of all of humankind "by what was written in the book of life, by what they had done." (Revelation 20:12) "And if any one's name was not found written in the book of life, he was thrown into the lake of fire." (Revelation 20:15) I said in an earlier chapter and I'll say again—the God I know, the God I worship who created us all, is perfect in His kindness, His forgiveness, His wide-open arms, and his absolute, unconditional love. I cannot and will not conceive of a God so cruel, spiteful, and merciless that he would condemn any of His children to an eternity in a "lake of fire." Even the Dark Entities who've turned away from God, while He continues to love them and wait for their return to Him, will become a part of Him when life on Earth ends. So unless Jesus would appear in the clouds to deliver all of us, without judgment or discrimination, I can't imagine the Revelation version of the Rapture. And as you'll read later in this chapter, no one judges our lives on Earth but us, after we've arrived on the Other Side.

There's also a simple matter of logistics, by the way. While Jesus can obviously appear anywhere and everywhere he wants, I repeat—from personal experience, my Spirit Guide Francine, and more study and research than I can possibly describe—that the Other Side is three feet above the ground level of Earth. So why our spirits would be drawn all the way up into the sky for our trip to a Home just three feet above us I can't imagine.

I promise, the true Rapture is going to be far more spiritually enormous, and far more Godly in its universal, unconditional love. A beautiful story, not a biblical one, that illustrates that unconditional love so eloquently: the end of days had arrived, and the righteous who were gathered in anticipation of the Rapture finally asked God about Jesus's whereabouts. "Jesus is outside the gate," God replied, "waiting for Judas."

The true Rapture will be the increasing groundswell of deep spirituality that will be pervasive throughout the world by the end of days. It will supersede individual religions, politics, racial differences, anything and everything that stands in the way of humankind finally understanding that because we all share the same Father and the same Home, what separates us pales in comparison to what unites us.

The true Rapture will be the subtle lifting of the veil between our dimension and the dimension of the Other Side, so that we on Earth will have easy access to the spirit world that waits to celebrate our return.

The true Rapture will be a diminishing fear of the end of days, as our memories of our previous lives and deaths become clearer to us and we know beyond all doubt that we are eternal, that death is nothing but an illusion and that a simple step through the veil between dimensions will bring us the peace and joy and is our birthright as God's children.

The true Rapture will be the understanding that God is not vengeful and cruel, so that at the end of days all of us—*all* of us— will be safe and loved in His arms forever.

The Antichrist

We might as well get the subject of the Antichrist out of the way while we're at it, since being braced for his arrival seems to be as essential to the end-of-days anticipation as the Second Coming and the Rapture.

It will be a brief discussion, because we can officially stop watching for the Antichrist.

The Antichrist is already here, in human form.

The Antichrist has a name.

The name is apathy.

It's a fact that "evil prevails when good men do nothing." Too many have been doing nothing for far too long, and what could be more "anti-Christ" than to take the position that poverty, hunger, injustice, and abuse of the planet and its inhabitants are none of our business, or that we're just too busy to do anything about it? Apathy is a luxury we can't afford any longer, nor do we want to, because in the end it will destroy us.

As spirituality on Earth takes firm root in this century and begins to thrive—as each of us finds our God center and, by definition, we become more Christlike—the Antichrist of apathy will be driven away. A day will come when we can't imagine not taking care of each other and this world that's been entrusted to us.

And it's completely up to us how far in the future that day is, and how long we're going to tolerate the Antichrist in our midst by doing nothing.

Arriving on the Other Side

We hear so often about the tunnel and the brilliant white light at its end we have to look forward to when we die that it almost creates the impression that our journey Home stops there. But of course the journey only begins there. And I think it's unkind at the very least that so few discussions of the end of days address the question, "And then what?"

The answer is, "And then we pick up our *real* lives again, right where they left off."

Just as all roads lead to Rome, according to the old saying, all tunnels lead to the entrance to the Other Side. No matter where on this earth we leave our bodies, we all take exactly the same trip to exactly the same place. We emerge from the tunnel to find ourselves in a breathtakingly beautiful meadow. Waiting there to greet us are deceased loved ones from the life we've just left behind, as well as friends and loved ones from all our past lives, on Earth and on the Other Side. Our Spirit Guides are there. Our true soul mates are there. And best of all as far as I'm concerned, every animal we've ever loved from every lifetime we've lived is on hand, with such pure, urgent joy that the people waiting to welcome us have a hard time making their way through the happy crowd.

Beyond the meadow, and our glorious "welcome Home" party, is a gleaming cluster of massive, gorgeous structures that are essential to our transition from Earth to the Other Side:

+ The Hall of Records, with its towering marble columns and glittering dome, which contains, among other things, every chart of every incarnation of every one of our lives on Earth;

+ The Hall of Justice, pillared, domed white marble, most revered for its impossibly beautiful gardens and its treasured statue of Azna, the Mother God;

+ The Towers, twin monoliths of white marble and blue glass, where extra care is provided for arrivals from Earth who need special psychological and emotional help with their return Home;

+ And the Hall of Wisdom, with its vast marble steps and massive entry doors, to which most of us directly proceed from our thrilling wealth of reunions.

I promised earlier that I would describe the only judgment we'll face at the end of days. It's the same judgment we face every time we finish an incarnation and return Home, and it's undoubtedly the harshest judgment we could ever imagine.

It takes place in a gigantic room in the Hall of Wisdom. Our Spirit Guide accompanies us to one of the countless white marble benches that surround the room. We take a seat by ourselves, with our Spirit Guides looking on, and begin a process that many near-death survivors recall but few remember in enough detail to understand exactly what happened.

You've heard those who have had a close brush with death describe feeling as if their whole life flashed before their eyes. The truth is, they didn't just imagine it. What they actually experienced was an abbreviated trip to the quiet stillness of that room in the Hall of Wisdom where the Scanning Machine sits waiting.

The Scanning Machine is a huge convex dome of blue glass. And through that glass dome, we watch each and every moment of the life we've just lived unfold before our eyes. Rather than appearing like a movie, our life plays out in the form of a three-dimensional hologram, so that no matter where we move around the Scanning Machine, we can see every detail, good or bad, right or wrong, with perfect clarity. We review our lives for as long as it takes, even "re-winding" as much "footage" as we want as often as we want.

Obviously our encounter with the Scanning Machine is more than just an entertaining way for us to make the transition from Earth to the Other Side. It's an essential step in the eternal journey of our spirits. As we trudge along through our lives on Earth, we have no significant memories of the charts we wrote for those lives to help us accomplish the specific goals we came here for. But the moment we return Home and arrive at the Scanning Machine, we have total recall of our charts. So it's not just a matter of watching our last incarnation unfold in three-dimensional detail for the sheer nostalgia of it, it's a matter of seeing how that incarnation stacked up against the detailed plans we laid out for it ahead of time. And make no mistake about it, it's the toughest judge of all who ultimately evaluates our success and failure—not our Spirit Guide, not God, but *us*. Us as our spirit selves, mind you, from the perspective of the Other Side, where not only is there no negativity but there's also no defensiveness and no ego-driven self-justification to prevent us from facing the truth of our actions and being accountable for them.

During our lives on the Other Side, the Scanning Machine is one of our most valuable research tools. In the same way we study our just-completed incarnation when we first return Home, we can also study every other incarnation we've spent on Earth, and, for that matter, every incarnation of anyone and everyone who interests us, by essentially "playing" any chart we choose through the hologram "projector" of the Scanning Machine. We can be an eyewitness to any event in our spirit's history or the history of humankind, or if we prefer we can even "merge" with that event, becoming a part of it, feeling all the emotions its actual participants felt, without altering its dynamics or its outcome in any way.

The Scanning Machine is one of our most cherished destinations when we return Home and as we proceed with our busy lives there. But its value will only intensify when the end of days comes and our time on Earth is through. It will allow us to revisit as often as we like the lives we lived and the lessons we learned on that planet we'll never see again. And, more than that, it will provide our souls with the immeasurable growth that learning from our earthly mistakes can offer as the reincarnation phase of our eternal lives draws to a close.

Life on the Other Side

By no coincidence, I've written an entire book called *Life on the Other Side*, which I hope you'll refer to every time you find yourself becoming even slightly anxious about the end of days. If you come away with nothing else from that book or this one, I hope you'll remember and believe this one simple truth: our lives on Earth are nothing but sleepwalking compared to the blissful, divine exhilaration of being alive in that sacred place that's our *real* Home.

Never doubt that the Other Side is every bit as real as Earth. In fact, my Spirit Guide Francine insists it's far more real, and that *we* are actually the ghosts in *their* world rather than the other way around.

The landscape is exquisite—again, identical to Earth as it was before erosion, pollution, natural disasters, and human destruction took their toll. Atlantis and Lemuria thrive in clear blue oceans. The Parthenon, the Great Library of Alexandria, the Hanging Gardens of Babylon, the Venus de Milo, all earthly wonders and treasures look brand-new. Coastlines and mountaintops are as sharply defined as the day they were created. And everything thrives in weather that is a perpetually calm, pure seventy-eight degrees.

There is no day or night, no time at all on the Other Side. All that exists is "now." In our spirit identities, which are the finest of all our personality traits on Earth, we never need to eat or sleep. We have careers that reflect our greatest passions and talents, and our social lives are as busy as we choose, with the widest possible variety of friends since everyone at Home knows and loves each other. We create our homes through thought projection, just as travel involves nothing more than thinking ourselves wherever we'd like to be.

While God's presence fills the very air we breathe, there are magnificent houses of worship everywhere, with all religions shared and celebrated. The angels walk among us, never speaking to us or to each other, making no sounds at all until they join in a massive choir to perform indescribably thrilling concerts of hymns in a revered structure called the Hall of Voices.

There is no negativity, no sorrow, no illness, no pain, no imperfection of any kind on the Other Side. No matter what age we were when we left our earthly bodies behind, we're all thirty-three years old at Home, at our perpetual peak of vitality. We are pure love and purely loving with every breath we take. Our eternal lives are a constant celebration of the joy of living in our Creator's holy presence.

All of which leads to what may be the most significant point of all about that time when life on Earth ceases to exist: with so much sacred, peaceful joy waiting for us on the Other Side, maybe we should stop calling it the end of days and start calling it the *beginning*.

THE BENEDICTION
from the Inca Q'ero shamans

Follow your own footsteps.
Learn from the rivers,
the trees and the rocks.
Honor the Christ,
the Buddha,
your brothers and sisters.
Honor your Earth Mother and the Great Spirit.
Honor yourself and all of creation.
Look with the eyes of your soul and engage the essential.
Amen.

ABOUT THE AUTHOR

Sylvia Browne is the accomplished author of forty-six books, including twenty *New York Times* bestsellers. As a highly acclaimed psychic, Browne consults with police and the FBI to help solve missing persons and other high-profile cases, in addition to her work providing private readings. Browne also founded her own church, the Society of Novus Spiritus, more than twenty years ago. She appeared regularly on the *Montel Williams Show* for seventeen years, is a frequent guest on *Larry King Live*, and hosts her own live show at the Excalibur in Las Vegas. Her son, Chris Dufresne, is also a psychic. Browne and her family live in California.